LOST MEN OF AMERICAN HISTORY

Books by *Stewart H. Holbrook*

BURNING AN EMPIRE. *The Story of American Forest Fires*

ETHAN ALLEN

HOLY OLD MACKINAW. *A Natural History of the American Lumberjack*

IRON BREW. *A Century of American Ore and Steel*

MURDER OUT YONDER

NONE MORE COURAGEOUS

TALL TIMBER

LOST MEN
OF
AMERICAN
HISTORY

BY

STEWART H. HOLBROOK

With an Introduction
By ALLAN NEVINS

THE MACMILLAN COMPANY
NEW YORK • 1946

COMPOSITION BY THE MAPLE PRESS COMPANY, YORK, PA.
PRINTED AND BOUND BY COMAC PRESS, INC., BROOKLYN, N. Y.

For

Nelson Horatio Holbrook

Introduction

Mr. Holbrook has hit upon a fresh approach to American history. He carries his reader down many a novel byway which somehow turns out to have an interesting relation to the main highroad; and he does this by an expedient as simple as it is sound. He has pursued the significant event and the important personality without regard to their celebrity—with an eye rather to the striking figure who has somehow missed fame, and the memorable occurrence which has somehow escaped memory. A great part of the real history of the country, as he demonstrates, is summed up in the careers of its secondary and tertiary personages. In a remarkable panorama, he shows how fickle and fortuitous is not merely contemporaneous fame, but the kind of fame conferred by Clio in all her grandeur.

It is not hard to say why every schoolboy has heard of Eli Whitney, whose one great (and rather elementary) invention transformed the industry of a section and gave slavery a new basis. But why has scarce a single schoolboy heard of Elkanah Watson, who not only dreamed of the Erie Canal but promoted the idea, and who performed services of the most solid kind to American agriculture? The Underground Railroad is picturesquely famous; but why then is old Levi Coffin, its most redoubtable conductor, and the author of a stirring book of reminiscences, totally forgotten? In the decade before the Civil War, *Uncle Tom's Cabin* stirred the multitude; and so did another book called *The Impending Crisis*, which was scattered broadcast by the Republican Party as a campaign document, and which figured in stormy debates in Congress. Yet for every thousand persons who have heard of Harriet Beecher Stowe, catching up her pen in the Maine parsonage, is there one who has heard of Hinton Rowan Helper, the North Carolina spokesman for the poor-white sufferers from slavery? Most people can name the James B. Eads who bridged the Mississippi and built the jetties that liberated the port of New Orleans. But who can name the builder of the far more influential Soo Canal, an epic feat which furnishes the theme for some of Mr. Holbrook's best pages?

This book, with its melange of material old and new, raises some questions which students of history will find worth pondering. There is always danger that the story of the nation, at least in its briefer versions, will become conventionalized. We take it up in familiar categories like the winning of independence, the westward movement, and the rise of industry; and we humanize it by bringing in a well-canonized set of heroes. Some students will not be willing to accept all Mr. Holbrook's personages at his estimate of them, but he at least raises the question whether a periodical revision of our calendar of great men would not be profitable. And he also touches on a deeper question. The United States is a great mass democracy, where equality of opportunity is emphasized; and it was for generations a new country, where frontier conditions stimulated individual enterprise. In view of these facts, have we not made a little too much of the very great men, the primary figures; and too little of the serried ranks of talent and achievement just behind them, the host of men whose labors were the main element in progress? The illustrious hero unquestionably counts for less in America, measured by realistic tests, and the secondary figures count for more, than in older lands of restricted opportunity, strong class lines, and settled economic conditions.

Whatever our view of these matters, Mr. Holbrook's volume is worth reading. Some of it will be new to everybody, even the specialists; and most of it will be both new and very entertaining to the great body of ordinary Americans.

ALLAN NEVINS

To the Reader

THE United States of America is to me incomparably the greatest story on earth, a tremendous drama, arranged with scenery and props such as no director could visualize and with a cast of characters superb beyond imagination. It is a story filled with thunder and lightning, with vast movements of men and machines, with the smells of coke, of dust, of sagebrush and balsam. It is a story shot through with knavery on a stupefying scale, yet leavened with sufficient stark honesty, courage and determination to keep the faith.

There is a surge in our history like the surge of the sea, and as blind and powerful. And like the sea, the heavings of my country have often tossed men and events to symbolic peaks as high as Ararat and there left them, to remain for the most part secure and shining in the beautiful mellow light of History. The same heavings, too, have tossed other men and events of importance onto remote and obscure shores, then ebbed to leave them as forgotten almost as if they had never lived or occurred. I found many of them to be covered with the sand and silt of a hundred years and more. It is the modest intent of this book to make known a number of these men and women, and a few events, that are quite unknown to most Americans today.

By now we all are familiar with the theory, so highly thought of in recent times, that conditions, and chiefly those of an economic nature, are the dynamic force that makes History move. To my mind, this theory is tenable only in part and to a certain point, beyond which volition takes over. I believe that men, even one man or one woman, often have had immense effect in slowing or hastening the forces that are said to make history; that they have had the ability, sometimes of genius, to catch and direct as through a funnel the great currents that were flowing and ebbing around them. Many just such men and women have been slighted or wholly ignored in our history books. They are in large part the people I want to tell about.

It may be charged that in putting undue stress on these mostly forgotten men and women I have put other and allegedly more important men and women out of focus. This is true. But I fancy it will accomplish no immeasurable harm. The other great Americans, the secure and patented stock characters of our history books, will not suffer from my treatment; I cherish them as much as any man, and you will find no lines in this book seeking to detract from their stature in order to build up the size of the others.

It may also be charged, and with even less accuracy, that certain characters in this book are not important at all. This charge cannot be proved any more than I could prove the contrary; and I do not wish to prove anything at all. I am content to give some sort of historical recognition to these worthies and to let the reader judge of their importance as he will. I will rise to remark, however, that the taproots of America are in such people as are stressed in this book. They make a pattern of our genius, a genius for the unpredictable that no other nation can match, a right, almost a duty, to be original and to break all the rules. Let our native cynics believe, if believe they do, that we are the most herdlike of all herdlike peoples. We do have a herd, and our masters of advertising and ballyhoo lead it by the nose, as it deserves to be led; yet, no herd ever had so many bellwethers, so many mavericks who struck out for new pastures.

There is another thing, too: Since 1939, or thereabout, it has been much the style in the United States to praise democracies, and especially our own. Strong men have become tearful and their voices have broken, as well as their prose, with emotion, as they reflected aloud, and often too loud, that we are a nation in which anybody may become

President, that we achieve our laws by open discussion, and
that the rights of minorities are often respected. Some of
these strident writers and orators have sounded as if only
then had they discovered what a truly wonderful place is the
United States of America.

All of this has left many of us, including this American,
quite calm, even uninterested, for never since I was born
have I thought otherwise than that my country, for all its
imperfections, was the finest place on earth. If this sounds
smug, then let it stand. I have been around considerably in
the Republic, and I figure I know America's sores as well as
its glories, yet I have as much need of "inspirational" reading about America as I have need to be told that the sun
rises and sets. Indeed, I should as soon think of seriously
heeding these special pleaders as I would of wearing a button
that said I-Love-You-America on it.

I suspect that many of these suddenly patriotic pleaders
for American democracy must at some time or other have
lost faith in the United States, or never understood it anyway; and, when the dark clouds began to gather, hurried
like sinners at a revival down the sawdust path, to stand at
the testimonial bench and give cry to their conversion and
salvation. In any case, the things they are trying to shout
have been obvious truths to many of us since we were born.
We did not have to learn them, either, for we drank them
in with the air we breathed and have never since had cause
to doubt them, not for a moment. Not even, I repeat, in the
Harding Era.

No authentic American, native or adopted, need pay any
heed to the tub-thumpers for American democracy. All he
needs know is something of the men and women who made
this country what it is today. He can learn about them in
countless and excellent histories and biographies, and they
will tell him it took a vast number of all sorts of able and
earnest men and women to bring the United States into
being and to make it great.

Yet, as I have said, many a worthy American has for one reason or another never been given his just due. A majority of them were mavericks, malcontents, unorthodox thinkers— men and women who were going against the wind and the tide. Often they were preposterous. More often they were genuine prophets ahead of their times, perhaps the most lonely sort of people there are. Right or wrong, every last one of them had some influence in forming the character of the American people. It is of them I sing.

Portland, Oregon,   STEWART H. HOLBROOK
March 1, 1946.

Contents

Illustrations

CHAPTER I

Ye Very Roote

WHEN stout old William Bradford sat him down to compose his *Of Plimouth Plantation*, the first good history
written in what is now the United States, he remarked right
away, in his quaint manner, that he "must begine at ye very
roote & rise of ye same." What Bradford considered of basic
importance were the actions of theologians and the liquida-
tion of the redmen. Most writers on the period since Bradford's day have merely continued the tradition, and thus our
histories of colonial times are still filled with theological
bickerings, with massacres of Indians, and the interminable
warfare that resulted in the eventual exclusion of the French
from the American provinces.

There is no doubt but that these men and events were of
considerable importance, yet they pale into insignificance
when put alongside the arrival of the first company of Scandinavians, an incident that fails to rate so much as a line in
most general-history books. It was the first Swede in America who brought the first log cabin, and I believe *that* to
have been the most important single event between Columbus and the beginning of the American Revolution, a period
of two hundred and eighty years.

The early American settlements were composed almost
wholly of people of English stock. 'Tis a pity, too, for they
would have had a much better time of it, during the early
hard years—and many more of them would have lived beyond

childhood—if their companies had numbered a Scandinavian
or two, who knew how to build the only fit house for pioneer
settlers in a new and wooded land. But not until the Swedes
along the Delware had fully demonstrated the surpassing
utility of their kind of house did the log cabin, that most
cherished of "American" institutions, appear widely in
North America. And this is a good place to remark that it
was not the English who first adopted the cabin from the
Swedes. The English preferred to live pig-headedly in their
sties of huts, drenched and frostbitten, until the swarming
Scotch-Irish, after 1718, had distributed the Swedish cabin
to all parts of the new colonies.

Neither Captain John Smith, that stocky, cocky, and
competent pioneering genius, nor the courageous and able
Governor Bradford of Plymouth ever lived in a log cabin,
and probably neither of them ever saw one. The first settlers
of all, those at Jamestown, lived in tents, in caves, or in what
were called English wigwams. So did all other English settlers, during their early years, for a century to come. The
English wigwams were patterned after two similar but
slightly different abodes—the huts in which many miners in
Wales made their homes, and the true wigwams of the
American Indian. They were constructed of woodbine or
grapevine, steamed and bent to form a skeleton shaped something like the frame-top of a covered wagon. The skeleton
was then covered with thatch made of such reeds or heavy
grasses as best came to hand. Heat for warmth and cooking
came from an open fire, not a fireplace as we know it, inside.

Thomas Studley, one of the Virginia pioneers of 1607,
set down, with praise for Captaine Smith, how they went
about making their miserable huts. "Captaine Smith," says
he, "by his own example, good words and faire promises,"
put some of his crew to binding thatch, some to erecting the
vine poles, others to putting the thatch on the poles; "and
always did Smith bear ye greatest taske himself," neglecting
a hut for Smith until all others were under cover.

In such hovels did our goodly forefathers live during their first year or two in the New World. Then, as soon as they could, they set about building the only kind of real houses they knew, which were frame houses made of timber, deals (boards), and clapboards, together with two chimneys in the houses of the Virginia settlements, one chimney in those of the New England towns.

Captaine Smith was adept at getting out logs from which to make lumber for the newer homes, and Amos Todkill left a graphic account of logging operations under the doughty Captaine. Todkill was thrilled to hear the trees thunder as they fell, and enjoyed the bustle and danger of it. There was danger not only of being killed or maimed, but worse, of losing one's soul by reason of cursing, which somehow has always accompanied logging. Felling trees, as many a man has learned since, brings blistered hands; and Todkill soon heard many Greate Loude Othes that drowned even the echo of the crashing trees. But Captaine Smith was no man to let his loggers lose their souls; he was ready with "a remedie of this sinne." He set a spy to listening to the loggers and making count of their oaths; and at evening a Canne of water was poured down the sleeve of every man for each profanity uttered. This was Spartan treatment, and apparently it worked. "Within a week," says Todkill, "a man could scarce hear an Othe."

When at last the Virginia settlers had built their own frame houses, they "wrought upon Clapborde for English." In other words, their first exports were in the form of clapboards, or siding.

Even when frame houses had been erected there were great troubles because of the thatched roofs catching fire, yet it was many years before the English would adopt shingles or shakes. One more reason for the many fires in the early times was the type of chimney used. It was made of wood, then smeared with clay, and the smear did not always stick. As early as 1631 this fire menace had become so great that in

the Massachusetts Bay Colony, Deputy Governor Thomas
Dudley ordered that no man should build his chimney with
aught but stone or brick, nor cover his house mõre with
thatch. Although there appears to have been no public protest against this sensible order, nevertheless many of the bull-
headed settlers continued to use thatch for several years, or
probably until they had been burned down once or twice.

Now, for the arrival of what has been for two hundred
years the symbol of pioneer America—the log cabin,
cherished as a symbol second only to that of the much newer
Stars and Stripes.

The log cabin's first appearance in North America was in
1638, when members of the Swedish West India Company
set up a trading post and village on the shore of Delaware
Bay. It was the kind of house the Swedes had known in their
homeland, and it was exactly the thing needed to settle
America. With no tool save an ax a Swede could strike out
into the forest and within a short time have a most service-
able abode. Never was the theory of adapting a house to the
land better exemplified. Yet, the English settlers who lived
almost side by side with the Swedes on Delaware Bay were
slow to copy the Scandinavian boon to pioneers; as late as
1680 the Delaware English were still living in their English
wigwams or in frame houses. The English here and elsewhere in the American colonies often complained of illnesses
which they laid to "wett lodging." The Swedes never did,
for their homes were tight and dry, almost mansions compared to the leaky hovels put up by all except the more
well-to-do of the English.

There were probably two reasons for this failure to adopt
at once the most suitable home yet devised for pioneering
people. One was that the migration by sea from England
did nothing to change the habits of the English; they landed
on the American shore with an unbroken, unadulterated

cargo of craft culture. The other reason was the ingrained habit of centuries; to the English, frame houses were the only sort of houses. They knew of none other, save mere huts. Habits are most difficult to change, even unto craft culture, which seemingly has a good deal of the persistence inherent in such institutions as legal concepts, forms of greetings, superstitions, and language.

The North Germans who arrived in 1710 also brought the log cabin as they had known it at home. By the beginning of the Revolution, but not much before, the log cabin typified all American frontier settlements. What spread its use was migration by land, the migration inland from the coast. The new settlers had to pass through successive zones of earlier settlements, and these scenes helped to break the patterns of behavior brought from the Old Country, and to form new habits. The utility of the log cabin must have been obvious at once, on sight. Building it called for no saws, no hammers, no nails, no pegs, no plaster. A log cabin required no laborious sawing of boards, no long process of drying them. A log house could be constructed quickly by one man, and with incredible speed if a few neighbors helped.

It was the so-called Scotch-Irish, who began arriving in great numbers after 1718, who took the log house which the English for a hundred years had refused to adopt, and spread it to all parts of the frontier of the colonies. These Scotch-Irish found the choice tidewater lands occupied by families who had been settled for two generations or more, so the late-comers had to strike inland. On their way from the shore to the Appalachians these people were exposed to all the different kinds of housing in the many settlements, and with unerring judgment they chose the one best suited to the time and place. Westward into the hills they took with them the Scandinavian cabin. The log cabin also spread eastward, into the new colonies of Vermont and Maine. By the time of Lexington and Concord, the log cabin, substantially as we know it today, was the classic dwelling of the American frontier, well on its way to becoming a hallowed national institution.*

It is usually a poet and an artist, a painter, who work in combination to give us Americans our classic heroes and revered institutions. In the case of the institution of the log cabin myth the combination was of a historian and subsequent artists. It turned out to be just as effective as the more usual poet-artist combine.

There is no evidence whatever to show that the American log cabin became a sacred symbol until 1840, or more than two hundred years after its arrival on our shores. Significantly, 1840 is also the year in which the myth itself was conjured up by an honest and well-disposed historian who did not reflect on the fact that the meanings of many words change with the centuries. The historian was the Reverend Alexander Young, his book the *Chronicles of the Pilgrim Fathers*. The word whose meaning he misunderstood, with such lasting consequences, was "daub."

In composing his book Young consulted all of the old books and letters and journals written or kept by the ancient men of Plymouth, among them the journal of Pilgrim Fathers Bradford and Winslow, commonly known as *Mourt's Relation*, in which a storm of February 4, 1621, is reported to have "caused much daubing of our houses to fall downe." Young believed the daubing to indicate use of log cabins, bringing to mind the chinking of the space between the logs with moss, and daubing the moss with clay to keep it in place, which was a common practice in Young's own time. But in the English speech of an earlier century "daub" meant to plaster; and the daubing which "fell downe" in the big rain of February 4, 1621, was clay plastering smeared

---

* For an excellent and detailed account of the subject see Harold R. Shurtleff's *The Log Cabin Myth*, edited by Samuel E. Morrison and published by Harvard University Press in 1939.

over the clapboards or interior sheathing of the Plymouth hovels—not log cabins.

The Reverend Mr. Young finished his book in 1840. Mr. Young, it should be added, was politically a Whig. The Whigs in 1840 were running William Henry Harrison for President. An opposition (Democratic) newspaper sneered editorially that the White House was too good for Harrison, who would doubtless be content—continued the editorial— with a log cabin and plenty of hard cider. In this editorial was the death rattle of the Democratic candidate, Martin Van Buren by name. With whoops of delight the Whigs grabbed at the phrase about a log cabin and hard cider. They went to work with a will to show that Harrison's opponent, Van Buren, was a horrible dude, an aristocrat who loved silks, gold spoons and such trumpery; while good old Harrison, the plain, honest backwoodsman, was content with a log cabin and cider.

Once the Whigs saw that they really had a fine issue, they carried it to the extremes of political imagination. They erected huge log cabins in towns and cities as rallying places where the thirsty were regaled with oratory and cider as free as it was hard and which the Democrats weakly alleged had been spiked with clear spirits. Log cabins were carried as floats in parades. Badges and replicas in miniature of the sturdy homes of American pioneers were distributed by the many thousand. Songs on the subject appeared.

Consider that in 1840 hundreds of thousands of Americans actually had been born and reared in log cabins. They liked the idea that the log cabin had come straight down to them from the immortal hands of the Pilgrim Fathers. It is wholly understandable that Whig Young, writing his history, leaned strongly to the theory—which he alone invented—of log cabins at Plymouth in the day when the moss was green on The Rock.

Then, on August 19, 1840, the great Dan'l Webster, speaking at Saratoga, felt it meet to apologize for *not* having been born in a log cabin. But his elder brothers and sisters had been, he averred, and he was glad, for the Webster log cabin had been "raised amid the snowdrifts of New Hampshire, at a period so early that, when the smoke first rose from its rude chimney, and curled over the frozen hills, there was no similar evidence of a white man's visitation between it and the settlements on the rivers of Canada." The remains of this log cabin, Black Dan'l went on, still existed, and "I make to it an annual visit. I carry my children to it, to teach them the hardships endured by the generations which have gone before them. . . ."

So, the myth got away to a fine start. It had first appeared, in all the authority of the printed page, at a period when Americans had begun to marvel at their own progress. They had come a long way in a short time. Now living in frame houses, many of them in mansions, they all liked to make virtue of their early struggles or those of their parents, with the savage wilderness. They had tamed it while they lived in log cabins; and forever more the log cabin, the true frontier abode, was the symbol on their coat of arms.

Webster was not the only great man to speak of the crude dwelling of his fathers. From 1840 down through the years to the present day Presidents, Vice Presidents, and lesser candidates for office have let it to be known, with varying degrees of truth but always with sonorous words, that they had been born and reared in the classic house of the old frontier. It was considered a wonderful advantage in attracting the vote of the common man.

Graphic art, as usually happens, presently came forward to make the log cabin myth even more real. In 1858–75 appeared John G. Palfrey's huge *History of New England*, and in it the author included a right pretty drawing which had been made by Washington Allston, one of the best-known artists of his time. The drawing was of a handsome log cabin, and Palfrey captioned it "House of an Early Settler," by which he meant the days of the Pilgrims and Puritans. Palfrey's history immediately took its place as the great authority in schools and libraries, not only in New England but in many other states. Then, in or about 1887, a series of pictures by W. L. Williams started to appear. One of these pictures was of an all-log-cabin Plymouth, as of about 1620. It is beautifully done, and is clear and sharp down to the finest detail. It shows a pioneer village such as any American would be glad to think of as the home of his forefathers and the germ of the United States. This picture of an idealized Plymouth was reproduced in thousands of copies and framed and hung in almost every schoolhouse in the North and West, and in many in the South. The same picture was made into a postcard, and millions of them have been mailed home by tourists in the past half century.

From the period of the appearance of the Williams picture to the present, there is no telling how many artists have made free with early colonial settlements and their mythical log cabins; but as late as 1925 the group of high-toned Yale professors who edited the handsome *The Pageant of America*, included in its pages not only the all-log-cabin Plymouth, but a brand new all-log-cabin Jamestown by Artist H. A. Ogden.

Thus has one of our most popular historical myths been both preserved down to the present day and enhanced. In 1945, a weekly news-magazine, in a story about a family of scholars, pointed out with pride approaching awe that all of the members of this remarkable family had been born in a log cabin. One feels certain that this fact made of them better, truer Americans than would have been the case had they been born in a city flat or in a gaudy horror of the mansard era. The magic still prevails.

For a hundred years pictures of log cabins have been used on flags, posters, cards, letterheads, coats of arms, tableware;

in advertisements of patent medicines, groceries, undertakers, banks, trucking concerns, hotels; and made into registered trade marks.

For all these things, Americans may thank Historian
Alexander Young, who knew not the seventeenth-century
meaning of "daub," plus the Presidential campaign of 1840,
and subsequent artists and orators. For the log cabin itself,
however, we must thank those Swedes who unwittingly introduced what Americans to this day believe to be, and hail
with pride as, the one distinctive and unique American contribution to architecture, other than the steel skyscraper,
and possibly the silo. Its arrival in 1638 was perhaps the
most influential single event, and certainly the least known,
to occur in the American colonies until Samuel Adams staged
the Boston Massacre, one hundred and thirty-two years later.

CHAPTER II

The Great Agitator

IT WAS commonly believed by boys and girls of past generations, and the belief is still widespread and very deep —for such is the power of accumulated indoctrination—that the American Revolution was caused chiefly by a mob of Boston patriots who, for some vague reason having to do with taxes, boarded a ship in the harbor and tossed into the sea countless chests of tea belonging to nobody but George the Third of England, a bestial character without parallel in all history. The king, not liking to have his tea destroyed, thereupon hired a pack of mercenaries called Hessians, added millions of his own redcoats—barbarous fellows to a man—and sent the lot of them over here to put the poor and honest colonists in their place.

The canon continues along the classic line, and most of us have come out of our school days with the general impression that the Revolution was a spontaneous uprising of embattled farmers, a sudden combustion of patriotism and pitchforks, when every rustic became a Minute Man, every Minute Man a hero (except notably Benedict Arnold), equal to six Hessian soldiers or ten British redcoats, and who sprang to arms at the first alarm. (*"If they mean to have a war,"* said Captain *John Parker, "then let it begin here."*) Not only did they fairly leap for their muskets, but they continued to fight day and night until the glorious Republic was an accomplished fact.

This pleasant imbecility, which I have enjoyed as much as the next man, has been kept alive through a century and a half by poets, by historians, editorial writers, artists, and orators, much to the detriment of the United States of America. It is the chief reason why our country has never yet gone prepared into a war. And it was possible to impose the imbecility on us because we Americans, as perhaps no other people on earth, much prefer romantic fiction to fact.

Actually, the first certainty about the Revolution is that it was carefully planned by a few shrewd men and carried out by homemade and talented and ruthless agitators, whom historians have seen fit to call statesmen, and by military leaders of little experience but of great adaptability. The second certainty is that the great mass of American colonists were either passive to the revolt, or actively opposed to it. John Adams, no man for overstatement, estimated that throughout the war not more than one-third of the colonists were heart-and-soul in the Revolution; and this number was unquestionably much smaller previous to the Declaration. Hence, our glorious revolt in the cause of pure Liberty was in reality a struggle, on the part of a few able and active minds, to impose an idea on the mass of the people and to make them fight and if necessary die for it; and finally to make Great Britain recognize it as fact. This took, as they say, some doing.

The staging of "popular" revolts since the times of ancient Greece has always been accomplished by the use of propaganda in word and deed, sometimes known in the trade as "agitating." The American colonies were fortunate in having a number of agitators fit to compare with the best in world history, and the foremost of these Americans was Samuel Adams, a man who has been ignored or cavalierly treated by too many writers. The reason for this treatment, I suspect, probably stems from the typical American desire to have America's heroes unadulterated, to ignore such realistic methods as Adams propounded and used. *This* Adams, a poor relation of John and John Quincy and the least known of the Historical Adamses, was the one who stopped at nothing. Lies, subterfuge, misrepresentation of all sorts, and violation of confidences were his common practice in anything dealing with the Crown, or with Tories, or with anybody he said was a Tory. He would as lief slug, figuratively of course, a man from behind as in front. No fencer saw and took advantage of an opening, a dropped guard, more quickly. And when he thought it necessary, Samuel Adams did not stop short of cold-blooded arrangements for producing thoroughly dead Patriot Martyrs, a useful commodity in any agitation program.

Son of a Boston family dating from Genesis, graduate of Harvard, where he discovered that theology bored him, Samuel Adams failed as a counting-room clerk, then ran his father's prosperous brewing business into bankruptcy. He dabbled too much in politics to run a business. With the help of his many friends in Boston's political clubs he was elected to the General Court, as Massachusetts Bay Colony termed its legislature; and then was made tax collector of the city, a job he permitted to get out of hand to the amount of five thousand pounds and which brought him no end of embarrassment. Meanwhile, however, he absorbed many ideas of government from local politicians, especially from the tragic and able James Otis, soon to die a madman.

No matter what Adams seemed to be doing, he was playing politics, seeking to bring about a revolt of the American colonies, and their eventual independence. The dirtier the politics, the better Adams liked it. He enjoyed hearing an opponent grunt, when Adams landed one well below the belt. No man to strut, he preferred to pull the strings, to direct others in carrying out the plan he had in mind many years before other patriots had even conceived of such an idea.

There can be little doubt that Adams was the first man in all the colonies to have the idea of a United States, free and independent; and to carry it into execution he bent his every effort and talent, which was a talent for propaganda and subversive organization that approached genius. If George Washington was the Father of his Country, then Sam Adams was assuredly the Father of the American Revolution, and 'tis high time we added his birthday to our list of holidays.*

Adams began his subversive work in the 1760's, when the mercantile and navigation acts were bearing down hard on Boston's shipping and business generally. Middle-aged now, stricken with palsy, dressed in clothes rusty with age and giving to many "a misleading air of infirmity," he frequented the Green Dragon, the Bunch of Grapes, and other taverns where, as his tart cousin John remarked, "both bastards and legislators are often begotten." When he heard mechanics or laborers or businessmen complaining about hard times, Adams promptly told them the fault was England's. And gradually he imparted his ideas to John Adams, his lawyer country cousin, and to other professional men like Dr. Joseph Warren. He worked subtly and with great success on John Hancock, one of the town's wealthiest young men, and made of him, if Tories of the time are to be believed, the "Milch Cow of Whiggery." Hancock's money paid for many of the broadsides and posters that Adams put out to inflame the populace; and the same source bought the oats needed by P. Revere and other couriers dispatched on subversive rides by Adams.

Adams had long been friendly with Paul Revere, the silversmith. Nor did he neglect the lowly; one who claimed Adams as a friend was Andrew McIntosh, a truly frightful thug, illiterate, brutal, savage, who was the leader of a gang of waterfront toughs. Adams was a thorough organizer who knew he needed intellectual lieutenants no more than he did a goodly mob of shoulder-hitters and eye-gougers.

---

* Samuel Adams was born in Boston on the "sixteenth day of Septbr at twelve of the Clock at noon, being Sabbath day, 1722." This was Old Style. The corresponding date on the present calendar is September 27.

One of Adams's earliest moves was to amalgamate two or more of the local gangs of rowdies and impress on their leaders that fighting for what Adams called "Liberty" was much better than fighting each other. He promised he would find them plenty of outlet for their notable brawling tendencies. The opportunity soon arose.

At this period Boston merchants had agreed not to import any British commodities for sale, but at least eight of them were known to have broken their word. One of these was Theophilus Lilly. Street toughs presently placed a pole with a wooden head at its top in front of Lilly's house. From the pole a wooden finger pointed accusingly at his store. Merchant Lilly was much disturbed. A friend, one Richardson, variously described as "a stout man" and an "infamous informer," attempted to pull down the pole and effigy. The toughs pelted him with stones. Whereupon Richardson went into Lilly's house, reappeared with a musket and shot into the crowd. Christopher Snyder, aged eleven, was killed.

It is now possible to see plainly the hand of the Great Agitator at work. The boy's funeral, arrangements for which were unquestionably made by Sam Adams, was of the stuff that enshrines martyrs. The coffin, on which was inscribed "Innocence Itself is not Safe"—hyperbole of the worst sort —was taken to the Liberty Tree, says an old account, and there a great concourse assembled and followed the remains to the grave. Six of the dead boy's comrades supported the coffin, and in their wake marched some five hundred school boys and girls, followed in turn by "nearly fifteen hundred of the inhabitants." It was probably the biggest funeral Boston had seen.

It was also the most impressive. While the silent procession made its way, the deep bells of the city's churches tolled mournfully, being answered by those of meetinghouses in Cambridge, Dorchester, and Charlestown, for among Adams's friends were the parsons of local and near-by congregations.

It was a solemn occasion, and political too. The *Boston Gazette* discovered, surprisingly in one so young, that "The Little Hero had Shewn signs of Martial Genius and would have made a Clever man." Sam Adams had long been a leading contributor to the *Gazette*. Other papers took up the cry and within the week had apotheosized young Snyder into the First Martyr to American Liberty.

Such was the way in which a master of propaganda handled a street row.

Right on the heels of the Snyder incident came the "Bloody Massacre in King-Street." Its immediate inception was a drunken row between the King's soldiers and workers in a ropewalk near the waterfront. Noses were bloodied. Small mobs gathered in many parts of town. A particularly large mob gathered near Faneuil Hall and listened to a harangue by a "gentleman in red cloak and red wig." This may have been Adams. There is no record of what the man said, but it must have been enough, for as soon as he was done his audience began to shout "To the main guard!" and "Kill the lobsterbacks!" They struck out immediately for King (now State) Street where the Customhouse and a guard of the soldiery were located.

It was night now, the 5th of March, 1770. The moon was up, lighting the snowy streets. The little square around the State House, near the Customs, was already packed with civilians when the mob from Faneuil Hall arrived. Among them was Crispus Attucks, an enormous mulatto with white, Negro and Indian blood in his veins. A crowd of sailors and ropewalk workers followed Attucks, who carried a wicked club and shouted that he was going to remove some of the claws from the lobsterbacks. He poked a red-coated sentry in the ribs. The sentry called the guard. The guard turned out under Captain Preston, fighting its way through the crowd to the sentry's side.

The crowd pressed harder on the soldiers. Preston gave orders to prime and load, and there was a moment of silence, except for the metallic rattle and solid thump of iron ramrods. Preston took his position in front of the soldiers to prevent them from firing without orders. It was a tight spot. The vast dusky Attucks came close, swinging his big club. He made a swing at Preston, missed, but knocked down one of the soldiers. Gunfire echoed in the narrow streets.

The mob heaved backward, the stench of black powder in their noses, stumbling over one another to get out of there as quickly as possible. Those who lingered saw five bodies on the hard-packed snow, which was now running red in the bright moonlight. Crispus Attucks was dead. So were Sam Gray and James Caldwell. Sam Maverick and Patrick Carr moaned and shuddered. They were carried away to die later of their wounds.

Such was the Boston Massacre itself. Tried in a Boston court and courageously defended by John Adams and Josiah Quincy, six of the soldiers, including Captain Preston, were freed. Two other soldiers were found guilty, not of murder, but of manslaughter. They were branded on the hand in open court, then discharged.

Evidence at the trial, in spite of John Adams's care not to probe too deeply into the origin of the riot, indicated the affair to have been carefully planned by unnamed civilians.

The freeing of the soldiers by a jury of citizens seemed at first a blow to the so-called patriot cause. So it would have been except for Sam Adams, who was equal to the occasion. In the *Boston Gazette's* next issue he shouted to ask if this was "ye only satisfaction the publick has got for the MURDER of 5 men?" He recalled that the very dogs of the town had been seen "greedily licking human BLOOD in King-Street." Before this maddening thought could sink into public consciousness, he had Paul Revere, the local engraver, silversmith, dentist, and Son of Liberty, prepare cuts of "5 Coffings for Massacre" which appeared in the *Gazette* along with some rousing prose by one Vindex, who was

Samuel Adams.* The dead mobsters became heroes without peer—pure, patriotic, Christianlike martyrs. Adams sent copies to tavern keepers all over New England and New York. He reminded his readers, too, that it had been a vile Tory who had butchered the innocent lad, Christopher Snyder. But, weep not, said Vindex, weep not for that martyr of tender age. Revenge him. Vindex thought it was time for action.

Paul Revere and Henry Pelham, half brother to the artist John Singleton Copley, now got busy. Between them they concocted an engraving for a broadside that was on sale by March 26. This was a print of "The Bloody Massacre perpetrated in King-Street Boston on March 5 1770 by a party of the 29th Regt.," and it was probably the greatest single piece of propaganda put out during the entire era. It was of the stuff to inflame the weak-hearted, to send stout Whigs into spasms of hate. The drawing, like all such propaganda since, has little or no bearing on fact. As a "representation of the Horred Affair" nothing could well have been more inaccurate; here was subversive genius at work.

The picture shows seven lobster-coated soldiers, dressed in perfect line, shooting into a gathering of exactly nineteen civilians. (Contemporary accounts indicate the mob to have numbered more than a thousand persons.) The face of each redcoat is carefully shown, and no face fails to reveal either arrogance or hate, or both; and behind them their captain, Preston, waves his sword in the air, apparently shouting orders to fire and meantime retaining a casual sneer on his cruel face.

As for the "patriots," they are shown dying like flies, and bleeding like stuck pigs. Never has patriot bled so as these sanguinary men. The blood appears to be gushing from

---

* In that era nothing was better to rouse emotion than a nice row of black coffins reproduced with a newspaper article. The same idea was used later, after the battles of Lexington and Concord. Patriots eyed the grim containers and fumed for Tory blood. *Vindex* was Adams's most favored pseudonym, but he also used *Candidens* and *Valerius Poplicola*.

wounds, veritable holes, that could have been made with nothing less than a ship's auger. Attucks, the big colored man,
is down in the snow. In the background is the Customhouse,
labeled Butcher's Hall. Beneath the picture are three
strophes of doggerel beginning:

Unhappy Boston! See thy Sons Deplore,
Thy hallowed Walks besmear'd with guiltless gore.

Sam Adams's propaganda took effect. The troops were
moved to Castle William, in Boston Harbor. In England,
Parliament canceled the hated duties on everything—except
tea. Merchants of Boston voted to lift the boycott on British
goods. Shipping picked up. Employment increased. The affair had sort of boomeranged on Adams, and the ensuing
period of surface calm obliged the old agitator to produce
new "menaces" and remind his public of old horrors. He
must prevent the slothful colonists from reverting to their
peaceful and, to Adams, their sheeplike ways.

Adams was equal to it. He staged a monster observance on
the anniversary of the Massacre, when all church bells were
tolled, this time for a solid hour; and funeral orations, filled
with more politics than theology, were made by the many
Congregational ministers whom Adams called his Black
Regiment. In the evening there was "a very striking Ex-
hibition at the Dwelling House of Mr. Paul Revere, fronting
Old North Square," and "at one of the Chamber Windows
was the Appearance of the Ghost of the unfortunate
Snyder." Adams was bound that young Snyder's ghost
should walk until and if he could arrange for newer martyrs.
The Boston papers, including the red-hot *Massachusetts
Spy* edited by Isaiah Thomas, gave this and later anniver-
saries of the Massacre much prominence.

Governor Francis Bernard of Massachusetts had given up
his distasteful job and returned to England; and presently
Thomas Hutchinson, the lieutenant-governor and a native of
Massachusetts, was appointed governor. Hutchinson was a

well-disposed and able man, and the country people of the province, especially, welcomed him to the post; they considered him a true native son who could do no wrong. Sam Adams set out immediately to prove how mistaken they were, to prove, no less, that Hutchinson was the most horrible tyrant since the Roman Empire. He raked up "horrid examples" from Roman history to show how natives of Rome had always been the worst tyrants of their home province, and applied the analogy to Hutchinson. He did everything possible to blacken the new governor's public and private character and wound up by calling him an "oligarch," which doubtless sounded to the simple countrymen of the province like a combination of horse thief, sodomist, and Tory.

Adams also began organizing committees of correspondence, a euphemism for an undercover movement that was to completely wreck the complacency of the colonists, not only in New England but elsewhere. Tried and true patriots in every town and community were to keep each other informed of any action of Crown officials, or other Tories, and to be ready to act as "a band of brothers, which no force can break, no enemy destroy." Such committees had been used in the colonies since the beginnings of the controversy with England, but they had been rather pale and innocuous. These that Adams was forming were to be subversive and downright revolutionary. He took pains that they should be.

Now another incident occurred to rouse the sluggards. In spite of the general lightening of customs duties, smuggling was going on at a great rate. In June of 1772 the Crown's revenue cutter *Gaspée*, stationed in Narragansett Bay expressly to hamper Rhode Island's leading industry, fired on a packet which failed to stop, gave chase, and ran aground at Namquit, where a fast-ebbing tide left her high. The packet continued on to Providence and brought news of the affair to "Mr. John Brown, a leading merchant of that place."

John Brown was not only "a leading merchant" of Providence. Two years before he had laid with his own hand the cornerstone of Brown University's Hall; and he was ever a man of action. He thought that the *Gaspée's* plight delivered into patriot hands a fine opportunity to put an end to that "vexatious ship"—which no doubt had caused trouble for some of Mr. Brown's own vessels. So, Brown sent Daniel Pearce along Providence's Main Street, beating the life out of a drum, shouting the news, and inviting all stout-hearted men to join in a voyage for Liberty. Meanwhile Brown prepared a fleet of longboats. That night sixty-four men set out. As they approached the beached *Gaspée*, her commander challenged, then fired a pistol. Thomas Bucklin, one of the patriots, or pirates, returned the fire against orders and wounded the *Gaspée's* captain. The seagoing mob then boarded the revenue ship, took off her crew, and set her afire. She presently blew up and sank. Her crew was set on shore and the wounded captain given medical attention.

Large rewards were offered by the Crown for information leading to arrest of the pirates. Brown was arrested, but no witnesses could be found. He was released. The inevitable broadsides appeared at once, placing further curses on the Crown and its revenue boats. And these new inflammations had in no manner subsided when the Crown resolved to pay the salaries of Massachusetts judges, heretofore paid by the province. Samuel Adams, happy at this turn of events, now opened up with all of his horrors. "A bribe," he shouted from broadside and newspaper. He demonstrated, at least to his own satisfaction, that this "bribery" would make the American colonists "as complete slaves as the inhabitants of Turkey or Japan." It was time, he went on with great choler, to "strike a home blow, or sit down under the Yoke of TYRANNY." He was very fond of capital letters.

The Adams yeast was working famously in this year of comparative surface calm. One thing and one thing only seems to have driven this middle-aged man from the mid-

1760's to the end: the overthrow of English government in the colonies. It was his mainspring, his whole drive, his life. No one has been able to find an ulterior (commercial) motive in Adams's desire for an independent country. In this respect he stands almost alone among his fellows, the archetype of the revolutionary agitator.

Now that he had turned his sardonic powers on the committees of correspondence, the results soon became apparent. Marblehead, Newburyport, Charlestown, and many smaller towns throughout New England appointed committees. It was the same in other provinces. Intercolonial underground was established with committees as far south as Charlestown in Carolina.

To keep the always suspicious countrymen from thinking that Boston city men were *leading* them into trouble, Adams put out a lot of sheer pap about "his sensible Brethren in the country" and how the Boston folk were "imitating" the resolution of the small villages to "oppose TYRANNY in all its forms." This sort of thing, done with complete cynicism, flattered the rustics all the way up-country to Bennington in the New Hampshire Grants.

Adams also made certain that the committees in all of the colonies were given regular dosages of raw, red meat in the form of new horrors. He drew up a truly staggering list of "repressions" from which he said the honest colonists were suffering at the hands of cruel Ministerial Tools, and sent it broadcast. Few of the honest colonists had any conception of the irreparable injuries being perpetrated on them by the Crown until they read Adams's seething and all-but-groundless indictments.

By 1773, at least, it was apparent that these committees of correspondence were the answer to an agitator's prayer. Isaac Sears and John Lamb of New York, Patrick Henry in Virginia, and the notable Christopher Gadsden in South Carolina, all left-wingers in their respective regions, were quick to circulate the Adams brand of poison, and to elaborate on it—if that were possible. It seems hardly too much to say that the committees of correspondence were the genesis of the United States of America.

Late in 1773 Adams created a tremendous noise in New England when through Benjamin Franklin he got hold of letters written years before by Hutchinson, now royal governor of Massachusetts. Paying no attention to Franklin's admonition not to make them public, Adams promptly had them read to the General Court, then published and broadcast. There was really little in the letters to give offense; little, that is, until Adams gave them his own interpretation. He intermingled his own remarks with the text of the letters to such an extent that the total effect of the concoction was to ruin any influence Hutchinson may still have had with half-hearted patriots.

Adams followed this blow—one of the dirtiest pieces of fighting possible—by having the Massachusetts General Court address the King and request Hutchinson's removal. (This was the period that caused Hutchinson to refer to Adams as "The Grand Incendiary of the Province.")

Now came the celebrated Tea Party about which every American has heard, and about which almost no American knows anything. This is not strange, for few if any general histories have gone into the elaborate preparations made by Adams to bring it about.

The Party, like the Massacre, was no sudden and accidental clash between the Crown officers and the so-called patriots. It was manufactured to order, custom-built, with a genius that overshadowed Adams's comparatively simple if bloody plans for the Massacre. The Tea Party, in fact, and although it has become one of our symbols, is of importance to political history chiefly because of the malignantly clever methods used by Adams to stage it. The opportunity was furnished free by England; the great East India Company, virtually a part of the English government, found itself short of cash and long on tea. It had applied to Parliament for aid and had been granted a monopoly on all tea imported by the American colonies. The company, fully as ignorant of the American colonies as were the King and his ministers, decided in an extremely unfortunate moment to peddle its wares in America through its own appointed agents, thus eliminating independent merchants. The decision caused colonial businessmen, many of whom heretofore had been staunch Tories, to ally themselves with the Whig radicals. Here was government monopoly in all its brazen hideousness—as Sam Adams took pains to point out.

In late November (1773) three ships loaded with the East India Company's product arrived in Boston harbor and anchored below Castle William. They were thus not yet officially in the Port of Boston, a measure Governor Hutchinson had ordered because of conditions in the city. These conditions amounted to an impasse: Adams and his crew feared that if the tea were landed, the Yankees would buy and drink it, thus paying the tea tax, and in so doing "would drink themselves out of their liberties." Or, at least so Adams informed them.

Governor Hutchinson demanded of the East India Company that the tea be landed. But by this time he knew that Adams would stop at nothing to prevent it. So, he had the ships anchor just outside the port where, if things went badly in the town, they could return to England with their cargoes intact. If, however, the ships once actually docked at Boston and were then unable to discharge their cargoes, they would be liable to confiscation on their return to England. This was the law, made so by an act of Parliament providing that no dutiable merchandise could be returned to England *in the same ship* it went out in, without a pass or certificate from the governor of the colony to which the cargoes had been consigned. The governor, in turn, could not give such a pass without a receipt from the Customhouse that the duty had been paid. Governor Hutchinson, in holding the three East India Company's ships away from the port, was simply playing safe.

Safe? Not with Adams loose. Adams had his Liberty Boys board the ships and summon their captains to appear before the Boston committee of correspondence. There he ordered the skippers to bring their ships alongside Griffin's wharf, unless they wanted, he told them, a coat of tar and feathers. That was the kind of gangster old Sam Adams could be. The captains must have taken the order to heart, for the ships were docked at once, as ordered; and now Adams had meetinghouse bells rung and boys sent through town distributing incendiary handbills. But this was not enough. Adams sent couriers, including the ever-ready Revere, to committees in other parts of New England. His message was to the effect that if this tea were landed, it would be a mere opening wedge for England to tax everything needed or used by the colonies.

Governor Hutchinson refused to give the ships clearance to return to England until the Customhouse gave him a receipt for the duties; the Customhouse refused to give the governor such a receipt until the duties were paid; the consignees of the tea did not dare, what with Adams ringing bells and passing handbills, to pay the duties and attempt to unload the tea. Instead, the consignees were so frightened at the uproar that they left town and took refuge in Castle William. Sam Adams had now brought about a dilemma that made his heart glad.

Setting muscular patriots to watch the moored ships to prevent unloading of the tea—or departing—Adams called a "general muster" in Faneuil Hall where he told a large crowd about the dangers to liberty inherent in taxed tea. He intimated strongly there was only one thing to be done with such tea, and left it to his audience to figure out what he meant—which was not difficult, even for the dim-witted. Daily meetings of this sort continued in the Hall. The muscular Liberty Boys still watched the ships. The 17th of

December was a sort of deadline, the day on which the ships would become liable to seizure by customs officials for non-payment of duty.

Adams hardly slept during this period. He still feared that if any of the tea were landed at all, it would somehow get into colonists' teapots and be drunk, thus corrupting them beyond mending. On the 16th he called a meeting that brought several thousand persons, too many for Faneuil Hall; the meeting adjourned to the Old South Meeting House, and overflowed into the street. Josiah Quincy and others addressed them. At a quarter to six, just as candles were being lighted, Sam Adams stood up and took the floor. "This meeting," he declared in his palsied voice, "can do nothing more to save the country."

It was a prearranged signal. It set off immediate shouting. "Boston harbor a teapot tonight!" Adams's mob was well organized. Down through the narrow streets groups of men and boys moved swiftly and silently to Griffin's wharf. There they divided into three companies, boarded the three ships, and tossed overboard all of the tea. When the tide rose that night, and fell, the shore from the wharf to Dorchester was one long windrow of the East India Company's best bohea tea.*

Other cargoes of the East India Company's vile product were rejected at New York and Philadelphia and returned to England intact. Another consignment, to Charleston, South Carolina, was landed and stored in damp cellars where "it soon became worthless."

It was the job at Boston that echoed in Parliament. England closed the Port of Boston to all commerce, and did so effectively. It moved the seat of provincial government from Boston to Salem. It altered the charter of the colony and provided that henceforth certain important officials should

---

* A small vial of tea, said by the Bostonian Society to be the authentic article, is to be seen in a room in the Old State House, Boston.

be appointed by the Crown, instead of elected by the people. Lastly, it sent General Thomas Gage, commander in chief of the British forces in America, to be governor of Massachusetts Bay colony.

These measures were exactly what Samuel Adams wanted. He promptly called them the Intolerable Acts, and went into a fury in his correspondence with other committees. Here, he said, was what ye cruel Ministerial Tools would impose on honest and patriotic men. Were other colonies going to stand idly by while Liberty was taken away, first from one, then another? Rhode Island proposed a continental congress to discuss matters. Connecticut and New York offered the idea of "a congress of deputies from all the colonies." Virginia's House of Burgesses was dissolved by the governor for its radical acts, but met again without the governor's sanction and declared boldly that an attack on one colony was an attack on all. . . . The committees of correspondence were beginning to function in the manner Sam Adams had meant them to.

Adding blunder to blunder, Parliament next passed the Quebec Act, guaranteeing by statute the freedom of worship to the Catholics of that province. Adams hit the ceiling. "They would make us papists," he shouted; * and the committees of correspondence were presently notified that the Pope and his minions might land at any time and take charge of all theology in North America. It was a thought, said Adams, to make men shudder.

Although Adams made a good deal of a bogey out of the papist menace, of greater interest to the colonies was another clause of the Quebec Act—the one that extended Quebec's boundaries southward to the Ohio River. Such a division would conflict with claims of Massachusetts, Connecticut,

---

* It is obvious that when Samuel Adams called anyone a papist he meant one or more of several things—a communicant of the Church of England, a Roman Catholic, or simply anyone, even a Freethinker, who was opposed to anything that Adams favored.

and Virginia to lands in the west. It will be remembered, also, that a number of large land companies thought they owned great hunks of the land which would be alienated by the Quebec Act.

The colony of Virginia now presented a specific plan for a Continental Congress, a suggestion that had been made by Adams a number of times, both in spoken word and in writing. The Virginia plan was heartily endorsed by other provincial legislatures, and on September 5, 1774, fifty-three delegates representing all colonies except Georgia met at Philadelphia. Among them was Samuel Adams.

It is indicative of the man, of his fanatical one-mindedness, that when he was elected as a delegate to the First Continental Congress, Adams did not possess sufficient decent clothing to appear in a public gathering. He probably would have gone as he was, attired in seedy coat and patched breeches, had not his fellow delegates made up a purse for the explicit purpose of buying presentable clothing for the Great Agitator. He did buy it, including some new shoes and buckles, and away they went to Philadelphia.

The First Continental Congress drew up a Declaration of Colonial Rights, both moderate and dignified, and sent it to the King. It also formed an American Association, by which the colonies expanded the idea inherent in the committees of correspondence and agreed among themselves not to import or consume British goods until redress for grievances was obtained. Committees of safety were to be appointed in every town, and among their duties was that of noting and reporting any citizen who refused to abide by the Association agreement.

The First Continental Congress adjourned after making provision for a second meeting on May 10, 1775, unless redress had been made before that time. Sam Adams returned to Boston with a determination to prevent any such calamity as redress being given to anyone. At this period, a truce, a concilation with England, would have been welcome to a large majority of the Continental Congress delegates, but not to the Old Roman of Boston. On his jolting way homeward from Philadelphia, Adams must have been turning over in his mind the several possibilities for further subversive work.*

In the meantime, General Thomas Gage had arrived in Boston with four regiments of troops; and a small British navy, guns ready, rocked at anchor in the harbor. Gage had been given orders to put down the rebels in Massachusetts, to discipline the people there, and specifically to arrest Samuel Adams and John Hancock and to send them to England to be tried as leaders of the rebels.

Adams had now almost achieved the war that he, and he almost alone, had been working up to for these past ten years. It was now time for the shooting to begin, and begin it did. This first brush of arms was not on Lexington Green, nor at Concord Bridge, but in the wilds of New Hampshire, where no poet caught the echo to tell of the shot that was heard round the world. Yet the Battle of Fort William and Mary deserves better treatment than it has had.

Early in December (1774) some alert undercover agent for Adams learned that General Gage was about to send an expedition to Portsmouth, New Hampshire, to strengthen Fort William and Mary there. The fort contained "goodly store of powder and ammunition." Gage well knew that militia companies were drilling everywhere in New England. The Portsmouth fort was isolated. The colonial militia, Gage knew, had little powder of its own. The fort was manned by a small company of soldiers.

Adams made an effort to forestall Gage, and presently Paul Revere was pounding north through a wintry night on the most important of all his many rides. On the next afternoon, December 13, he arrived at John Sullivan's home on

* Remarked a fellow delegate, Joseph Galloway, of Adams: "He eats little, drinks little, sleeps little, thinks much."

the Oyster River in Durham, near Portsmouth. Sullivan, a lawyer and farmer, had been drilling the local boys for several months. He had also written Samuel Adams and others urging the colonies to take action for complete independence. He was a born leader of men, and spoiling for war. Revere's message was all he needed.

Sullivan sent his hired man around to muster a select group of his militia boys. After dark that night they floated down the river in short, squat boats called gundalows to Portsmouth, poled their awkward craft as close to the fort as they could, then waded ashore, and Sullivan demanded surrender. The commander of the fort, Captain Corcoran, although surprised, refused surrender and he and his men began shooting. They hit nobody, and presently gave up. For the rest of the night Sullivan and his men worked like beavers, wading waist-deep in the cold water to transfer to their boats ninety-seven kegs of gunpowder, a few small cannon, and a number of muskets. The weather had turned what even residents of New Hampshire allowed was cold. The river froze solid. For the next two days and nights the expedition slowly cut a channel upstream through the ice in order to get its booty to Durham and hide it. Gunpowder was to be a tragic shortage to the Americans in the opening days of the war, and the powder that brave Sullivan and his men took at William and Mary was used to good advantage a bit later at Bunker Hill. It had been a close shave, too, for the powder had scarcely been landed up-river and hidden when the British frigate *Scarborough* arrived at Portsmouth expressly to take the fort's supplies to Boston.

Revere waited at Durham until he knew the outcome of the expedition, then returned to Boston with the good news. Henceforth Revere was a marked man, under suspicion of Gage. He could no longer get a pass out of the city. From now on he kept a small rowboat hidden in North Boston, close by the Charles River.

King George in England was greatly vexed when he learned of the raid on his fort of William and Mary. He sent orders to General Gage to arrest and punish every man connected with it and to seize immediately all war supplies of the rebels.

This peremptory order doubtless reminded Gage that he had not yet been able to arrest Sam Adams, for whom he had been looking, in his casual sort of way, for several months. Gage had a pretty smart spy system of his own, and he was soon informed of two things: One, that the rebels had gathered a sizable supply of military stores at Concord; and two, that Sam Adams and John Hancock were in hiding outside Boston, probably in Lexington.

Dr. Joseph Warren was now acting as chief of the Liberty Boys in Boston. On March 5, in keeping with Sam Adams's old custom, he had gone to the Old South Church and there, under the noses of many British officers who had been sent to listen for subversive utterances, Warren had given the anniversary sermon on the victims of the Boston Massacre. The meeting came off without incident.

Then, early in April, Warren learned that Gage was to send an expedition to capture the patriot stores at Concord and to arrest Adams and Hancock. Warren sent Revere to warn those two men of their danger and to suggest hiding the stores in a new place. Revere made this daylight ride on a Sunday, April 15. The stores were moved and re-hidden. Adams and Hancock promised to be on guard. On the 18th, when British troops were actually moving out of Boston, Warren sent Revere riding again, and also Billy Dawes, one of the best horsemen in the colony. This, incidentally, was the ride—the least important of all Revere's many rides—that made both Revere and Henry W. Longfellow famous, by a poem as inaccurate as it is blood-tingling. The poem had no effect on Dawes.

Both Dawes and Revere reached Lexington, where they roused Adams and Hancock, and found the local Minute

Men, under Captain Parker, already alert and drinking rum in the Buckman tavern, hard by the Green. They, too, drank, and then, joined by young Samuel Prescott, who had been courting his girl, they started for Concord. On the road they were stopped by British troops. Revere was captured, and his horse was taken from him. Dawes escaped, but was thrown from his horse. Only Prescott got through to Concord with the alarm. By now, in any case, all of Middlesex county was aroused. Candles flickered in farmhouses all the way from Boston to Lexington, and on to Concord. There were shouts and noises of men getting their gear together. Women and girls were melting lead and running bullets.

Midnight had long since passed. It was the 19th of April, 1775. The main body of redcoats was moving out of Boston on the road to Lexington and Concord. It should not be forgotten for an instant that Sam Adams, the old agitator, was still in Lexington.

CHAPTER III

The Strange "Battle" of Lexington

In an inspired moment Ralph Waldo Emerson termed it the Shot Heard Round the World. He could also have called it, and with more accuracy, the triumph of Sam Adams's brand of agitating, but that would hardly have been poetry. Old Sam would not have cared, anyway, just so long as the shooting began. . . .

So, with mounted scouts well in advance, the British foot column moved quietly and swiftly out of Boston, then marched on through the night along the road to Lexington. In that hamlet, meanwhile, Captain John Parker, after consultation with Adams and John Hancock, roused his drummer boy, William Diamond, and the two went to the Green. The handsome village common was silent. All was still dark, and the air was damp with morning mist, but the drumhead was taut and true and the lad beat a long alarm roll that soon pounded into the ears of the sleeping militia, the Minutemen.

Although they scarcely could have known that the day was to make them, alive or dead, American heroes with few peers, the militia were fairly prompt. They rolled out of their straw ticks, took their muskets or fowling pieces, and congregated at the Buckman tavern, which stood square across the road from the Green. It was yet night, though the faint twilight of early morning was beginning to show when the last man appeared. Parker put them into company formation. They stood there a bit. Then Parker dismissed them, some going to their homes, others to the tavern. Yet, a little later Parker assembled them again. Why did he do so?

There are times when the narrative of history should be halted briefly to consider, on the spot, so to speak, the actions and also the possible motives of certain of the actors. The so-called Battle of Lexington is one such moment, for it was one of the oddest moments in our history. For well over a century a cloud of doubt has misted this minor yet celebrated action, and little wonder.

Captain John Parker, he who called the Minutemen, dismissed, then re-assembled them, was a soldier of considerable rough-and-tumble fighting experience in the French and Indian War. The Green where he stationed his handful of farmers was smack on the road down which the British must pass. Hills and thick woods, ideal for observation, were hard by; or, they could have served for ambush cover. Yet Parker chose the Green—open, level, and so close that his men must almost be brushed by the passing regulars, who were known to be on their way. Why did Parker pick this suicidal spot? It was merely asking for trouble, he and his rustics, all armed, standing by the wayside, inviting insult and molestation.

Was Captain Parker acting under orders, possibly orders from the Great Agitator, Sam Adams? Adams had been hiding in Lexington for days. He was the dynamo that started the revolutionary idea and kept it in motion. He had ably used the blood shed in King Street to rouse sluggards. He had diverted or perverted every possible incident in a successful effort to inflame the colonies. Now, on the 19th of April, 1775, did he feel it was time to draw the British fire again, to make some more Patriot Martyrs?

Here on the Green was a scattering of farmers, commanded by an experienced soldier who would be the last person, under ordinary circumstances and acting under his own free will, to oppose a long column of professional troops

THE HISTORICAL MUTATIONS OF A BATTLE
IN FOUR SCENES

BATTLE OF LEXINGTON AS REPORTED IN 1775

BATTLE OF LEXINGTON AS PAINTED IN 1830

The Battle of Lexington
From the drawing by Hammatt Billings

LEXINGTON AS IT APPEARED IN 1855

The Dawn of Liberty
From a painting by Henry Sandham

ALL RESTRAINT HAD VANISHED BY 1886

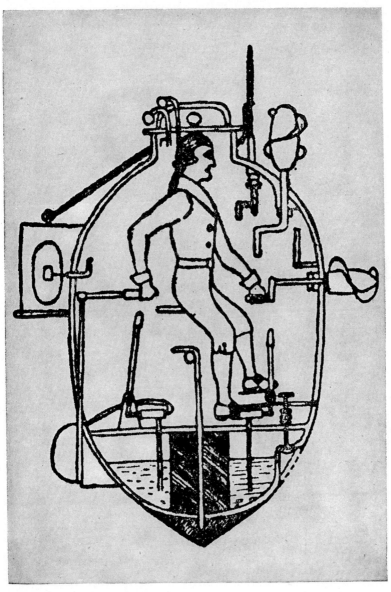

SERGEANT EZRA LEE GOES TO SEA IN THE *TURTLE*,
FIRST SUBMARINE, AUGUST 1776

GENERAL WASHINGTON ORDERS GENERAL CHARLES LEE
OFF THE FIELD IN LANGUAGE NOT REPORTED BY
PARSON WEEMS

with a squad of rustics. Yet there he and they stood, looking
squarely into the face of death. They must have been powerfully urged, more likely ordered, to take their impossible
stand. Any old Indian fighter like Parker would automatically have picked the nearby woods.

On came the British, and Major Pitcairn of the column
saw the assembled Minutemen. He ordered them to disperse,
calling them rebels, which they were. They started at once
to disperse. Pitcairn wished to surround them in order to
take away their arms. Killing, even wounding one of them
was his last thought. But as the militia were dispersing,
Pitcairn saw the flash of a pan from behind a fence. Another
flash. Pitcairn's horse was hit, and it reared, throwing the
Major to the ground.

Now the British began firing—without orders, Pitcairn
always maintained—and Americans fell on the Green. The
"battle" of Lexington was over, and without further ado
the British column moved on toward Concord.

Let them move while we consider briefly the history *of* the
history of the affair on Lexington Green. I cannot name
another incident which has undergone so many mutations,
and they are mutations, moreover, that can be accurately
measured. It all began, did this oddly changing history of
the Battle of Lexington, in 1824, almost fifty years afterward, when the Honorable Samuel Hoar, in welcoming the
Marquis de Lafayette on his visit to Concord, Massachusetts, spoke of the Battle of Concord, which occurred *after*
the Battle of Lexington, as being "the first forcible resistance to the Crown."

The people of Lexington did not take kindly to the reference. They objected to being thus nosed out of first-blood
honors; and an endless controversy with Concord began at
once, and with odd and fascinating results. These results
are to be seen in a succession of prints of the Battle of Lex-

ington, made between 1775 and 1886, which shows a remarkable and steadily increasing resistance on the part of the
Lexington patriots.

The first print, made by Doolittle and Earle in 1775, and
after consulting the Americans involved, shows the Minutemen dispersing in every direction. Not one of them displays
an attitude of fight; those farmers are getting out of there
as quickly as they can. The second print, made about 1830—
or six years after Samuel Hoar's famous oration on first-
blood—by Pendleton, shows that although the Minutemen
may still be said to be dispersing, yet nine devoted souls are
facing the foe, and of these seven are firing, two loading. The
third sketch, made by Billings in 1855, shows the dispersing
to be confined to the extreme left of the line, while the firing
and loading have been extended to no less than eighteen
stout-hearted patriots. And now comes the mural, done in
1886 by Hy Sandham, expressly for the Lexington town
hall. This throws off all restraint. There is no dispersing,
not even a shadow of wavering. *Here* is battle. The patriot
line holds from end to end, like a stone fence. Some of the
Minutemen are dying, but all others are either loading or
firing—emptying their muskets into the glittering target
offered by the British light infantry. . . . Let them who
will, write a nation's history. Give me the boys who draw
the pictures.

Few of us ever question the authenticity of a historical
picture, unless it conflicts with our desires, or preconceived
views. Yet of all the pictures of the Battle of Lexington,
that first print by Earle and Doolittle, drawn from information given the artists themselves by the obviously truthful
men who were present when the shooting started, must be
accepted as the most accurate; and it would seem also to
give weight to the supposition that the Minutemen were stationed on the Green, not with the idea of attempting battle
with the great column of British regulars but to provoke

the regulars into an "incident." I believe the affair was
staged in cold blood by Samuel Adams.*

It of course matters little who fired first at Lexington.
What matters is that this little band of farmers stood there,
insultingly close to the road, and precipitated bloody shooting. It should be remarked, too, that it was the rattle of
British and not American musketry on that hot dawn which
brought from Adams his oft-quoted line: "Oh what a glorious morning is this!" It is a grand, a stirring line, one
eminently fit to be cut in marble, one that came from deep
in the soul of him who felt that at last his mission had been
accomplished. He had supplied the formal battle, the
martyrs, to fan the Revolution into intense flame. The smoke
had hardly cleared when Adams and his crew of propa-
gandist helpers had dodgers, well bordered with the inevitable
black coffins, in circulation. Adams's version of the fray,
characteristically enough, was that it had been a wanton
and brutal and unprovoked assault on a few peaceful vil-
lagers.

The British only paused at Lexington that morning. On
they marched to Concord, and there still more patriots met
them at the famous bridge that arched the flood. Here there
was real fighting. And fighting continued. As every schoolboy knows, the embattled farmers gathered from a dozen
towns, following the British out of Concord, back to Lexington, and on half a mile to the Monroe tavern. Here Lord
Percy, with supporting troops for the harassed light infantry, made a brief stand, but the farmers were becoming
thick—and ornery as hornets. Percy formed his troops into
the classic hollow square, planted two small cannon on high
ground above the tavern, and received the retreating British
within his lines. They needed this respite, too, for many had

* For a thorough résumé of the Lexington prints, see Harold Murdock,
The 19th of April, 1775, Boston, 1923.

their tongues hanging out, says an old account, like those of dogs after a chase. Percy stood long enough for "light refreshments" to be served; then, after firing a salvo from his battery, the combined British forces started back to Boston.

On came the farmers, who pressed so close at West Cambridge that Percy stood about and a sharp skirmish ensued. Dr. Joseph Warren, Sam Adams's noted lieutenant, was in this fray and barely escaped with his life when a British bullet knocked a pin out of an ear-curl in his hair. Harassment of the miserable British continued until they reached the safety of Boston, after dark.

It had been a great day for the Americans, this 19th of April in '75, and out of it has issued some of the most glorious bombast we possess. Listen while Benson J. Lossing, one of our early historians, sums it up for posterity: "The events of that day," says he, and echoes can still be heard in our holiday oratory, "formed the first disruption of the chrysalis of old political systems, whence speedily came forth a noble and novel creature, with eagle eye and expansive wings, destined speedily to soar far above the creeping reptiles of despotism that brood amid the crumbling relics of old dynasties." Then, in full cry, Lossing reaches his climax. "These events," says he, "formed the significant prelude to that full diapason, whose thundering harmony, drawn forth by the magic touch of the new spirit of Freedom, filled the nations with wonder, and ushered in the New Era so long predicted and so long hoped for."

Lossing, like many another American writer since, then went on to indicate that the embattled farmers, dead shots to a man, had all but wrecked the British army in America. This cherished idea that Americans are by nature and practice veritable marksmen is a belief that has caused the United States incalculable harm, this past century and a half. Because of it we have believed that our citizen army, which

would magically spring to arms instantly—and which is another greatly cherished fatuity—would be composed almost
wholly of men who could shoot the eye out of a squirrel at a
hundred yards.

If the battles of Concord and Lexington proved anything,
they manifestly proved that our farmer-militia were anything but accurate with a gun. That they wreaked as much
destruction as they did was because there were so many of
them shooting. The British lost 73 killed, 174 wounded, and
26 missing, or a total of 273. The American losses were 49
killed, 39 wounded, and 5 missing, or a total of 93.

The British engaged numbered 1,800 men, while no less
than 3,763 Americans took part. Not one American in ten
hit a redcoat that seething day, and this is certainly not the
sharpshooting related in so many American history books.
It was no discredit to the Americans that they were rather
poor marksmen. They hardly could have been otherwise.
Powder had been uncommonly scarce for about five years.
The muskets used were not dependable above eighty yards,
and the best range was sixty yards; no rifles were in use.
There had been ho good hunting in eastern Massachusetts
for many years. And when farmers there did see and shoot
at a deer they used buckshot—much different than using a
ball in a smoothbore. Moreover, true shooting men are made
by constant practice. The yearly musters in Massachusetts
had long since degenerated into convivial gatherings, hardly
distinguishable from mass drunks. It is true that by 1774,
considerable attention began to be devoted to these musters,
but habit was still strong and powder was still scarce.

What these brave farmers used was a firelock gun. A flint
struck the lip or frizzen of the lock, the spark went into a
covered pan of powder; a slow flash set off the charge; slow-
burning powder sent a slow bullet along a heavily dropping
trajectory. In other words, a man had to aim very high over
his target if it were more than eighty yards distant, and
probably if it were more than sixty yards away.

There was no uniformity of powder or bullets. The bullets were made at home, usually by the women folk. A few of the Yankee farmers may still have carried the romantic powder horn as late as 1775—and to the glory of all Revolutionary murals since—but those of the so-called organized militia used cartridges made of a roll of paper containing ball and powder. Holding the cartridge by the bullet end, the soldier bit off the paper at the other end; he shook enough powder for priming into the pan, then poured the rest of it down the barrel, dropped in the ball, then stuffed the paper after it as wadding, and rammed it home.

That these farmers did so much damage on the 19th of April was due to their numbers and to the fact that they did take aim. British regulars were drilled in the French and Prussian school, which did not go in for aiming a piece. The British Manual of Arms said nothing about aiming; only "leveling." The priming and loading was accomplished "by the numbers," requiring eight different commands, which were to be executed in twelve movements. Used to close fighting in Europe, the British still clung to fire by volleys.

The stone walls along the roads from Concord to Boston were responsible for most of the casualties inflicted on the British, and for many of those on the Americans. Israel Putnam remarked more than once of Americans that while they were anxious about their legs, they had no fear for their heads. Cover them up to their shoulders, said Old Put, and they would fight forever. Thus the second line of stone fences (the first line was too close to the road) back from the British march were the places favored by the Yankee bushwhackers. And it was also back of the fences that the bushwhackers fell prey to British flankers, who came upon them from behind.

All glory and credit to the gallant farmers of Essex and Middlesex, but let us not call them sharpshooters. To do so, in the face of the record, is to imply that their aim had been affected by what a good many of them, if tradition be correct, were drinking that day.

As for Samuel Adams, Lexington was doubtless the high point of his life. He was of little help in prosecuting the war, or in forming the colonies into the United States. He served in Congress, was Governor of Massachusetts, and lived unblemished in "honorable poverty" until his death in 1803. His real work was done when the shooting began at Lexington. If George Washington was the Father of his Country, then Samuel Adams was assuredly the Father of the Revolution.

CHAPTER IV

Hardly a Man Is Now Alive

OFTEN a century or more must elapse before anything approaching a true history of a war can be written. The folklore of a war, of course, begins long before the fighting is done; and, by the time the last smoke has drifted away this folklore has congealed into "truth" of a neolithic hardness.

Folklore is aided and abetted by poets, by phrasemakers, by orators. It is enriched by them, too. I can believe only by a form of romantic hypnosis that Captain Parker, when he and his farmers faced the redcoats on Lexington Green, said not to fire unless fired upon and that if the British wanted a war, then let it begin here. It is a grand sentence, a glorious line, and I am happy it has been cut into stone. But neither Parker, nor anyone else who was present that day, heard such resounding words.

Parson Weems, the genial book-selling-and-writing liar, founded a mythical Washington, fantastically bloodless and good, who in spite of much corrective writing largely endures to this day. That is the way it is with folklore, and historians good or bad can do little but dent it here and there, and gnaw away at the edges.

Factual history, that which is spread in the documentary evidence, is often subject to revision, as new discoveries of material are made, or old material is subjected to critical interpretation. Not until 1941, as an instance, when Carl Van Doren's *Secret History of the American Revolution* appeared, did the general public get the detailed truth of the enormity of Benedict Arnold's treason.

Novelists in recent years had conjured up a sickly senti-mental Arnold who was, they make out, really a pretty fine and honorable sort of fellow. They have it, these novelists, that Arnold was driven into his sell-out because of the shabby manner in which those responsible for conduct of the war had treated him; they make out that he sold himself to the enemy because he felt it was for the good of his fellow Amer-icans; they suggest that any decent and intelligent man would have done what Arnold did, given the circumstances.

Then, along came Mr. Van Doren's sound study, grounded in the hard, cold records of the time, and here is the sort of fine American who emerges: To begin with, it was Arnold and not the British who was first to propose the treason; he started his overtures as early as June 1779; the treason was not done on the spur of the moment, a moment of dissatis-faction and disappointment, but with extremely cool cal-culation, for Arnold went cynically into treason as a busi-ness, carefully surveying the ground and estimating the possible profits; he haggled over the price of his treason; and, in addition to selling out his country, he made an extra effort to betray Washington in person into the hands of the enemy—Washington, the man who had helped and de-fended Arnold at every turn.

Nor is that all about Arnold. For a long time the bounder had been selling Continental Army commissary rations of pork, salt, and wine for cash, and putting the cash in his pocket.

As for Arnold's beauteous wife, the pathetic Peggy, over whose "cruel fate" at least two generations of American women have wept, she was a cool-headed partner in her venal mate's treason within a month of their wedding, and perhaps before.

More than a century had passed before all of this addi-tional documentary evidence regarding the Arnolds was col-lected and put together in a book. It is an effective sample of cumulative historical research and writing, and it should

remove forever the figure of Arnold as one meriting pity, or
even consideration as anything but the cheapest kind of
traitor.

Another story that had to wait a long time before its many
component parts could be fitted together into a coherent and
important narrative is that of the treachery of General
Charles Lee of the American Army. Not until 1858, on the
eve of the next great American conflict, was it possible to
confirm with proof the suspicions that brought Lee a court-
martial on less serious charges than the one of which he unquestionably was guilty.

This soldier of fortune was a swashbuckler who seems to
have been able to impose on others the values he set upon himself. He was born in England in 1731, entered the British
army, and saw service in America in the French and Indian
war; and later fought in Portugal and Poland. After taking
part in revolutionary uprisings in the latter country, Lee
served in the Russian army against Turkey, then returned
to service in England. In 1775 he came to the American
colonies, as a half-pay British officer, and took up land in
what is now West Virginia. The war was just beginning.

A loud and able self-advertiser, Lee insinuated himself
into the councils of the Continental Congress and on the
strength of his military experience, which he painted in
glowing and heroic colors, was appointed the second major-
general in the American Army. But he would not accept the
commission until Congress had officially resolved to indem-
nify him for any loss of property he might sustain as a
result of taking up arms. Nor did he renounce his half pay
as a colonel in the British army until he had received his
commission as a major-general in the Continental Army.
Lee was a man who looked both ways.

General Charles Lee served without distinction at the
siege of Boston, and later was in charge of the defense of
New York City, where he seems to have had much trouble

and bickering with civilian officials. Next he was ordered to the Southern department, to oppose the British in Virginia and the Carolinas. Here Lee appears to have devoted much of his energy in trying to discourage Colonel William Moultrie from defending Charleston. The British, Lee told Moultrie, would demolish all defenses and slay the defenders, to a man.

Colonel Moultrie, however, was no man either to be discouraged, or intimidated by a superior officer. He threw up his dirt-and-palmetto defenses, and when the British arrived he gave them such a warm welcome that they withdrew. It was one of the most courageous and successful engagements of the war, and it was carried out while General Lee was planning a route for what he said must be Moultrie's line of retreat out of Charleston.

Lee was not yet under suspicion. Ordered to the North, he took command of a corps in New York, and soon turned out to be extremely dilatory in regard to Washington's order to him to join his troops with those of the commander in chief. He was cocky, even arrogant, and in a letter to General Horatio Gates remarked that Washington was "not fit to command a sergeant's guard." Lee was soon captured— in a manner that has a haze of doubt about it; a small raiding party of British suddenly came upon Lee's headquarters, and took him away, a prisoner, to New York City. It was here that he performed the treasonable activities that did not come to light for generations.

For the British high command Lee prepared a plan of campaign which he told Lord Howe would bring an early capitulation of the Americans. Lee's written plan of campaign, which was dated "29th March 1777," involved certain movements of British troops, which need not be gone into here, and was founded on Lee's undisputed knowledge of the American forces, their numbers, equipment, supplies, and even of certain American plans for future campaigns. And Lee recommended his plan highly to Lord Howe. "I am so confident of the event," wrote this American general to the commander of the British army, "that I will venture to assert with the penalty of my life, if the plan is fully carried out and no accidents (such as a rupture betwixt the powers of Europe) intervenes, that in less than two months from the date of the proclamation not a spark of this desolating war remains unextinguished in any part of the continent." The proclamation referred to was one Lee proposed Howe should make, promising good treatment and pardon to all Americans, either soldiers or civilians, who should immediately surrender on a day named for the purpose.

Lee also wrote to Washington, inclosing a letter for transmission to the Continental Congress. In this letter he informed Congress that he had important proposals to make and asked that they send a committee to wait on him, under a flag of truce. Just what proposal Lee intended to offer the Americans is not clear, but unquestionably it was defeatist in purpose. Congress refused to send the committee.

In 1778, in an unfortunate moment for the Americans, Lee was exchanged. So far from being considered a traitor, or even under any suspicion, Lee rejoined the American Army at Valley Forge in the role and style of a great hero. General Washington rode out four miles to meet him. Lines of soldiers were drawn up all the way back to Headquarters, and saluted as Lee and Washington passed. The drummers and field music let go Ruffles & Flourishes. And a room back of Mrs. Washington's sewing room was assigned to General Lee.

Within two weeks of this day, as documents have since made clear, General Lee was secretly in friendly correspondence with both Lord Howe and General Clinton. And it is interesting to note, in light of subsequent happenings, that the battle of Monmouth was only a month in the future.

General Lee, the exchanged prisoner, complained to Congress because that body had seen fit to promote other generals while Lee was in the hands of the British. He was running true to form.

Now came a military crisis. British troops began moving north through New Jersey. The Americans followed, with Lafayette leading the advance. Because of his seniority Lee was offered command, but refused. Now came orders from Washington to Lafayette to attack the British at Monmouth. Lee suddenly asserted his seniority and the right to command the attack. Lafayette gracefully yielded, and Lee set about, either by design or else because of cowardice, which latter seems unlikely, to lose the battle.

Anthony Wayne's division began the American attack at Monmouth, and soon that brave officer saw to his horror that Lee's corps, which composed the main part of the army, had at once started to retreat, to retreat behind Wayne and without any warning. Wayne had to fall back at once to protect his own flanks. The retreat was swiftly becoming a rout when Washington came up with Nathanael Greene, Baron von Steuben, and Henry Knox. The first thing Washington did was to order Lee off the field, doing so in language that was not reported by Parson Weems and would not have been approved by him. Reforming the leaderless and fleeing troops, Washington fought the British to a standstill until dark, when they decamped. What began as a rout engineered by treachery was turned into, if not an American victory, then at least a draw.

Without waiting for a reprimand from his commander in chief, Lee wrote an arrogant letter to Washington demanding an apology for the rough language used in ordering him from the field. Washington naturally enough refused to apologize, and said so curtly in a note. Lee demanded a court of inquiry. Instead, he got a court-martial which found him guilty, not of treachery, but of disobedience of orders, misbehavior in front of the enemy, and disrespect to the commander in chief. He was given the incredibly mild sentence of suspension from the Army for twelve months.

The remaining few years of Lee's life—he died in 1782—which were largely spent in futile attempts at self-vindication, are of no importance. That he was as great a traitor as Arnold would appear sufficiently proved not only by his actions in the field, at Monmouth and elsewhere, but also by the contents of the Strachey Papers, discovered in 1858 and published for the first time in 1860. Even at that time, hardly a man was then alive who could have remembered General Lee and Monmouth.

Lee and Arnold were not alone in their infamy, for there were other murky and often treasonable doings of men high in what at the time were fondly thought to be the *secret* councils of American leaders. Indeed, they were so numerous as to constitute a hidden war, far more dangerous to the patriot side than was realized for many years afterward, going on beneath the open warfare of the Revolution. One of the most disheartening cases of traitors in high places was that of Dr. Benjamin Church who, before discovery of his treason in part, was unanimously elected director and chief physician of the first American Army hospital.

Born at Newport, Rhode Island, Church was graduated from Harvard in 1754, studied medicine in England, married an English girl, and in 1768 built a fine mansion in Raynham, Massachusetts. This same mansion, which put the doctor deeply into debt, may have had a bearing on his subsequent actions. Just when his treason began is not certain, for the record has clouds in it. He was an able pamphleteer and his articles, in the troublous days just before 1775, seemed to support the patriot cause, although there is some reason to believe that he was at the same time contributing material to a Tory sheet in which he ridiculed the efforts of Whigs.

Yet, he must have been careful and clever, for at the time of the Boston Massacre he was in the inner councils of Samuel Adams's crew of revolutionaries. It was Doctor

Church who examined the body of Crispus Attucks, killed in the Massacre; and it was Doctor Church who on March 5, 1773, delivered the memorial address of the Massacre which Adams had arranged in order to keep the patriots from getting sluggish. Moreover, Church was a member of the Boston committee of correspondence, and as such knew all of the plans of Adams and his men.

Suspicion seems to have first been present when in 1774, after a "secret" meeting of the Boston revolutionaries, it was learned that the proceedings had become known almost immediately to the Tories. It was Paul Revere who apparently first voiced suspicion of the doctor, and ever after Revere felt uneasy. Yet Church remained in the confidence of Samuel Adams, of Warren, Hancock, and other radical Whigs.

Deeper suspicion centered on Church right after the battle of Lexington. The doctor had flown Boston along with almost all other prominent Whigs before April 18, 1775; and now, after the battles of the 19th, he said he must return to the city in order to get medicines needed to care for wounded Americans. He did so. On his return to the American lines he reported that he had been arrested on the trip and taken before the British General Gage. Within a few days the Americans learned, through their own spy system in Boston, that Church had gone voluntarily to Gage. Still Church was not arrested by the Americans. In May of 1775 he attended the Continental Congress at Philadelphia and consulted about methods for the defense of Massachusetts. He was here elected, unanimously, director and chief physician of the Continental Army, at four dollars a day, and sent to Cambridge.

While in charge of the Cambridge Army hospital, Church sent a cipher letter to the commander of a British vessel at Newport. This was intercepted and taken to General Washington. Arrested at once and tried by a court-martial, General Washington presiding, Church was found guilty of holding criminal correspondence with the enemy. In addition to the incriminating letter, it was strongly believed, on fairly good evidence, that for at least six weeks prior to the battle of Lexington, Church had kept General Gage well posted on all movements and plans of the patriots. But this belief was not documented by sound evidence until almost a century and a half afterward. And hardly a man was then alive who . . .

Doctor Church was put in prison at Norwich, Connecticut, but because of ill health was removed to Massachusetts and placed on parole. In 1778 he left Boston on a ship bound for the West Indies. Neither the ship nor Church was ever heard of again. It is significant that Church's family, like Benedict Arnold's, was pensioned by the British Crown.

Another long-kept secret was that of Metcalf Bowler, chief justice of Rhode Island, who for two years acted as an informer for Sir Henry Clinton, the British commander. Nothing came of it, but Bowler tried; and he received cash from Clinton and was always wanting more.

There were weevils everywhere at work attempting to wreck the American cause. Edward Fox of Maryland, a trusted clerk in the Continental treasury, was in contact and in correspondence with Major André and other British officers and was paid British guineas for his treachery. William Heron, member of the Connecticut Assembly, secretly served the British for more than a year, and was paid by them. Heron was petty. Down in Pennsylvania was a man who would do treason in a big way. He was Colonel William Rankin, a commander of the American militia in York county, who proposed and attempted to raise an army of 7,000 Americans that would fight the rebels. Rankin also planned to blow up a patriot powder magazine at Carlisle.

These were a few of the American traitors. There were many more whose work has been uncovered from time to time in the past one hundred and sixty years, as old letters and documents came to light. Some of these men sold out for money, others because they thought the rebels could not

win, and wanted to be on the winning side. Had they and
their widespread treachery been known at the time, many a
patriot might well have thought the cause was hopeless.

Only the treachery of Arnold is yet generally known to
Americans, who still use his name much in the manner Norwegians, and much of the world, now use Quisling. This is
well enough, for Arnold was crafty, unscrupulous, unre-
pentant. Only General Charles Lee approached him in character.

Following the War of the Revolution came many another
good story, not dealing with treason or treachery, which for
one reason for another, and often for no discernible reason
at all, had been withheld during the contest, or was known
only to a few. Three of these now-it-can-be-told incidents are
in such contrast to the records of Arnold, Lee and other
knaves, and so little known today, that they serve to restore
one's possibly decaying faith in human nature. One concerns what in olden time, when titles were written with stark
directness, might have been called The Story of Christopher
Ludwick and the Hessian Soldiers. It appears to have been
pretty much buried since the year 1801, when Ludwick died.

When the Revolution broke out into fighting, Christopher
Ludwick was a prosperous baker of Philadelphia. Born in
1720 in Hesse-Darmstadt, Germany, he joined the Prussian
army and served against the Turks, later was a baker aboard
a British East Indiaman, and in 1753 arrived in the American colonies to seek his fortune. He opened a bakery that
was immediately successful, and was famous for its special
breads and cakes. Well liked by his fellow Philadelphians,
he was appointed both to the local committee of correspondence and committee of safety, which were carrying on activities subversive to the Crown.

Tall and erect, with what a contemporary described as a
commanding presence, Ludwick had considerable influence.
He was hot for the Revolution. When a collection was to be

taken up at a meeting, for the purpose of buying arms for the local militia, Ludwick arose to his full height and in badly accented but perfectly plain English told the chairman that "although I am but a poor gingerbread baker, write me down for two hundred pounds." Ludwick was frugal enough so far as himself was concerned, but open-handed, then and later, in anything for the good of his adopted country.

In 1776 the British moved into New York harbor, driving the Americans northward, then into New Jersey. It became known that on Staten Island, in New York harbor, the British had quartered several thousand of their mercenaries, mostly Hessians. Hearing of this, Ludwick went to General Washington with an idea. Let me, he said to the commander in chief, dress myself in the garb of a deserter from the Americans and go to the Hessian camp at New York. Let me talk to them, Ludwick went on, and see if I cannot convince them they would be better off as good farmers in Pennsylvania than as cannon fodder at a few pfennigs a day.

Washington agreed to the novel plan. Disguised in dirty Continental uniform, Ludwick somehow made his way through the British lines and got to Staten Island. He must have had eloquence as well as considerable imagination, for the Hessian forces soon began melting away. Speaking the language like one of them, Ludwick first called them fools for risking their lives so cheaply, and to the profit of a crowned prince; and criminals for fighting a nation that merely wanted freedom.

This was dangerous business that Ludwick was on, perhaps as dangerous a mission as any man had during the Revolution. One whisper to a Hessian officer, and Ludwick would have been strung higher than Nathan Hale. But he talked on, day after day, living with the Germans in their quarters.

Get out of here, ye clods, he told them. Get over to the mainland. Then make your way to wonderful Pennsylvania, a heaven for Germans, where so many of our former coun-

trymen are now prosperous and independent farmers and
traders and merchants. Land down there is to be had for the
asking. Go get it. Two Pennsylvania cabbages will serve to
fill a bushel basket. The turnips are enormous. The cows all
give ten quarts of milk twice a day.

The poor Hessian slaves listened to their countryman.
They began to slip away in the night, first a couple or so,
then a dozen, then by the score. Ludwick never ceased talking. Doubtless he mixed his facts with imagination bordering
fantasy, picturing the affluence of German farmers in Pennsylvania and their idyllic life. It was strong meat, and it
fetched them. Within a few days Hessians were moving off
the island by the hundred, and Ludwick escaped with them.

The exact number of desertions brought about by Ludwick's one-man attack isn't known. A nearly contemporary
figure sets it at "several hundreds." What is more, many
and perhaps most of the deserters did go to Pennsylvania,
did settle there, and did become prosperous farmers, just as
their descendents are today. At the time of Ludwick's death,
Dr. Benjamin Rush wrote * that the former soldiers of
Staten Island were "now in comfortable freeholds or on
valuable farms, with numerous descendents, and they bless
the name of Christopher Ludwick." Thus did the "Pennsylvania Dutch" colonies gain hundreds of new recruits who no
longer fired their muskets at American soldiers. It was a
notable battle that Ludwick won single-handed.

More Hessians were captured by Washington's army at
the battle of Trenton, and Ludwick came forward with another idea. "Let us take these prisoners to Philadelphia," he
told the Continental Congress in session, "and there show
them our fine American churches. Let them see how our
tradesmen eat good beef, drink out of silver cups every day,
and ride out in chairs every afternoon; and then let us send
them back to their countrymen [who are still fighting for

---

* *American Daily Advertiser,* Philadelphia, June 30, 1801.

the British] and they will all soon run away, and come and settle and be as good Whigs as any of us."

Congress liked the idea, and sent Washington a letter asking that he not exchange any of the Hessians taken at Trenton. Washington had already seen what the genial Ludwick could do. He held the prisoners and put the provisioning and transportation of them into Ludwick's care. Ludwick took them first to Philadelphia, then into Birks, and Lancaster, and Lebanon counties. Whether or not the indoctrinated Hessians were then sent back to their fellows still with the British is not clear.

Ludwick did not rest on his reputation as a master of desertion tactics. In 1777 he was made Superintendent of Baking—Baker-General, he was usually called—to the entire Continental Army. Here he performed prodigious feats of organization and efficiency. Until Ludwick took over, the Army's baking department had been a. scandal. The bread was seldom good, and generally very bad. Congress had finally had to recognize as custom a piece of graft that had grown into the Army, and stipulated that only one hundred pounds of bread need be furnished for every hundred pounds of flour. This is wrong, said Ludwick. The proportion is incorrect. For every hundred pounds of flour the ovens operated by Baker-General Ludwick turned out 135 pounds of bread, good bread. He said that he did not wish to enrich himself "out of my Government." He often spent his own money, to buy brick and mortar and to pay incidental expenses. At times, when Congress was slow with cash, Ludwick even paid his bakers' wages out of his own pocket.

The bread Ludwick's ovens produced was so good that it may have been a factor in the greatly improved morale of the Continentals which was apparent soon after the German baker took charge. He was greatly liked by both officers and men. He was a favorite of General Washington, who gave orders that his gallant Baker-General was to be admitted to his quarters at any time—a privilege no general officer seems to have enjoyed. Often Washington and Ludwick were

closeted together, says an old account, for as long as two
hours at a time; and the General liked to drink toasts with
him, always closing with a couplet: "Health and long life,
to Christopher Ludwick and wife."

The genial baker closed the war with an almost herculean
feat. On Cornwallis's surrender, Washington asked for six
thousand loaves of bread to feed the British. It was a stupendous order for the equipment which Ludwick had in the field,
but he met it within twelve hours.

So highly did Washington hold his Baker-General that at
the end of the war he wrote and presented to Ludwick what
amounted to being a certificate of high character and a cita-
tion for all-around patriotism and gallantry. Possibly this
unusual paper was of consolation to the old baker when
Congress repaid the hard cash Ludwick had expended—some
said to the extent of thirty-five hundred pounds—with paper
currency of little value. Ludwick's plight after the war was
such that he "slept in coarse blankets rather than to go further into debt for sheets," for he was penniless, his business
was gone, and old age was upon him. Yet he never soured,
and he managed to redeem enough of his property to enable
him as his last act to buy the freedom of three African slaves.

Not so important to the winning of the war as Ludwick,
but just as gallant and as heart-warming, is the story of her
who appears to have been America's one female soldier. This
was Deborah Sampson, a rather startling amazon from
Massachusetts. Calling her the sole authentic female soldier
of the war is not loose talk. The lesser known Margaret
Corbin had smelled the smoke of battle. So had a number of
women water-and-cider carriers who were known generically
in the argot of the day as Molly Pitcher, among whom was
Mary Ludwig Hays McCauley.* But none of these were
soldiers. Deborah Sampson enlisted as a man, was mustered

* Although a number of Molly Pitchers performed during the war, and
some were of doubtful character, the title was particularly appropriated
by the oaklike Mrs. McCauley, who served a cannon at Monmouth.

in as such, fought as and like a man, and in her later years drew a regulation soldier's pension from the federal government. Her descendants are alone in that they might, if they cared to, join the D. A. R. solely on the strength of a female ancestor.

Deborah Sampson was born in Plympton, not far from Plymouth, and among her forebears were the doughty Captain Myles Standish, the hesitating if celebrated John Alden, William Bradford (the first American historian), and the charming Alice Southworth and Bathsheba La Broche. She had a bit of schooling, but her parents were poor and when still in her teens she became a hired girl for a family in Middleboro, also in the Bay Colony. It was here in 1782, when she was approximately twenty-two years old, that Deborah got the idea of enlisting in the Continental Army.

To have an idea, for Deborah, was apparently tantamount to acting. She cut her hair. She "borrowed" a suit of clothes belonging to one Sam Leonard—who never got over it—and under the name of Timothy Thayer enlisted with the Continental Army's recruiting officer at Middleboro. She was paid the enlistment bounty, probably of "one hundred paper dollars," which however was not a great deal of money in actual cash. It was nevertheless sufficient to get Deborah-Timothy into trouble, for closely afterward she was seen at a tavern, two miles east of Middleboro Four Corners, where she called for and presumably drank spirituous liquors and thereupon "behaved in a noisy and indecent manner." Some loathsome acquaintance, no doubt a draft-dodging patriot, recognized and reported her, and she was unmasked and the remaining bounty money taken from her. She returned to her household duties in disgrace. As for Sam Leonard, he was so shocked "at the idea of his clothes having been worn by a woman that he never wore them after."

Middleboro itself was shocked, and the First Baptist Church of that village, of which Deborah was a member, held a meeting and voted to "withdraw fellowship," which meant excommunication. One doubts that the determined Miss Sampson cared greatly. By the time the Baptists had got around to their churlish act, Deborah had secretly spun and woven some fine Massachusetts wool into cloth which she took to a local man who made clothes, and had him fashion it into a suit for a man she described as a "male relative about my size." When she got the clothes, she disappeared from Middleboro, and long before the local Baptists had got around to unchristianizing her, she was away on one of the greatest adventures a woman ever had, before or since.

One night in May—it was still 1782—young Deborah got into her own coat and trousers. When the house had settled down in sleep, she tiptoed down from the shed chamber, out into the road, and made her way to Worcester, a distance in those days of not less than seventy-five miles. She went directly to the recruiting office there, and a day later she was Private Robert Shurtleff in Captain George Webb's company of the 4th Massachusetts Regiment of Foot, commanded at that time by Colonel Shepard, later by Colonel Jackson. Possibly she was put in a drill squad to learn the School of the Soldier and the Manual of Arms; but there could have been but little fuss about training, for early in June the 4th Regiment left Worcester on the long march to West Point on the Hudson. A week later the outfit was crossing the Housatonic at New Milford, Connecticut, and presently was arrived at West Point, with Private Robert Shurtleff, or Deborah, holding her own on the long and dusty march.

One wonders what good Captain Webb would have thought of a woman, a young woman, in his company? And what of Captain Webb's men? It is a subject that soldiers of all times and all nations have discussed, this possibility, this happy possibility, of a female soldier—a topic that has taken up endless hours of barracks-room conversation. But there seems to have been absolutely no suspicion of Private Deborah by her fellow soldiers, then or later, until an improbable accident, wholly beyond the girl's control, brought about the denouement.

What was she like, this authentic amazon, this Yankee girl who lived and fought with soldiers? Contemporaries agree that she was tall—five feet seven and one-half inches—muscular, of "good eyes and a not unpleasant voice." In movement she was quick, erect, and strong, as "fleet as a Gazell, bounding through Swamps many rods ahead of her companions." Whatever the case, she appears to have given serious thought to her general outline, her profile, for she bound a bandage tightly around her breast; and, wrote one who knew her well, "it is not improbable that the severe pressure of this bandage served to compress the bosom, while the waist had every natural convenience for augmentation." This is quite possible, for most women have found that the waist is given to augmentation, even if cared for. One can guess that when Private Deborah was encased in her bandages and the shapeless homespun clothes of the period, she had the shape, or lack of shape, of her indubitably male fellows.

Soon after arrival at West Point Deborah saw action in a sharp skirmish at Tappan Bay, during which she "suffered a slash from an enemy saber." This was close in-fighting. A bit later she was wounded in the side by a musket ball, in an engagement in East Chester. It felled her, but she got right up again and kept moving. She told an inquiring surgeon that it had been merely a scratch, that she would be all right, and then hid herself in the woods for several days, living alone and dressing the wound herself. She feared "discovery of her true Sex" more than she feared bleeding to death. Incidentally, the musket ball was never removed from her body.

Private Deborah had hardly recovered from her wound when she was sent with a small detachment to Fort Ticonderoga, then into western New York. There is no record of fighting on these expeditions, but Deborah must have continued to conduct herself well, for presently she was made an orderly on the staff of General Paterson, in Philadelphia. What was described as malignant fever was loose in the city and the hospitals were filled with stricken soldiers. The disease struck Deborah, too, and she was soon moved into the hopeless ward of an Army infirmary. As she lay on a pallet, unconscious and seeming hardly to breathe, Doctor Binney came through on his rounds. Seeing the motionless figure, he went over and put his hand on the patient's chest to learn if the heart was still beating. It was, and good Doctor Binney's heart must have skipped a beat or two. For a moment he stood in amazement at the discovery he had made; then he went to tell the head nurse about it.

Private Deborah Sampson was immediately moved elsewhere. When General Paterson learned about the kind of orderly he had on his staff, he delivered himself of his only line that has come down through history: "Why," he said, "this is truly theatrical!" But the General had a sense of humor. When Deborah had recovered he sent her to West Point, and there she was permitted to don female garb and to parade down the ranks of her former comrades in arms, the soon-to-be-sheepish men of Captain Webb's company of the 4th Massachusetts Regiment of Foot, not one of whom recognized the tall girl as the late Private Robert Shurtleff.

Little imagination is required to guess the remarks and barracks-room discussion that followed. Aye, that followed time without end whenever two or more veterans of Captain Webb's company were left to talk over old times and lost opportunities. All that has come down to us of these discussions is seemly and to the effect that Deborah was a rattling good soldier who never once acted otherwise than in a highly "military and courageous manner." Not once during her Army days was she found in liquor, which was something of a record in troops of the time. It was also recalled that she had never indulged in horseplay of any kind, and "never wrestled nor suffered anyone to twine his arms around her shoulders."

There is no record of a Welcome Home celebration for Deborah, who was honorably discharged in November of 1783. Middleboro missed a grand opportunity. But that town could not hold her. She married Benjamin Gannett of Sharon, Massachusetts, moved to that town, and became the mother of three children—Earl, Mary, and Patience.*

But the end of the war did not retire Deborah permanently to the fireside. In 1802 she became what must have been the first woman lecturer in the United States. Certainly she was the first female veteran to appear on the platform. Her talk was filled with noble abstractions about Liberty and Females and the rigors of war, but audiences loved it; and with good showmanship she kept her best bit for closing. In this she appeared in some sort of military garb, with a regulation Army musket, and went through the Manual of Arms— "briskly and with perfection," says one who saw her, "and she brought the musket butt smartly down to the floor with a Thud." If there were any other acts on the bill, this drill with Old Betsy must have stopped the show midstream.

Deborah lectured in Boston, Worcester and other Massachusetts towns, then toured upstate New York, appearing at Albany, Ballston Springs, and elsewhere. She kept a diary of her tour, and in good Yankee style kept account of her expenses. Soldier or no, she was still a woman; one item in her Albany expenses was $1 for Dressing my Hair."

After her lecture tour Deborah seems to have settled comfortably into life at Sharon and to have become in time a local matriarch, unique in that although she was female, she was a blown-in-the-bottle veteran of the Revolution. She

---

* In 1792 the Massachusetts legislature, taking cognizance of the Commonwealth's unique veteran, granted the sum of thirty-four pounds to Mrs. Gannett. In 1805 the federal pension office allowed her a pension of four dollars a month, increased to six dollars and forty cents in 1816, and in 1818 to eight dollars for life. In 1838 Congress by special act granted the sum of $466.66 to her heirs.

BENJAMIN GANNETT.

[To accompany bill H. R. No. 184.]

December 22, 1837.

Mr. Morgan, from the Committee on Revolutionary Pensions, made the following

REPORT:

The Committee on Revolutionary Pensions, to which was committed the memorial of Benjamin Gannett, have carefully re-examined the subject, and have resolved to adopt their report of a former session, viz:

That the petitioner represents that he is the surviving husband of Deborah Gannett, to whom he was lawfully married on the 7th day of April, 1784; that she died on the 29th of April, 1827. He also states, that in the early part of her life the said Deborah enlisted as a soldier in the army of the Revolution, under the assumed name of Robert Shurtleff, where she faithfully served her country three years, and was honorably discharged in November, 1783; that, on account of a wound received in the service, she received a pension as an invalid until the passage of the act of 18th March, 1818; and that she received a full pension under the act until her decease. The petitioner further states that the effects of the wound which she received followed her through life, and probably hastened her death. The petitioner represents himself to be eighty-three years of age, infirm in health, and in indigent circumstances. He states also that he has two daughters dependent on charity for support. The petitioner prays that he may receive the amount of the pension of his wife, from the time of her decease, and that it may be continued to him until his death.

It appears from a letter received from the Commissioner of Pensions, that Deborah Gannett, deceased, was placed on the Massachusetts roll of invalid pensioners at $48 per annum, which was afterwards increased to $76 80 per annum. This she relinquished in 1818, for the benefit of the act of March 18, 1818. She was placed under that law at the rate of eight dollars per month, from the 14th September, 1818, which she received up to the 4th March, 1827. It further appears from said letter, that the papers containing evidence upon which the original pension was granted, were burnt in 1814, when the British troops invaded Washington and destroyed the War Office with its contents.

On the 14th September, 1818, the said Deborah made her declaration, under oath, that she served as a private soldier, under the name of " Robert Shurtleff," in the war of the Revolution, upwards of two years, in manner following: Enlisted in April, 1781, in a company commanded by Captain George Webb, in the Massachusetts regiment commanded by Colonel Shepherd, and afterwards by Colonel Henry Jackson; that she served in Massachusetts and New York until November, 1783, when she was hon-

ed in writing; which discharge she had lost. She was at Cornwallis, was wounded at Tarrytown, and, up to the declaration, she received a pension therefor.

——— testifies, under oath, that she lived in the family of Benjamin Gannett ——— an forty-six years after he married Deborah Sampson; ——— knew that said Deborah was unable to perform any labor a ——— the time, in consequence of a wound she received while in the ——— , from a musket ball lodged in her body, which was never ——— He also states that she saw Benjamin Gannett married to ——— son at his father's house in Sharon.

——— oad and Jeremiah Gould, the selectmen of the town of ——— State of Massachusetts, certify that they are acquainted with ——— nett, now living in said Sharon; that he is a man of up ——— years of age; that he is destitute of property; that he has ——— ious man; that he was the husband of the late Deborah ——— sed, who for a time received a pension from the United ——— military services during the revolutionary war.

———, formerly a Senator in Congress, in a letter to the Hon. ——— on, now a Representative in Congress, states that said Gannett is a very upright, hard-laboring man, has brought up a large ——— a poor man. He further states that he has long since been ——— ed that said Gannett had been subjected to heavy expenses ——— for his wife, the said Deborah, for twenty years or more, ——— received a pension under the act of 1818, on account of wounds she received in the United States service.

There are other certificates among the papers in this case, showing the physician's bill alone, for attendance on the said Deborah, to be more than six hundred dollars.

The committee are aware that there is no act of Congress which provides for any case like the present. The said Gannett was married after the termination of the war of the Revolution, and therefore does not come within the spirit of the third section of the act of 4th July, 1836, granting pensions to widows in certain cases; and were there nothing peculiar in this application which distinguishes it from all other applications for pensions, the committee would at once reject the claim. But they believe they are warranted in saying that the whole history of the American Revolution records no case like this, and " furnishes no other similar example of female heroism, fidelity, and courage." The petitioner does not allege that he served in the war of the Revolution, and it does not appear by any evidence in the case that such was the fact. It is not, however, to be presumed that a female who took up arms in defence of her country, who served as a common soldier for nearly three years, and fought and bled for human liberty, would, immediately after the termination of the war, connect herself for life with a tory or a traitor. He, indeed, was honored much by being the husband of such a wife; and as he has proved himself worthy of her, as he has sustained her through a long life of sickness and suffering, and as that sickness and suffering were occasioned by the wounds she received and the hardships she endured in the defence of the country, and as there cannot be a parallel case in all time to come, the committee do not hesitate to grant relief.

They report a bill granting to the petitioner a pension of $80 per year from the 4th day of March, 1831, for and during his natural life.

died April 29, 1827, aged about sixty-seven years, and was buried in nearby Rockridge cemetery. A street in Sharon was named for her; and on April 10, 1944, a Liberty Ship, launched from the Bethlehem yards at Baltimore, honored her name. Were the Navy not so hidebound in the matter of naming its fighting ships, it could do worse than to have a cruiser *Deborah Gannett*, or at the least a destroyer.

Yet, Deborah was comparatively fortunate. Not even a rowboat, so far as I am aware, commemorates Sergeant Ezra Lee, the gallant and completely fearless captain, mate and crew of as odd a ship as ever went to sea. This was the *American Turtle*, and I can think of no act in all the Revolutionary war that called for more cold courage than that displayed by the *Turtle's* operator.

The time was late summer of 1776. The Declaration had been signed on July 4. Less than two months later the Americans were badly beaten on Long Island and forced to retreat to the mainland of Manhattan and present Westchester. Things looked dark for the Patriot cause, and it was then that the American high command made use of what newspapers of the time regrettably failed to announce as a secret weapon.

This weapon was really secret, and genuinely new. The *American Turtle* was conceived in the unusual mind of David Bushnell, a farmer boy of Saybrook, Connecticut, who had been graduated from Yale College in 1775. During his college years Bushnell had become interested in methods to explode charges of gunpowder under water, and promptly on his graduation he set out to devise an underwater craft to be used against British ships of war which were beginning to close American ports. With no little help and encouragement from another Yale man, Dr. Benjamin Gale (A.B. 1733), young Bushnell went furiously to work. Late in 1775 the *Turtle* was ready for its trial run in the Connecticut River near Saybrook.

Whether Bushnell himself operated the craft is not known. He was described by contemporaries as "frail." In any case, the trials must have been encouraging, for presently General Samuel H. Parsons of the Continental Army was calling for "two or three volunteers" to learn how to operate the Americans' secret weapon.

Among the volunteers was Sergeant Ezra Lee of Lyme, Connecticut, one of our really great forgotten heroes. Sergeant Lee, surely, was fit to command the first submarine ever on the water, any water; and one idly wonders what he thought when he first laid eyes on this floating coffin. The *Turtle* was made of oak frame timber in the shape of a round clam. It was bound with iron bands, the seams calked, and "the whole smear'd over with tar." The top or head was of metallic construction, hinged, with eight small windows of thick glass. "On a clear day," said Sergeant Lee later, "I could see to read at a depth of three fathoms."

But little reading was Sergeant Lee to do once he had been clamped into his primeval sub. There was too much to attend to. The craft was six feet high. A foot spring opened a cock which let water into a compartment, for submerging; two hand pumps were used, by nobody but Lee—the only man aboard—to empty the compartment, for rising. When on the surface, two small tubes let air into the vessel, but when submerged the operator had to get along with such oxygen as was present. The *Turtle's* inventor said that the vessel contained "sufficient air to support the operator for thirty minutes." Candles were tried for lighting, but they consumed the oxygen very fast, and resort was had to "two pieces of shining wood, or foxfire"—phosphorescent wood —to light the compass and the depth gauge. In the depth gauge was a cork that rose with the descent of the vessel, and fell with the ascent. "A one-inch rise of the cork," said Sergeant Lee, "denoted a depth of one fathom."

For ballast the *Turtle* carried nine hundred pounds of lead on her bottom, a part of which could be cut loose and lowered by cable to act as an anchor. For motive power, there were two sets of paddles—"like the arms of a windmill," says Lee—furnished with a crank for each set. The smaller set was at the *Turtle's* head, or top, and aided the vessel to ascend. The larger paddles, which were twelve inches long, were the lateral motive power. "By vigorous turning of the crank," Sergeant Lee reported, "I could make about three miles an hour." There was also a rudder, a sort of fin on the craft's rear.

Such was the *Turtle* proper; but there was still more rigging for Lee to operate, for the vessel carried a complicated boring machine, and a sort of torpedo, called a magazine, which was the craft's offensive weapon. What with holes all over the ship to permit entry of the various shafts of the propellers, of the rudder, the pumps, and the boring apparatus, it seems a wonder that Sergeant Lee did not operate in water up to his waist, but he never complained of bilge in his scuppers; and Dr. Benjamin Gale, who as related had a hand in the *Turtle's* construction, vowed that "all of these shafts are so curiously Fix'd as not to admit any water to incommode the machine." *

In November of 1775 Lee made several experimental voyages around Saybrook. Troubles developed. In late November the forcing pumps were not performing well. In early December Dr. Gale was writing Silas Deane to say that the shining wood or foxfire failed in frosty weather, and asked to learn if "Dr. Franklin might know of any kind of phosphorus that will give light in the dark and not consume the air." Gale had met Sergeant Lee, whom he found to be "no enthusiast, but a perfect philosopher, and by no means doubtful of succeeding." Any man who was going to put to sea in the *American Turtle* simply had to be a perfect philosopher. Otherwise he was beaten before he started.

* Good detailed descriptions of the craft are in a letter to Professor Silliman of Yale from Charles Griswold, in *American Journal of Science*, Vol. 11, No. 2, 1820; and in a letter from Dr. Gale himself to Silas Deane, in Collections of Connecticut Historical Society, 1870.

The experimental voyages apparently continued throughout the spring and early summer of '76, mostly in Long Island Sound. Meanwhile, the British had taken possession of Long Island, Staten Island, and Governors Island. The Sound was getting too warm for any vessel that was made "to produce astonishment in those against whom it is designed"; so Lee and his helpers hauled the *Turtle* out of the Sound at New Rochelle, took it overland to the Hudson, and launched it in the river. The time had come for the first U-boat attack in history.

It was now August, 1776. A sizable British fleet lay in New York harbor just north of Staten Island. With it was a large number of transports. Soon came a favorable night, and at eleven Sergeant Lee and party set out. They were in two whaleboats, towing the *Turtle*. At a point described as Whitehall Stairs—near the Battery—the expedition halted. Lee crawled into his one-man sub, the head was clamped tight, and away he went down the dark waters alone.

Here was a voyage for a man of cold courage, a hero by the standards of all times and places. Even in the quiet waters of Long Island Sound, in broad daylight, and with no lurking enemy, a ride in the *Turtle* was something akin to suicide. There were so many things to go wrong with the bungling and complicated mechanisms. Should the lead weight on its bottom drop away, the operator might find himself standing on his head. Too, the vessel was really a sieve, with its countless openings plugged hopefully, even though it were "smear'd over with tar"; should a leak start, the operator could do little but drown where he was, for he was clamped in from outside. A floating log might break one of the eight windows. A good stiff jolt could set off the devilish infernal machine that rode on the *Turtle's* back. It is questionable that any other ship ever put to sea was so open to fatal accident. But there is nothing in the record to indicate that the daring young Nutmegger from Lyme gave it a passing thought.

Now it was night, and down below him somewhere in the misty dark, as Lee knew, was the fleet; and in the fleet the *Eagle*, sixty-four guns, the mighty flagship of Lord Howe. Sergeant Lee had understandingly set his heart on the *Eagle*.

Turning his crank "vigorously," Lee went on toward the great armada, rocking at anchor in the stream. The tide was in ebb, "very strong," and before he was aware of the speed he was making, he had passed the men of war and was heading out to sea. This was bad, for dawn was soon coming and the *Turtle* was no craft to approach the British navy in daylight. What was worse was the tide. Lee had to work like a nailer to get the awkward craft turned about, and then by great labor at the crank "for the space of five glasses by the ships' bells, or two and a half hours," he at last arrived under the stern of what he felt certain was the *Eagle*, looming up big and tall and sinister in the twilight that precedes early dawn.

Lee's task now was to attach the torpedo or magazine to the bottom of the man o' war. This magazine was an oak container shaped like an egg. It was attached to the *Turtle* by a large screw, a little above the rudder. In the oaken egg were 130 pounds of gunpowder, a clock, and a gunlock provided "with a good flint that would not miss fire."

The method of attaching the bomb to the ship's hull was this: a long sharp screw, worked by hand from inside the submarine, would penetrate the hull—theoretically—then be disengaged, and left sticking out from the hull. Attached to this spike was a line for holding the torpedo firmly against the ship until the magazine should explode. So, all that Sergeant Lee had to do, now that he was under the *Eagle's* hull, was to hold the *Turtle* steady, bore into the ship, disengage the screw, plug the hole in his own craft, loose the powder magazine from the *Turtle*, attach it to the screw in the *Eagle's* hull, then to get out of there as quickly as possible. Incidentally, the clock was set for running twenty minutes

from the time the magazine was unscrewed from the submarine—which automatically set the infernal machine in
motion—until the lock struck and fired the powder. Lee, the
perfect philosopher, figured that twenty minutes would
give him time to get clear.

Well, here he was at last, under the gently rocking flagship of the British fleet. One can wonder what his thoughts
were, this perfect philosopher, this first submarine commander. But he had little time for reflection. He opened the
sea cock and let more water into the submerging compartment. The *Turtle* slowly yet surely sank. Lee felt it rubbing
against the underside of the big ship. All was dark as pitch,
except for the foxfire glowing on his compass and gauge.
He started the boring machine, and although it turned perfectly he soon saw that it was not boring anything. What
Lee had run into was the hard fact of thick copper sheathing
on the hull of the *Eagle*. He paddled along a few feet, then
tried again. Same result. After more futile attempts, Lee
put the *Turtle* into a dive, going under the ship and coming
up on the other side. This was clever if dangerous maneuver-
ing, but Lee was a determined man. It was still copper, however, and he could do nothing against it with his wood-
boring bit.

Dawn was coming. Lee noted that he could now see the
machinery and his own hands. He could hear orders being
given on the decks above him, but he did not think they applied to his attempt, for he was certain he was as yet undis-
covered. But he was in a notably tight spot. It was getting
daylight by the minute. Lee knew he had before him a voyage of four miles before he could consider himself anything
like safe.

Sergeant Lee pumped water out of the compartment, and
rose to the surface to take his bearings. He had to do this
because the foxfire had failed again and he could not read
the points of his compass. Getting his bearings he submerged
again and started north toward the Battery on Manhattan.

turning the crank as fast as he could. The tide, praise be, had turned and was now with him again. Governors Island, which he would have to pass, was his gravest danger. He had to rise to the surface every little while to make sure of his course; and presently he came abreast of the Island and could see hundreds of troops down near the shore. They had seen him, too, and were obviously trying to make out what the strange craft could be. Lee saw a big barge push off from shore and start toward him. He turned the crank for dear life, but the barge was coming swiftly, bearing down on the *Turtle*.

Sergeant Lee was no man to take a torpedo to sea and bring it back. Just as the barge filled with British marines got within good shouting distance, Lee pulled the pin of his torpedo and cut the thing loose, expecting that his pursuers would seize it, as well as himself, and that they and he would be blown to atoms. Providence, however, directed otherwise, as Lee related the incident; for the enemy "after approaching within fifty or sixty yards of the machine, and seeing the magazine suddenly detached, began to suspect a *Yankee trick*, took alarm, and returned to the Island." It was well for them that they did.

As for Lee, he knew what was in that lethal egg-shaped thing, and he paddled like a beaver to get as far away as he could. He made his escape. The magazine had barely drifted past Governors Island when it went up in one big blast, tossing large columns of water and hunks of wood and iron high into the air. The force of the explosion—"a report like thunder"—was noted at the Battery on Manhattan's tip. It was the Black Tom Explosion of '76.

General Israel Putnam, General Parsons and other American officers saw the explosion, and were on hand to welcome the intrepid Lee when he crawled out of the *Turtle* and came ashore at Whitehall Stairs.

Sergeant Lee must have loved his strange and dangerous craft and been a glutton for punishment as well. A few days later he made another attempt, this time on a frigate off Bloomingdale, but the watch gave the alarm. A year later the British frigate *Cerberus* lay in Black Point Bay, west of New London, Connecticut, holding a prize schooner. One of the crew found and hauled at a long line which seemed to have fouled on the schooner. At the end of the line was "a machine up to one hundred weight" which the curious tars hauled aboard. It promptly blew up with a roar, killing three men and blasting the schooner to bits. Sergeant Lee was at work again, and this time he had drawn enemy blood. The incident understandingly made Captain Symons of the *Cerberus* pretty angry, and in reporting the event to Admiral Parker he referred to the barbarous "mode these Villains must have taken . . . the ingenuity of these people is Singular in their Secret modes of mischief."

The *Turtle* seems to have later been moved to the Delaware river where it helped to plant the river with floating kegs of powder and to send them bumping, and sometimes exploding, among the British fleet there. This event was celebrated in doggerel as "The Battle of the Kegs," by Francis Hopkinson, which made sport of the terror of the British sailors at this new kind of atrocity.

As for Sergeant Ezra Lee, his cold-blooded courage had taken the eye of General Washington himself. The commander in chief congratulated him in person, and later employed him in some sort of secret service, probably as a spy. Lee also served bravely at the battles of Trenton, Brandywine, and Monmouth. He died at Lyme, his home town, in 1821, aged seventy-two, full of honors as an outstanding hero of the Revolution. Had a Longfellow fastened upon him, he would be as well known today as Paul Revere, and it is a pity that he isn't.

In the United States, at least, David Bushnell is considered the legitimate father of the submarine. Nor had Sergeant Lee failed him. Only the sturdy copper on Lord Howe's flagship prevented Bushnell from joining the ranks of Eli

Whitney, Samuel Colt, and Thomas Edison.* Long after the
war, in the letter to Jefferson, President Washington wrote
of the *Turtle:* "I then thought and still think it was an effort of genius."

---

* American military intelligence in 1775, of course, was not function-
ing to any extent. Yet it seems strange that Bushnell and his advisors do
not seem to have known about the sheathing of hulls of the British navy,
which had begun to use copper as early as 1761, according to E. Keble
Chatterton, *Sailing Ships and Their Story.*

CHAPTER V

Daniel Shays & Noah Webster

THE war was over in 1783, but not the Revolution. The new United States of America, as Thomas Paine had toasted the far from united colonies, was attempting simultaneously three political and highly dangerous experiments. Independence, which many good Americans were presently to think resembled anarchy more than anything else, had been won. Republicanism had been nominally achieved by the constitutions of the various states, adopted during and after the war. And since 1777 the states had been loosely joined by the Articles of Confederation and Perpetual Union, a leaky vessel at best.

The Confederation had served to hold the fiercely individual states together while the actual fighting was on; but once peace had come, the thirteen jealous republics, soon to be joined by new states, devoted their efforts to passing laws against each other, and to internal bickerings. They refused to grant Congress any sanction of federal power. Vermont had set itself up not merely as a new state but as an independent republic, a nation, and appointed a backwoods ambassador to treat with Great Britain. Rhode Island defeated a proposal to provide Congress with a customs duty. New York defeated a later and similar plan. Maryland and Virginia were fighting each other. All of the states were fearful of giving any power whatever to the federal government.

Thus the great weakness of the Confederation and Perpetual Union was that it rested solely on the good will of

71

the sovereign states. Congress might requisition and be damned to it—the states often could not and more often would not honor the requisition. But Congress could not tax. It could not lay customs. It had no money. It could enforce none of its laws. The end of the war cut all connection with a great trading empire. Times were hard and getting worse. Anarchy seemed to many to be just around the corner—and so it was.

Given certain conditions, either political, military, or economic, a man of the hour is likely to arise. Ordinarily he has nothing to do with the conditions, but he "does something" about them, brings them into such sharp focus that the imperative need for a remedy is apparent to all. In the predicament of the United States at the end of the war such a man did appear. He was Daniel Shays. As much as any other man, and more than most, Shays was responsible for the Constitution of the United States and all that it implies.

Born of humble parents in 1747, Daniel Shays responded to the call for fighting men in April of '75. He was among the troops that pot-shotted the British on their retreat from Concord. A man of gigantic stature and great strength, he was cited for gallant action at Bunker Hill and promoted to lieutenant. He went on to perform so well at Ticonderoga, Saratoga and Stony Point that he was commissioned a captain in the 5th Massachusetts. No braver man ever fought with the Continentals. He proved an efficient officer, and later events were to certify the trust placed in him by common soldiers.

A brief period of postwar prosperity led to the inevitable depression which, seemingly, the returned soldiers of all wars must face. In those days most returned soldiers were farmers, and farmers everywhere found themselves heavily in debt to the merchant and trading class. The commercial interests had largely succeeded in shifting the weight of state taxation to the land. Courts were bogged down with suits for debts against farmers. The veterans of the war returned to civil life to find that their pay—when they got it at all—was in worthless paper money and heavily taxed land.

The conditions in Massachusetts probably were no worse than they were in the other states, but note that it was to Massachusetts that Daniel Shays returned from the war—to the manifest confusion of those historians who assert that individuals can never affect the flow of history. Shays was a completely disillusioned veteran who already had been forced to sell a handsome sword, given to him by the Marquis de Lafayette, to buy food for his family. Shays said aloud that the war might be over but the rights of man, about which he had heard so much, had not yet been achieved.

Throughout the summer of 1786 popular conventions and town meetings demanded reforms in the Massachusetts administration. No reform came. Even Samuel Adams, now grown old and conservative, was against any reform. He thought things about right as they were. His arteries were hardening. He curiously held that the demands of Massachusetts farmers were the work of British subversive agents, intent on wrecking the Republic piecemeal by state revolutions. As summer moved into autumn, desperate farmers and laborers gathered in scattered groups to prevent the sitting of county courts, the dockets of which were stacked high with debt cases, including hundreds of evictions. At Springfield Shays appeared at the head of some eight hundred men and in an effort to get more arms attacked the arsenal. Another force under Luke Day had planned to attack at the same time, but did not. Local militia defeated Shays's men, who "retired to the hills," and months of chase and guerrilla warfare began.

The Massachusetts legislature roused and sent General Benjamin Lincoln and troops to put down the rebellion. In February of 1787, Lincoln marched his men through a blinding snowstorm and fell suddenly on Shays at Petersham. Armed for the most part only with staves and pitchforks, the rebels were routed by gunfire, and dispersed, and had to be hunted down one by one in the deep snow, like so much game. This was work that the militia under General Lincoln did not like, for there was much sympathy for the Shays mob.

After the debacle at Petersham Shays and several of his followers fled to Vermont, where Ethan Allen first bade them welcome, saying that the Massachusetts government was manned by a pack of damned rascals anyway. A bit later two of Shays's trusted lieutenants, Luke Day and Eli Parsons, approached Allen with an invitation from their leader. If Allen would proceed to Massachusetts and take command of Shays's army—which by then must have been non-existent, or underground—a second rebellion would be staged which, with Colonel Allen's undoubted leadership, would unquestionably be successful. There had been a time when such an adventure would have been exactly to Allen's liking. But now he was newly married, the Republic of Vermont was doing well, and he had a deal of real estate on his hands. He would not listen to the proposal.

In a general pardon of the rebels, Shays was specifically excepted. In a fact, he was condemned to death by the supreme court of Massachusetts. A few months later, however, Shays petitioned for a pardon, and it was granted. He returned to his home, and soon moved to New York state, settling in Sparta, where he carried on a farm and died forgotten in 1825.

The effects of Daniel Shays's uprising were tremendous. Although the rebellion pleased Jefferson, who thought that a little bloodletting was a good thing for a republic, it frightened Washington and nearly everyone else of any standing, economic or political, in the United States. Washington wrote that there were combustibles in every state like those in Massachusetts, that only a spark was needed to set them off into explosions. He said he felt infinitely alarmed at the disorders and wondered what would become of the Republic if they continued.

A number of the conservatives among the Founding Fathers felt deep despair, and some of them turned to the idea of monarchy. The President of Congress went so far as to sound out Prince Henry of Prussia, to learn if he would be interested in becoming king of the United States of America. Daniel Shays had indeed given reflective Americans a vision of dreadful disorder, perhaps of final disintegration of the Republic. Shays had also done something else; he had shown that a government, itself founded on rebellion, could also deal with rebellion.

From the emotional surge of fear that swept the squabbling and chaotic states came presently the convention that drew up and put into force the great Constitution of the United States. Politically the country became of age. But not culturally.

Building a distinct culture, a national character, a way of living, cannot be done by an Act of Congress, nor yet by an Army and Navy. It must come from many sources. It does not happen instantaneously. It is gradual and is conditioned by climate and topography, by native population, and in the case of the United States it has always been greatly influenced by immigration. Perhaps the greatest single influence of all has been the American frontier, the ever changing pioneer regions. As the succeeding waves of migrants tamed and conquered the frontier, the frontier also did something to the pioneers. It had a hand in forming their characters. The use of Indian corn and the rise and dominance of the log cabin are two instances.

It has been the general habit of American historians to show that the War of 1812 started the flowering of a national character and set us up as a really independent and world-respected nation with a culture all our own. A good case can be made out for this contention, yet between the end of the Revolution and the year 1812 there came many and notable stirrings of a distinct nationalism, stirrings that

were vigorous and lasting. Out of them came ideas and institutions and ways of living and working that were of the
greatest influence in forming what are today accepted as
distinctly American characteristics.

Before these largely indigenous American ideas could be
worked out, it was of course imperative that the dominance
of the Christian theocracy be broken. Up to the time of the
Revolution the colonial parsons ruled autocratically in most
matters and were obeyed by a people who had observed what
happened to witches like Goody Bassit, who was properly
hanged, to dissenters like Anne Hutchinson, who was banished,
and skeptics like Ethan Allen, whose dreadful book, *Reason
the Only Oracle of Man,* was largely destroyed by fire from
God's lightning, and who himself died in liquor "and in
Hell lift up his Eyes being in torment."

But the powers of the parsons pretty much passed with
the Revolution. The Deists who did much of the drafting of
the Constitution left God and the Powers of the Air out of
that document.* And the First Amendment, added in 1791,
declared that Congress could make no law respecting religion. Even the tombstones in the churchyards of the several
states recorded the changing belief. Those old slate and
granite markers, indeed, trace as nothing else now can the
breaking down of Puritan theocracy.

Consider the earliest stones. They have a skull and crossbones, symbol of men who looked the King of Terrors fair
in the eyes and asked no quarter. There was no hope. Death,
rather than life, was their obsession. Within fifty years, however, the crossbones have disappeared entirely, and now the
skull is winged, indicating how the stern Calvinism has been
corroded, softened, for the winged skull can mean only death
and resurrection. In the third phase, the winged skull re-

---

* And Paul Revere, now a caster of fine bells, left God out of his first
job, which he inscribed "The first bell cast in Boston 1792 P. Revere." Up
to this time, most if not all bells carried some devout legend, like "Man
made me to show forth the Glory of God." Revere was abreast of the times.

mains, with an addition; the face now has two mouths, one for the skull, one with lips for the cherub. What can this be except death, resurrection, and salvation? And by mid-eighteenth century all sign of the grinning skull has disappeared, and in its place is a veritable cherub, smiling, flying. Then, quite suddenly between 1775 and the end of the century—a matter of twenty-five years at most—all symbols of Christian theology disappear, and in their place are the cinerary urn and a cypress or weeping willow—pagan devices both. Americans had ceased to be obsessed either with death or with the hereafter, and had turned their energies toward worldly affairs.*

The worldly affairs of Americans of the time were largely maritime and agricultural. As farmers they had not yet hit their stride, but on the seas they were as good as they came. From the mass of rough and uneducated American sailors now arose one who was touched with genius. He was Nathaniel Bowditch of Salem, Massachusetts, the frail son of a cooper and shipwright. He taught himself mathematics, taught himself Latin for the sole purpose of reading Newton's *Principia*, and sailed on East Indiamen out of his home port. On his second voyage he spent every spare moment making observations and teaching the crew how to take lunars, the only method of getting longitude without a chronometer, an instrument which no Salem shipmaster of the day thought he could afford.

With Bowditch on all his voyages went every scientific book he could borrow. He discovered some eight thousand errors in the navigation tables then in general use, and began work on a new set of tables. It appeared in 1802 as *The*

* Odell Shepard of Trinity College has an interesting study of Yankee gravestones in his *Connecticut Past and Present* (New York, 1939). His researches show a lag of from ten to twenty-five years as the freshening wind blew inland from the port cities; viz., the urn and cypress might appear at Saybrook, Connecticut, as early as 1775, but at Bennington, Vermont—far inland—not until 1790.

New American Practical Navigator, being published simultaneously in America and England, and since has been known as the seamen's bible, as it is to this day.

Bowditch's book speedily made this Yankee mathematician known around the world, for the book was soon in the sea chest of every American captain and seaman—men who were to become fabulous on the oceans. Bowditch himself was something of a practical mariner. On Christmas day in 1803, returning to Salem from a long voyage in the *Putnam*, he ran into a blizzard. All other ships on the coast ready to make port were standing off, waiting for the snow to cease. Trying to make harbor was too dangerous.

Bowditch kept the *Putnam's* bow heading in, and one of his crew was heard to remark that "Our Old Man goes ahead as if it was noonday!" The crew thought themselves as good as lost, but the frail young skipper plowed ahead for the rocky harbor. Bowditch knew where he was—apparently he always did, no matter the weather. And he got a break just at the entrance of the port, when the snow let up for a moment and he could confirm his position. The moment was enough. The ship went safely in, to dock at 9 o'clock at night in one of the worst snows of record.

The story of this master feat of navigation grew and took on the usual exaggerations, until Bowditch became as fabulous as his book. But it was his book that told the world the United States was beginning to produce its own native geniuses. Bowditch became well to do but did not stop his scientific work. He spent many years in translating the first four volumes of Laplace's *Mécanique celeste*, which has been hailed by astronomers as an epoch in American science. He also contributed many and valuable papers to the young American Academy of Arts and Sciences, one of which, on the motion of the pendulum, anticipated discoveries of almost a century later. Bowditch left a legend, and for many years to come, "I sailed with Cap'n Bowditch, sir" was a Salem man's password to an officer's berth.

Another self-taught man of colonial birth who did something to give the United States a character of its own was Asher Benjamin, born in rustic Greenfield, Massachusetts, two years before the Revolutionary war began. Benjamin had a natural eye for the beautiful and the practical, and in a day and place where "architect" was a term unknown to most people, he became just that. With what must have been almost no encouragement, Benjamin in 1797 produced a book, *The Country Builder's Assistant*, which with its revised editions became of huge influence in the back country of New England and in upstate New York.

Visitors to interior New England and New York, even in late years, must occasionally be struck by one fact—for miles they may drive up the Kennebec, the Connecticut, the Merrimack, and other rivers, and pass countless farmhouses that may be neat but are nondescript and of no particular beauty; but every few miles they are sure to see a house of simple yet imposing design, so handsome as to catch and hold the eye in quick admiration. Such a house likely stems from Asher Benjamin's books.

What Benjamin did was to produce the first practical building guide in America. Page after page of carefully drawn and engraved plates, covering everything from trusses, keystones and modillions to plain and fancy designs for chimney pieces, went into the book. Other pages showed guilloches and frets and gave rules for drawing them in correct proportions. One diagram showed how to diminish the shaft of a column and how to set the flutes of a pilaster. Elsewhere the author told how to make stucco and mortar, how to lay a foundation, how to proportion outlines for the main structure.

The whole book was down-to-earth. A farmer about to build his own home found it a godsend, a whole course in design and construction. Carpenters of the day, whose knowledge of design was limited to saltbox-roofed and plain hip-roofed houses, got ideas from it—ideas for those wonderful fanlights so much admired today, for those classically simple doorways, for handsome fireplaces and their mantels; for the acanthus, the parsley and the waterleaf decorations.

Benjamin's first book and the revisions of it went through edition after edition, all to the glory of the American countryside, where no architect could hope to earn a living. More than Charles Bulfinch, more than any other one or score of men, Asher Benjamin influenced the country scene in Northeastern United States. Although the bases for his designs came from England, from Rome, from Greece, they underwent considerable modification in his hands, and were further modified in the hands of those who used Benjamin's books to build their homes. By the time the finished product stood on an elm-shaded hill overlooking the Merrimack, or the Kennebec, or Lake Champlain, it was a house of a distinct character, a house that reminded nobody of houses seen in England, Italy or Greece. Asher Benjamin helped to build America as a nation.

What Benjamin did for the countryside, the better known Charles Bulfinch did for Boston and other port cities. Of a wealthy Boston family, Bulfinch went abroad to study architecture and returned to design mansions for rich traders of Massachusetts. He also designed the Bay State's capitol, many fine business blocks, and the celebrated India Wharf. His influence traveled far through his disciple, Samuel McIntire of Salem. And it was Bulfinch who took charge, at the resignation of Latrobe, as architect for the national Capitol in the District of Columbia, and finished the job. No longer would the United States have to engage Frenchmen or Englishmen to design their homes and public buildings.

But it was an English lad who founded the American textile industry. He was Samuel Slater, who served apprenticeship in the new English cotton-spinning mills and made himself thoroughly acquainted with the amazing machinery devised by Richard Arkwright and Samuel Crompton. In 1789, when he was twenty-one, Slater embarked for America. He was in disguise, since the emigration of textile mechanics was forbidden. So was the exportation of any designs of the closely guarded textile machinery. Not daring to be found with plans in his possession, young Slater carried all his information in his head. His mind must have been singularly endowed, for the machines of the period were huge and very complicated.

In Providence, Rhode Island, Slater met Moses Brown, who had capital, and a year later American-made cotton goods were on the market, the product of machines built by a man who had retained in his head the design and connection of thousands of minute parts. Slater married another textile genius. She was Hannah Wilkinson, who is believed to have conceived the idea of making sewing thread of fine cotton yarn. She fashioned the first samples with her own hands. Hannah's brothers went into this end of the business, and cotton thread largely supplanted linen for sewing.

If the end of the Revolutionary war brought a revived interest in matters of industry and intellect, it also brought the usual reaction against all things military. With the coming of peace the genial and profane General Henry Knox drew up a comprehensive plan for a national militia, what in time became the National Guard, but the plan could find no favor in 1790. It must wait a bit. It was General Knox, too, who broached the idea and made the first move for establishment of the United States Military Academy at West Point. The General said that he did not think the Revolution would be the last war fought by the American people, and he felt that if wars must be fought, Americans should have a professionally trained leadership.

Even with peace and the reaction, the United States needed firearms, and two of the men who started making guns for the government devised a process that is still hailed as

America's first great contribution to industry—that of interchangeable parts and mass production. The two men were Yankees, Eli Whitney and Simeon North.

Whitney has come down in history as the inventor of the cotton gin, the machine which had such influence on the economy of the entire country and, most ironically, fettered the slave to Southern soil and presented the problem that was to split the Republic in twain. The cotton gin and its results have always and properly been given prominence in our history books. Not so with Whitney's other contribution. Whitney was no moony dreamer of perpetual motion. He had both feet on the ground. When he ran into the usual troubles of inventors—those of imitation and infringement—he fought successfully to protect his patent; and he also began to make ten thousand stand of arms for the government. No gunsmith, Whitney proposed to make the rifles by a new method which he described as follows: ". . . to make the same parts of different guns, as the locks, for example, as much like each other as the successive impressions of a copper-plate engraving." There in one sentence was the idea of mass production, a titanic conception.

At this period gunsmithing was a trade, and the making of one rifle a long and careful task to be done only by an experienced workman who made every part himself. Whitney soon devised machinery that could be operated by anybody possessing eyes and hands; it reduced an extremely complex process to a succession of simple operations. Ridiculed, of course, as a visionary and all-around crackpot, Whitney went ahead and made good rifles with unskilled laborers—made them so fast that the government men half-suspected some trickery. Whitney's process did not go begging to American industrialists; they adopted it as quickly as machines could be made to handle their various products. It was the same process that Henry Ford applied a century later to the manufacture of automobiles.

Simeon North, born the same year as Whitney (1765) in Connecticut, was a maker of scythes until 1799, when he got a government contract to produce five hundred horse pistols. These were probably made by the old hand process, or at least in part so; but in a later contract for twenty thousand pistols North had the government put a clause in his contract that shows he had independently hit on the same method Whitney was to use. "The component parts of the pistols," said the contract with North, "are to correspond so exactly that any limb or part of one Pistol may be fitted to any other Pistol of the twenty-thousand." They did fit, too, and the government found the North product to be exceedingly well made.

It is impossible to say which of these two men preceded the other in devising America's mass-production technique. Whitney's fame rests on the cotton gin, while North is wholly unknown today. Both men were of immeasurable influence in creating the United States as we know it.

Another contemporary prophet of things to come was not so successful. About 1811 Colonel George Shoemaker, of Centerville, Pennsylvania, hauled nine wagonloads of what he called hard coal into Philadelphia for sale. The Colonel had been experimenting with this fuel for several years, and had found it cleaner, hotter, and more lasting than the soft coal then in use. On this primeval selling tour, he managed to dispose of only two loads, for cash. The others he gave away, and for neither did he receive thanks. He was promptly denounced as an impostor who was attempting to peddle black stones. The Colonel was a little ahead of his time, but his idea soon proved sound when closed stoves came into use.

Elkanah Watson, however, found the times ripe for at least two of his new ideas. Born at Plymouth of Pilgrim stock, Watson did not serve in the Continental army, but his war years were nevertheless filled with adventures, many of them concerned with supplying gunpowder to the Americans.

He was a rattling good businessman. After making and losing two or three small fortunes he settled in Albany, New York, in 1789, and almost immediately began interesting the public in a waterway from the Hudson river to the Great Lakes. The idea became his obsession. Two years later he prevailed on several wealthy friends to accompany him on a tour through central New York, and during this trip he proposed what not long after was the Big Ditch, the Erie Canal.

It would appear that Watson was the first man to propose such a canal. He also interested influential persons in building it. And great as the influence of the Erie canal was to be for a period, Watson's other hobby had an even greater and much more lasting influence. He had moved to Pittsfield, Massachusetts, where he set up as a scientific farmer. He imported Merino sheep, special breeds of pigs, and prize bulls. In 1810 he staged a "Berkshire Cattle Show" which grew into the Berkshire Agricultural Society, which sponsored the first county fair in the United States.

Watson was a publicist of ability. He wrote and published countless articles about the county fair. He corresponded with farmers in all of the states. He traveled extensively, and always with an eye to promoting county fairs. He told farmers everywhere that they could learn much from each other and that the fair was the most practical method for the distribution of ideas and accumulated knowledge. So well did he work that long before his death in 1842, the county fair was a sound and valuable institution, of greater influence on American life, then and now, than scores of other and much better known events in our history.

Before getting on to the real giant of American intellectual independence between the wars, it might be well, for contrast, and amusing, too, to consider briefly the woman who seems to have founded a typically American religious cult. Possibly Jemima Wilkinson is not important to history, but she did set a style in religion that although not continuous has been a recurrent phenomenon with us, and is perhaps as characteristically American as anything we have. She was born in Rhode Island in 1752 of well-to-do parents. All authorities agree that she was extremely pretty. She was not fond of work. She loved to read, especially "frivolous literature"; but when she heard the great George Whitefield preach at a revival in about 1768, she was a changed woman. She fell into a coma of several days' duration, and reported, when she came to, that she had died, gone to heaven, talked with the Lord, and now here she was, Jemima Wilkinson no longer, but the Public Universal Friend, sent to earth to direct all good men and women in the path of Jesus Christ. Henceforth, she always referred to herself in the third person, as The Friend.

The Friend naturally went to preaching the Word at once. She dressed in a long, flowing robe of fine white material, mounted a horse, and rode through Rhode Island, holding meetings, founding churches. She seems to have been a remarkably fluent and effective preacher, and it probably did not hurt matters that she was very easy to look at. Tall, graceful, with raven hair and "dark hypnotic eyes," she was a woman to attract attention anywhere. And she did.

Because she preached celibacy and stressed the necessity of supporting her sect regardless of family or other obligations, she soon ran into opposition. She mounted her horse again and led a considerable band of followers into Pennsylvania, then into western New York. Here in 1790 on the wooded frontier she established near Seneca Lake a colony she was pleased to call Jerusalem. The colony prospered famously—and so did The Friend. Although everything was supposedly held as community property, The Friend managed to get 12,000 acres of land for herself, and she also had her followers turn to and build for her sole use what many a surprised traveler in that part of the woods, who came upon it suddenly rising among the trees, called a mansion.

Setting up her headquarters in pretty grand style, The Friend appears to have become dictatorial, and perhaps a bit grasping. "The Friend hath need of these things," was an expression she used often, just before she acquired something new. But when signs of revolt appeared, The Friend put on her lovely white robes and turned loose all the power of her great eloquence, which fetched them every time. She learned to like luxury, living in the uncharted woods of western New York like some oriental hussy. When the Duke de la Rochefoucauld visited her colony in 1796, he found that The Friend's house "resembled the boudoir of a fine lady, not that of a nun." Six handsome young girls were constantly in attendance on The Friend. She dressed in silks and her formal appearances, of which Rochefoucauld saw two, were conducted with superb showmanship. The Duke naturally enough had an eye for good-looking women, and he found The Friend to be "extremely well made," with fine teeth and beautiful eyes. She did not, said the observant Duke, look a day over thirty, yet she was forty-four when he saw her. He thought that although she aimed at simplicity of manner, all of her actions were as studied as those of an actress.

In time, it appears, as has so often been the case, The Friend felt the need of an Elijah, and Elijah appeared in the form of one Squire Parker of the colony. Suspicion seems to have crept into the breasts of certain female members of the colony, and watchful eyes and keen ears went to work. It was soon whispered that Elijah and The Friend were seen in what an unfeeling attorney might have described as *in flagrante delicto*, but which the handmaidens said was "blessing each other with repeated raptures."

In any case, Jerusalem in New York state, which had reached a peak population of two hundred and sixty gullible persons, began to fall apart. The Friend herself became fat and horrible with dropsy, her great beauty swiftly deserted

her, and she was left an embittered old woman. She died in
1819, and Jerusalem died with her. Yet she had labored to
some purpose, and Americans of more recent years will have
no difficulty in tracing The Friend's style and influence down
to their own time.

On another plane entirely was the intellectual genius of
America in the period between wars. Much as Watson and
Bowditch and Benjamin and Whitney and the others contributed to America's rising pride of nationalism, and they
each contributed a great deal, the forgotten or rather unknown giant of the time was Noah Webster. Of all the really
great Americans of this period Webster is the least known.
True, many Americans know that a Noah and not a Daniel
Webster compiled the Dictionary, but that is about all. It is
a case of a man being lost in the shadow of his work.*

Although Noah Webster's great Dictionary was published
after the War of 1812, he belongs to the period between wars
because it was then that he got the idea, and preached it, of
making the United States less dependent intellectually on
England and Europe. He was born in 1758, at West Hartford, Connecticut, of a father who apparently recognized
something unusual in his son. Webster Senior mortgaged
and nearly lost his fine farm in order to send the boy to Yale
college; and the young man found times hard indeed, after
the Revolution, for a man of intellectual bent. Young Noah
studied for the law, taught school, practiced journalism, and
in 1783 prepared and published his first Blue Back Spelling
Book, one of the great landmarks in the history of American
education.

The Blue Back Speller sold fifteen million copies within a
few years. What it did to the chaotic orthography of the time
can hardly be appreciated today. In eighteenth century
America there were few rules as to how words, even common

---

* I find, however, a goodly number of native Americans of old stock who
in 1945 are of the opinion that it was Daniel who "wrote the Dictionary."

words, should be spelled; anyone who has read old letters, or even official documents, knows the astounding attempts at phonetic expression our forefathers made. One finds *jinerll* for *general; Ffebrewarie* is a month; *toune* was *town;* and in the matter of spelling native American place names truly stupefying efforts were made.

Young Webster, who was a pedantic and choleric fellow, wanted some order, some rules, for orthography. Moreover, he was intensely patriotic. He wanted Americans to have their own particular ways of spelling. He thought, with good reason, that an American orthography would encourage the publication of American books. More important, he said, was that "a national language is a band of national union." Let us spell in our own way, he went on, for this will "inspire us with the pride of national character." He thought that Americans, no matter how they boasted of their independence, were sheeplike and slavish in their copying English terms and spellings. He did not like his fellow Americans' "blind imitation of English manners." All of this, he said, turned their attention from their own interests and prevented them from respecting themselves.

There was little ground to go on in the business of rules, and none at all in respect to the thousands of strictly American words and expressions of which no English scholar had ever heard, much less had attempted to spell. So, Webster spelled them one and all as he thought best. He threw out most of the *-our* endings, like *honour, labour,* and substituted the simple *-or.* He lopped off the *k* from *publick* and similar words; he transposed the second *e* in *theatre* to make it *theater.* And from here he dived into the mass of Indian words and made-up frontier words and wrote them out as he thought they should be. It was a tremendous job this young Yankee set out lonehanded to do. In subsequent editions of the Speller he added new words, and in every instance also gave the proper, or what he held to be the proper, pronunciation of each word.

With publication of his first Speller, Webster faced the danger of having his work pirated without compensation; none of the newly established states had given thought to copyright law, nor had the so-called federal government, which had little authority anyway. So, Webster deliberately started on a tour to visit the thirteen capitals and in each of them to interest the legislators in a copyright law. He also wrote pamphlets recommending a stronger federal union.

His tour of the states, as far south as Charleston, gave Webster a good realization of the nation being formed. He earned his way by giving lectures on the need for an *American* language, with its own rules and meanings and spellings; and by teaching school and holding singing schools. He often found the way difficult, for Americans were not greatly interested in acquiring intellectual independence. Yet it is surprising that even our great men did not always appreciate Webster's efforts. "I view Webster," wrote Thomas Jefferson, in 1801, "as a mere pedagogue, of very limited understanding."

During these years Webster was giving thought to the necessity of an American dictionary. Being a man of easy irritation, he became provoked at the English dictionaries, books which coldly ignored the United States and its thousands of new and unique words; and he swore, more than once, that he would produce an American dictionary. In 1803 he gave up journalism and teaching and shut himself away from the world, and three years later his first Dictionary was published. Although this book contained more than five thousand words that had never been in any dictionary, he thought of it only as a preparation for a larger work. So it was. For the next two decades he labored prodigiously at what in 1828 was published as *An American Dictionary of the English Language*, the grandfather of all American dictionaries.

Webster's work as a lexicographer has naturally put all of his other contributions in shadow, yet there were other works of this man which affected Americans. In the medical field he wrote a sound treatise on epidemic and pestilential diseases. He edited John Winthrop's *Journal*, a notable historical contribution. He compiled school readers that sought to indoctrinate young Americans with a love and respect for their native country, and probably were successful in doing so. The influence of Webster's readers was incalculable. He wrote pamphlets on banks, on insurance, on the decomposition of white-lead paints, on the rights of neutral nations in time of war. His monograph, *Experiments Respecting Dew*, begun in 1790 and published in 1809, still holds an honorable place among pioneer American essays in physical science. This and other of his pamphlets doubtless hastened establishment of the United States Weather Bureau and of the Bureau of the Census. His interests were as many and as diversified as were those of Franklin and Jefferson, but for some reason, and that possibly the monumental success of his great Dictionary, they have been forgotten.

A radical only in his lexicographical life, Webster remained a confirmed Federalist conservative to the end of his days, which came in 1843; and until the last he continued to wear the tie-wig, the small clothes, the low shoes with silver buckles, that men wore in his youth. Yet, though he would have no truck with the new-fangled trousers and such, his fanaticism in respect to speech and spelling was so radical and so competent that he, perhaps more than any other one man of his time, gave Americans a feeling of being something more or less original, and not merely a copy of an Englishman.

CHAPTER VI

With Her Own Wings

FOLLOWING the end of the War of 1812 our country went into half a century of astonishing growth and consolidation. Seen in retrospect, it seems a period of the greatest ferment and movement. It was as if a new machine, vast and complicated with countless wheels and parts, had at last started in motion with a force that nothing could stop. Not before since history was first set down on paper, perhaps, had a nation made such progress in material things—gains in territory, new inventions, internal improvements, new industries and kinds of businesses. And there were a few of the people who somehow found time for matters intellectual, some of them humane, although the true flowering of these things did not get under way so early as did material progress.

As the countless wheels of the new machine began to turn and pound and grow steadily into a thunder that was climaxed by the Civil War, the leisurely life of the Founding Fathers and their sons and daughters gave way to the swift tempo of civilization arriving and expanding with dizzy speed. Only a very few could see, or thought they saw, a dark cloud in the sky. As for the rest, it was clear sailing, all the long way from the Atlantic to the Pacific shore. Orators were constantly amazed at American Progress, and they said as much from a thousand stumps and platforms, while the people not only believed them but went ahead to prove them right. In the space of fifty years the people of the United States were to acquire half of the livable part of

North America, string it together with canals, rails and wires, and erect their outposts in every region. What is more, they were all unconsciously yet most effectively creating ways of living and of thinking that were putting a patent mark on the American character that had started to form with the end of the Revolution.

It was a great and wonderful drama that filled these years from 1815 or thereabout to 1865. Little wonder Americans contemplated the rising number of stars in the blue field with swelling pride. Both great men and great windbags were declaring that the national bird was no longer a fledgling but was soaring, flying with her own wings. Little wonder they and their hearers believed in the American Epic. They were living it.

Internal emigration was epidemic, emigration to newly acquired American territory, emigration to regions technically foreign, emigration to still other regions of doubtful sovereignty.

Opening of the Erie Canal sent footloose adventurers westward at once, among them landlookers for lumbermen. These taciturn, cast-iron men took one good look at the tall *Pinus strobus* that stood trunk to trunk from the western end of Lake Erie to the western end of Lake Superior—and God alone knew how much farther—then returned to their home stamping grounds in upstate New York and all parts of New England, to tell lumbermen they had discovered lumberjack heaven.

Maine and New York still had empires of spruce, but it was pine that America and the world wanted; and here in Michigan, Wisconsin, and Minnesota was pine without end —to be had for one dollar and twenty-five cents an acre. Soon the Erie Canal saw the advance guard of the men who were to make settlement of the deeply forested Lake States region both possible and sudden. These red-shirted lads, as Timothy Dwight noted, lived a life that seduced them to irreligion, immoderate drinking, and other ruinous habits not named, but they were the proper men to prepare a wild region for quick settlement. They hit southern Michigan with bawdy shouts and a clanking of saws and axes, and in almost no time at all they had made clearings for the restless farmers of New York and New England who followed closely in their wake.

The farmers were leaving the Eastern states in increasing numbers, driven from their poor land by lack of markets for their crops; either they emigrated, or the farmer and his womenfolk became hired hands in the new manufacturing towns of southern New England, where the fruits of Samuel Slater were becoming most apparent. Huge black wagons drawn by six horses toured the Yankee countryside in company with polite, smooth agents of textile concerns. These agents told glowing tales of the wonders of the new mills where children both male and female could earn as much as three dollars a week—but failed to say that many worked for eighty-five cents a week. The agents stressed the fact that morals of employes were carefully guarded by enforced attendance at church and Sunday school.

Thousands of Yankee families became slaves to the mills. More thousands packed up their household goods and struck west, and found Yorkers, Jerseyites and even Pennsylvanians on the move. Ohio was the first goal of many of these rural folk. They moved by Conestoga wagon, by buggy, horseback, and on foot. One who saw the procession in 1817 passing through western Pennsylvania thought that the Yankees could be known by the cheerful air of the women, who ordinarily walked ahead of the wagon, as though anxious to get to their New Canaan; while the Jersey people stayed within their wagons; and the Pennsylvanians lingered behind, as though regretting the homes they had left.

The overland trek was slow and difficult. The way eased when the migrants got to Pittsburg. Here they might build a craft and float down the big river. An observer along the banks noted how quickly the frontier changed the habits of the rank individualists of New England. At Pittsburg he saw several Yankee families prepare two large rafts which they lashed together, and begin their voyage. Each craft was ninety feet long, with a small house on the deck. On each was a load of hay, around which several horses and cows were feeding; and piled here and there was all the rigging of the barnyard—plows, scythes, wagons, rakes, hoes; while children and poultry moved about. Sitting in a chair at the door of one of the deck cabins was an old woman, engaged in knitting. Another female was at a washtub, under a line from which clothes were already flapping in the breeze. As for the men, they did not appear to be too busy. They were chewing tobacco, said the observer, as complacently as though they were still in "the land of steady habits."

Ohio, the Western Reserve, long claimed by Connecticut, was filling up, becoming an empire. Indiana, Illinois, Kentucky, all were being settled. So were Tennessee, Alabama, Mississippi, and the still somewhat vaguely designated land west of the Mississippi river. These regions were being populated by small farmers dissatisfied with both the land and the economic and political conditions in Virginia and the states farther south. Few slaves moved with these pioneers, who for the most part were very poor. But after the War of 1812 there began another sort of migration from the Old South. This was of the larger planters who first acquired huge tracts of rich new western land, then moved like barons of feudal days, with their troops of slaves, families, horses, cattle, silver plate, fancy furniture, and the contents of their wine cellars. With them, too, moved the dark shadow which as early as 1820 could be identified as a national problem by a stray prophet or two, who had almost no listeners.

One of the westward migrants, Moses Austin, mine owner of Virginia, did not stop at the Mississippi river. He arranged for a grant of land from the government of Mexico and founded an American settlement in what is now Texas. Moses Austin had a son, Stephen F., who carried out the undertaking by leading three hundred families into the new land. Meanwhile, a severe banking panic in 1819 had sent other restless Americans seeking new land where banks did not exist. Rumors got about that Austin could get Americans fine land at little cost, and thousands of footloose gringos invaded Texas without asking leave.

Austin was a great leader, an honest man who had no wish to remove Texas from Mexican rule. But the great tide of genuine settlers, plus thousands of wild men of extremely dubious character who wanted excitement more than they wanted land, soon put the situation wholly out of hand. Mexican officials became alarmed at the influx, and with reason. They then performed the mistake of declaring invalid many of the grants they had made to Americans. This was asking for the trouble that promptly followed.

In 1836 the Americans staged a series of revolts. Mexican forces under General Santa Anna were sent to quell the uprisings and were defeated by Americans headed by General Sam Houston. Texas declared itself an independent republic and hoisted a flag with one star in its field. It was admitted to the Union in 1845.

A year after the statehood of Texas was accomplished, the United States declared war on Mexico, allegedly because Mexican troops had attacked Americans under General Zachary Taylor, who had invaded Mexican soil. It was a shoddy war at best, made so not only by the patent hypocrisy of the American "cause" but by the tragic interference of Washington politicians, who did everything possible to hamstring the outstanding American commander, General Winfield Scott. Not even in his worst hours had General George Washington so much political skulduggery to contend with as did General Scott in the Mexican war. That Scott was able to win the fight in 1848 was due chiefly to his sheer ability in the face of criminal sabotage in high places.

The Mexican war did, however, force War Department brass-hats, many of whom were still thinking in terms of flintlock muskets, into tragically delayed acceptance of the "great tamer of the frontier." I mean the revolver or repeating pistol as invented by Samuel Colt, sometimes called Colt's Patent Pacifier, the deadliest weapon devised in the nineteenth century. Every American knows the Colt gun, and almost no American knows anything of Samuel Colt.

This lethal genius was born in Hartford, Connecticut, in 1814. The boy did not fit in well at school, and his continuous experiments with gunpowder, which fascinated him beyond control, resulted, after he had blown the windows out of Amherst Academy, in his being sent to sea for a regimen of discipline. On the brig *Carlo* in the Indian Ocean, and while watching the helmsman, young Colt, barely sixteen, got the idea of his life. He noted that no matter which way the wheel was spun, each spoke came directly in line with a catch that could be set to hold it. In his quick fertile mind, which was never far from guns and powder, the boy pictured a series of chambers coming successively in alignment with a stationary barrel. Before the voyage was done Colt had whittled out of wood a model of the revolver substantially as we know it today.

Home again, the young man had a mechanic make two revolvers from the model. One blew up the first time it was fired from a vise; the other failed to fire at all. Colt was not discouraged, for he felt that the mechanic was incompetent; a right smart workman must be found to make a new gun. Colt's father would not give him money for the job, so the boy went to work in the elder Colt's textile factory. Wages were small, so small that young Colt figured it would require twenty years of careful saving before he would have sufficient money to hire a good mechanic. He must have capital much sooner than that.

Working in the mill laboratory at odd hours, the boy devised an apparatus to make laughing gas (nitrous oxide), then so new that few knew of it. He gave a demonstration in the street, and took up a collection. It was not much, but it was better than textile wages. Young Colt began to advertise laughing gas demonstrations in the newspapers of Lynn, Lowell and Boston. With a true sense of ballyhoo, he billed himself as "Dr. Coult of New York, London and Calcutta." Crowds came to see the demonstrations. Sensing the animosity of preachers toward anything pertaining to entertainment, Dr. Coult's advertisements stressed the fact that the shows were "moral lectures of a scientific nature." Amusement was never mentioned. Young Dr. Coult gave free tickets to the parsons, who were loud in their praise. (It is possible that the great Phineas T. Barnum got a number of his ideas from Dr. Coult.)

Dr. Coult was doing fairly well, and now he sought new fields on the frontier in Ohio, showing in Cincinnati for several months, then on to New Orleans. When the tour was over, Colt hired a mechanic, one John Pearson, to make working models of the revolver. They performed beautifully. Colt, now returned to his real identity, borrowed a thousand dollars from an aunt, put his two guns in a carpetbag, and went to England. Getting English patents, he returned to the United States in 1836 and received American patents. A month or so later the Patent Arms Manufacturing Company was chartered in New Jersey, and an old silk factory building was taken over.

Colt adopted the production ideas of Eli Whitney and Simeon North, and refined them. "The first workman," Colt told his stockholders in the new company, "should receive two or three of the more important parts and he affix them together and pass them on to the next who would add a part and pass the growing article to another who would do the same until the complete arm is put together." All parts were to fit any Colt revolver. The completed guns were to be inspected by men who did nothing else. Here was the assembly line.

Colt's stockholders could not or would not invest sufficient capital to make guns the way Colt planned. The factory was soon producing, but on a tiny scale, and the product was so costly that few would touch it. Sensing that something must be done, Colt had two handsomely engraved revolvers made, and these he took to Washington and presented in person to President Andrew Jackson. The old fighting man tested the guns himself and was delighted with their speed and accuracy. He gave Colt a fine letter about the guns. A test was arranged by Army men at West Point. Now came the blow. The Army found the gun "too complicated for Army use." On top of this came the panic of 1837. The factory shut down, and Colt himself was forced to pawn revolvers for his board and room.

Colt made good use of his time during the ensuing depression; he invented a waterproof cartridge of tinfoil which made the loading of his revolver ten times as rapid as before. Still the Army was not interested. Colt went to Washington to lobby around, trying to find somebody with enough imagination to see what six shots in six seconds could mean to American soldiers fighting Indians. He got nowhere at all until a crew of Texans came to town to ask statehood for the Republic of Texas. Among the long-horned delegation was Captain Sam Walker of the Rangers. He had used a Colt revolver, and now he said in a loud tone that the Colt, so help him God, was the only gun worth a damn in rootin', tootin', shootin' Texas. Captain Walker meant it. He spent his time in Washington buying up every Colt arm he could find in the pawnshops, and went on to New York for the same purpose.

Colt looked up Captain Walker, and they had a grand visit. The Ranger officer made some suggestions for improvements which Colt saw were good and which he later adopted. Colt also changed, at Walker's suggestion, the caliber of the gun from .34 to .44, which endured for many years. The Colt factory managed to make up an order of one hundred guns, which Walker took with him back to Texas.

But this encouragement, the first he had had, came too late for Colt. The Patent Arms Manufacturing Company folded up and relapsed into bankruptcy. Inventor Colt reflected on the fact that although all who had used his gun swore mightily by it, it had failed to find a market. He came to the conclusion, which he put into writing, that the success of any invention, such as the revolver, depended only about ten per cent on its real merit, but about twenty-five per cent on the prominence and popularity of the inventor, and sixty-five per cent on the self-interest of politicians. He may have been somewhat cynical in these percentages, but what is important is that Colt acted upon them; he said he would make his name well known before he again attempted to do any·· thing with his revolver.

At this time Great Britain and the United States were having hot arguments over the Canadian boundary, especially in Maine where the "Aroostook War" was under way. Hostility was high. The American public, fearful of the British navy, demanded that our harbors be protected. At this instant Sam Colt came forward to announce that he had perfected a submarine mine system that would protect any harbor from any fleet. The announcement was perfectly timed. The newspapers gave it an immense hearing, and almost overnight Samuel Colt became a public figure. Congress made an appropriation of $20,000 for demonstration of what Colt called his harbor-defense battery. Now Colt would have to produce.

Prior to this, Colt had become friendly with Samuel F. B. Morse, who was trying to get government aid for his magnetic telegraph. Congressmen were scared to aid Morse because their vocally pious constituents, egged on by the divines, believed that sending messages over a wire was the work of Satan no less. "If God had intended words to be sent over a wire, He would have . . ." It was the same argument that had been used to stem nearly all progress; and it is significant that the first official message sent by Morse was "What hath God wrought," a concession to the fading yet still strong power of the parsons. Colt had given Morse powerful aid in promoting the telegraph, and now Morse helped Colt with his harbor-defense battery.

Heralded by the press, a huge crowd assembled at Coney Island and watched Colt blow what was described by an enthusiastic witness as "all hell" out of an obsolete gunboat, setting off the submerged electric mine from shore. The seeming magic took the public fancy. Newspapers raved about it. The governor of Connecticut, noting the sudden prominence of a native son of Hartford, made Colt a colonel in the Putnam Phalanx, a select militia company of that town.

Colonel Sam Colt went on with his public demonstrations. He blasted other boats clear out of the East River, another out of the Potomac. This was dramatic stuff. Colonel Colt became a military genius. And now came the Mexican war. Down in Texas, General Zachary Taylor was impressed to learn that the Rangers, in fact all of the hard-shooting Texas men, would use nothing but Colt's revolvers. Taylor sent Captain Walker to Washington with a hurry-up order for one thousand of the Colt guns. Finding none on sale anywhere, Walker looked up Colt again.

The Colt factory, as has been related, was in disuse, and rusting. If the guns were to be of any use they must be had at once. Colonel Colt himself had difficulty getting hold of one of his own revolvers. From this he drew certain specifications—barrel and cylinder—which he turned over to Eli Whitney's plant. He gave a contract for springs to another factory, for triggers to still another, and so on. The various parts were then assembled and put together, and Captain Walker went back to the war with a thousand Colts, weapons that changed the military thinking of two hemispheres, for observers from European countries were on hand to watch the butchery done by the Colt guns, and they sent word home that an American had invented the deadliest weapon imaginable.

By the end of the war, Colonel Colt knew that his hour had arrived. His fame was great. He had no trouble finding capital to start a new factory, which in 1848 he opened at Hartford. Before the building was completed, orders were pouring in from England, France, Russia, and Turkey, and success of Colt's Patent Repeating Arms Company was assured. The Colt revolver had become a part of History.*

Samuel Colt was merely one of scores of Yankees who were inventing things in early nineteenth century. The United States Patent Office opened for business in 1790, and it is related that a dozen men, all from Connecticut, were waiting in line at the door to register their gadgets. For some reason that not even Nutmeggers can explain, the men of Connecticut have turned out more useful inventions than have those of any other state, in fact, any two other states combined.

It is possible that the great exodus out of New England in early nineteenth century had something to do with the inventiveness of those who remained at home; that they found themselves in an economic backwash with few ways of making a living. But I believe that their inventiveness stemmed, in part, from their ingrained dislike to see anything go to waste. Take old Benjamin Gilbert of Georgetown, Connecticut, for instance, a tanner who contemplated the awful waste of horsehair around his plant, and got to worrying so about it that he up and made a machine for weaving the hair into the furniture-covering too well known to call for further

---

* As an employer Colt was as far advanced as he was in arms-making. His factory was kept clean. He supplied free soap, wash basins and towels, and installed hot water. He thought fourteen hours too long, and cut the workday to ten hours. He built the first employees' social center in the country and stocked it with books and newspapers, and encouraged his employees to hold debates and hear lectures. Other employers called Colt a dangerous man.

description. Likewise, the first calf-weaners and nutmeg graters were made of scraps of tin that were going to waste in a Connecticut tin-dish shop.

One of the most important of all Connecticut inventions was given to the world in 1832, when Thomas Ireland Howe of Derby got worried because his wife lost so many pins. Pins in that day were actually worth their weight in gold, or a little more. They were made by hand, and in two pieces. The head often came off and the pin was lost. Howe invented a machine that turned out fine pins *in one piece* and by the million and what is more, stuck them in neat rows in a paper wrapper. Let no woman forget Thomas Ireland Howe.

Sharon, Connecticut, became the mousetrap headquarters of the known world in the early part of the century, for John Bostwick there invented a dandy trap and would make it in any size wanted, from a one-hole triangular-shaped affair to a six-hole round job. Over in Glastonbury, J. B. Williams was noting the waste that went with use of cake shaving soap. He worried and ruminated about this for some time, then came out of his spell with a shaving stick that reduced the waste of the soap.

It was probably genius and not waste that inspired Thomas Sanford of Beacon Falls to invent, in 1834, a friction match. He knew he had something pretty good, something that would do away with flint and steel, and he moved to Woodbridge and there built a factory to make matches. To turn his machine he built a huge waterwheel that proved too big for the stream it was intended for, and the result so discouraged Sanford that he is said to have sold his "recipe" for ten dollars.

What inspired Linus Yale of Stamford is not known, but inspired he was and in 1848 he produced the first cylinder lock, a mechanism with which it was possible to use 32,768 different keys. Not long before Yale patented his lock, another Nutmegger, Charles Goodyear of New Haven, obtained Patent No. 3,633, one of the most important to history ever granted. It was, as almost everybody knows, for the vulcanization of rubber. More than ten years of starvation and hard work went into Goodyear's great contribution.

Many of Connecticut's inventions traveled West in the packs of Yankee peddlers, who became so widely known that they were long stock characters in plays, books, and songs.*

Following the Mexican war, the winning of which was much aided by the Connecticut invention of Samuel Colt, Arizona, New Mexico, and California were ceded to the United States. California was an American possession in fact before the Mexican war started, for far-ranging gringos on the heels of John C. Frémont, explorer, had settled in San Francisco and the Sacramento Valley. These men, egged on by unofficial and potent suggestions from Washington, staged a revolt, just as Texas had done, just as the Floridas had done, and hoisted a flag indicating independence. It was the old technique all over again, and it was still good. After a little shooting, which the local Mexicans felt was seemly before giving up, the Stars and Stripes was raised over Monterey on July 7, 1846. A little more than a month later, Commodore Robert Field Stockton, United States Navy, issued a proclamation declaring California a territory of the United States of America.

Meanwhile, another huge if vague region had come under the American flag. This was the Oregon country, comprising the present states of Oregon, Washington, Idaho and parts of Montana and Wyoming, in which the dominance of the Hudson's Bay Company had been successfully challenged by American settlers in the Willamette Valley of Oregon, among whom was the influential Reverend Jason Lee. It is

---

* Although he belongs to a much later period, Alfred C. Fuller, who opened a one-man brush factory in Hartford in 1906, was the father of the modern Yankee peddlers. Neither his product nor his men should need introduction.

of note that this great Oregon country became American territory by a treaty with England in which neither war nor purchase had any part. Nor was there very much chicanery used in the business.

Well, the borders had now been pushed through to the Pacific and the Gulf of Mexico. True, there remained thousands of native red men to be civilized in the style and manner made popular at Tippecanoe Creek by General Harrison; but continental expansion had come to an end. Seventy years after the Declaration, thirteen small and bickering colonies along the Atlantic coast had become a republic occupying approximately half of the North American continent. It was a stupendous meal in so brief a time, and little wonder that digestive pains soon became apparent.

While the colonies had managed to curb their jealousies long enough to win independence in the face of a foe, the years after 1815 swiftly brought into being three distinct regions with sharply opposing interests: the manufacturing North, the slave-holding South, and the pioneer West. Neither tariffs nor free trading could please all three. And early in the century the West came to feel, and doubtless with good reason, that both South and North were out to bleed and trim the new states and territories—a feeling, virtually a conviction, that prevails to this day.

New England and the Atlantic states in general fought any government aid to roads and canals that would help the West. The West retaliated by putting Andrew Jackson into the White House and urging all sorts of legislation to hamper the manufacturing and cotton-planting states; and laws to give the new states more weight in the national government. This battle raged without armistice until the Civil War, and was resumed on the day of Appomattox. It was being fought in 1945. But neither then nor now did it impede seriously the settlement and development of the country as a whole.

The various states could and did pass any crazy law that hatred of other states dictated, or that special interests desired; but after 1803, such laws had to pass muster before a formidable tribunal. In that year John Marshall, chief justice of the United States, laid down in the case of *Marbury* v. *Madison* the opinion that no legislative act, either of a state or of Congress, was a law if such act was contrary to the Constitution of the United States. And the good judge left no doubt as to who should pass on such matters. It was to be the Supreme Court of the United States.

Marshall's opinion in this case was as important to the nation as Bunker Hill, Saratoga, and Gettysburg combined; but it lacked the glamor of battle, and so thousands of us today speak of this or that as being "constitutional" without knowing what it means or the name of the man who first promulgated the theory. At the time of this epochal opinion on constitutional law Marshall was but forty-eight years old. Born a Virginian, he fought long and well in the Revolution, was admitted to the bar, and was appointed chief justice by John Adams in 1801. For the next thirty-five years he laid down the law with no precedents to guide him; and the law as he saw it was commonly that the Supreme Court could override acts of Congress and legislatures. It was a mighty thought at the time, an opinion that was to affect every resident of the United States for the next century and more.

The man who delivered this opinion on the rights and duties of the Supreme Court was one of the great judicial minds of the world, and 'tis a pity that so few Americans know of him. But courts of all kinds, as well as lawyers of any sort, except those dealing with sensational criminal cases, offer little of interest to the layman. John Marshall was a tall, meager, emaciated man, loose-jointed, careless in dress, and with a swarthy complexion. His eyes were his finest feature; they were black and possessed of "an irradiating spirit which proclaimed the imperial powers of the mind that sat enthroned therein." He possessed, said those who knew him, an almost supernatural faculty of developing a subject by a single glance of his mind. He liked good company, for he was far from austere when off the bench; and, like many a judge before and since, he enjoyed good food and hard liquor, went to cock-fights and horse races, owned a few slaves, and thoroughly enjoyed attending Masonic meetings. For all his intellectual powers, his manners were always most simple, and he was extremely good-natured. It is notable that he never considered himself a Virginian, or of any other state. He was, he said, an American. And he, perhaps more than any other one man, caused Virginians, Ohioans, State-of-Mainers and whatnot, to think of themselves first of all as Americans.

Neither Marshall's sound logic, however, nor the warnings and appeals of a few prophets, could do much to heal the fast-opening breach between the manufacturing North and the planting South with its black slaves. One of the earliest of these true prophets, a real fanatic who was willing to give his life to prevent his dire prophecy from coming true, was the tragic Jehudi Ashmun, a hero whose story has been successfully buried for one hundred and seventeen years.

Ashmun was a frail youth who liked books. Born of a numerous family in the backwoods settlement of Champlain, New York, he managed to work his way through Middlebury College in Vermont, then entered the Congregational ministry, becoming organizer and principal to the Maine Charity School at Hampden. In 1818 he went to Baltimore, where he engaged in journalism, and became editor of the *Theological Repertory*, a rather weak periodical of the Episcopal church. Soon the *Repertory* began to attract attention because of Ashmun's extremely able and appealing articles in support of a colony in Africa for freed slaves, later known as Liberia. This colony idea so captured the young man's imagination that he could think or write of little else. For the next several years he devoted much of his energy to interesting the public in it. It was an extremely difficult business, even for so eloquent a man as Ashmun.

The idea of a colony in Africa to be settled by freed slaves was apparently first suggested by Ezra Stiles, president of Yale College. Funds for such a colony were collected as early as 1776, and in that year several Negroes were being trained for the work at Princeton. But the war had to be won, and nothing came of the colony idea. Then, in 1817, the American Colonization Society was founded. The society, however, was by no means wholly humanitarian in purpose. It seems to have been formed solely for the sending to Africa of free Negroes, who were considered extremely dangerous and likely to breed uprisings among the black slaves.

Not long after the American Colonization Society came into existence, Congress appropriated a small and insufficient sum to provide a station in Africa for the return of smuggled Negroes taken and rescued from the slavers by revenue men; and two agents of the society, the Reverend Samuel J. Mills and the Reverend Ebenezer Burgess, were sent to prepare for settlement and administration.

Nothing much further happened. Neither the United States government nor the people appeared to be interested in the colony. The thing was dying of indifference when young Ashmun took hold. In his paper he spoke most eloquently for the colony, but he did not stop with the idea of shipping free Negroes. Ashmun said that slavery was both morally and economically wrong. He also said that slavery if continued was certain to overthrow the United States and bring it to chaos—which had not been said before. Ashmun had a plan to preclude the great struggle he saw ahead; he proposed the purchase of all American Negro slaves for cash. Then they were to be shipped to Africa and aided in settlement of what in good time should become a Negro republic, economically and politically independent.

A few kindly souls listened to Ashmun, and in time the federal government, never more than mildly interested in the project, appointed him its temporary representative to accompany thirty-seven free Negroes who were to be sent to Africa in the brig *Strong*. So, in 1822, when he was twenty-eight years old, the slight, tall, fine-featured and mild-mannered youth and his wife set sail from Baltimore, with the group of blacks who had been mostly taken from slave-runners.

Ashmun had intended to return on the same vessel, but he found the colony in such desperate straits that he resolved to remain. Death had taken a terrible toll of the first colonists. Of the 114 original settlers, about one-third were dead of fever. Most of the living were ill. The rainy season had begun. One of the white agents sent to aid the blacks was in his grave. The other had simply given up the whole thing and gone away.

Ashmun had barely time to take stock of conditions before he was warned, by a friendly jungle black, of an impending attack on the settlement by native tribes who resented Liberia, as the colony was becoming known. Ashmun was no soldier, yet he assumed leadership and prepared for the attack like a seasoned campaigner. He found two small brass cannon and a little powder. These would have to be his main reliance, for only twenty-seven men in the colony were well enough to bear arms. Ashmun set them to throwing up breastworks. He had them clear all trees and undergrowth for several yards in all directions from the homemade fortifications.

Now Ashmun collected such muskets and swords and pikes as he could, and drilled his pathetic force. The fever struck both Ashmun and his wife, who died almost immediately. Ill though he was and broken-hearted, Ashmun managed to keep his feet, and to keep his courage, which was very great and was going to be much needed. Then, one night, the surrounding jungles echoed with the rising thunder of drumming and the savage cries and exhortations of the chiefs, and the friendly native brought word that the attack was to be made that night.

On November 11, 1822, just before break of dawn, a screaming horde of between eight hundred and nine hundred savage blacks fell furiously on the little colony. Ashmun wheeled one of the tiny cannon to a slot in the breastworks, and brought it to bear on the advancing ranks. He stood with slow match burning until the howling blacks were within close range, then let go the grapeshot. It wreaked dreadful work, mowing down a score of the wild men. The black ranks broke, then rallied to the cries of their chiefs and came on again. Ashmun fired both cannon this time, and to good effect. But again the savages re-formed and came back to the charge. In the meantime one of Ashmun's men fell dead from a spear, then another and another. Ashmun paid no heed. He rammed another mighty load into one of his guns and touched it off. Every shot "found its way into the solid mass of human flesh," and this time the attack was stopped. With a yell of fear, the natives turned and like one man disappeared into the jungle, leaving more than one hundred dead on the field.

Ashmun took account of his own forces. He had lost four men; four others had been wounded. Nor was the war quite over. For the next three weeks Ashmun and his tiny crew mounted guard day and night. From the jungle came the almost continuous noise of the chiefs haranguing their men, and the drums beat constantly, as the savages got up steam for another attack. It came, again at dawn. Ashmun was ready with the same tactics he had used before. Holding his fire until the charge was fair upon his breastworks, Ashmun fired a volley from both guns. Again the cannon took great toll, and the wild men fled into the bush and kept going. Ashmun never again had to defend Liberia by force of arms.

The next attack on the colony came from within, in the person of one Doctor Ayres, sent by the American Colonization Society to replace the agent who had fled the colony before Ashmun's arrival. Doctor Ayres came soon after the second battle, and with him was trouble for Ashmun.

In the emergency into which he had run headlong as soon as he got to Liberia, Ashmun had naturally enough assumed responsibility and had successfully defended the colony. Doctor Ayres gave him to understand that he, Ayres, was now the head of things; Ashmun was without authority.

Ashmun's wife was dead. His drafts home for cash had been dishonored. His motives were being questioned by the society, and all of his great sacrifices were obviously not appreciated, if even they were understood. Doctor Ayres took over with a high hand, and after stirring the colony to near rebellion, got a touch of the fever—which so frightened him that he took the first boat back to the United States. Ashmun remained, and the poor Negroes, deserted again by one of their official agents, turned once more to Ashmun, who was fanatic enough to forget his wrongs.

With Doctor Ayres gone, young Ashmun had a free hand. He turned to with a will. He taught his charges how to clear land. He showed them how to build fences. He discussed with them the best crops, the use of kitchen gardens, and everything that pertained to what Ashmun hoped and believed would one day be a great nation of freed slaves from America. Every last black slave in the United States could be purchased for a few million dollars, Ashmun wrote in descriptive articles about Liberia. Let it be done now, and let the United States, which was responsible, see that the freed men were carried to the home of their fathers and there aided to build the Republic of Liberia.

It was a vision that in the 1820's could have been made a fact with comparatively little expense—perhaps less than the cost of one good battle, say, for instance, Antietam. But few men caught the vision Ashmun held before them. So, he continued his great work in the colony. He wrote an appealing little book, *The Liberia Farmer; or, Colonist's Guide to*

Independence and Domestic Comfort, which was later published; and for the next six years headed the enterprise with
great vigor and success, seeing the few shacks of 1822 grow
slowly into the neat village of Monrovia. Had he lived another score of years the sad story of Liberia might have been
different.

Ashmun had never quite recovered from his early attack
of tropical fever; and in 1828 he realized that his end was
not far off. He returned to the United States and died a few
days after his arrival, in New Haven. Many Yankees had
heard of the young man's noble work in the jungles of
Africa, and on the day of Ashmun's funeral "a large concourse of the citizens of New Haven and surrounding towns
united in a solemn tribute of respect to his memory and attended his remains to the grave."

Nine years later the Commonwealth of Liberia was formally organized, and in 1847 it adopted a constitution much
like our own. But at no time did the federal government,
nor the people of the United States, take much interest in
the project that might have saved so much tragedy—a
tragedy that did not end at Appomattox, a tragedy indeed
that is far from ended in 1945. Jehudi Ashmun, who died
worn out at thirty-five, was a great spirit, and he spoke with
prophecy to men who would not, or perhaps could not, hear.
Only *his* eyes, in 1822, caught the gleam of a terrible swift
sword. Only his ears heard the trampling of the grapes . . .

If men could not hear Prophet Ashmun speaking, they
were soon to be jolted out of their fatuous belief that American Negro slaves were happy in their Christian captivity.
In 1821, when Jehudi Ashmun was preparing to leave the
United States for Liberia, a carefully planned conspiracy
for a Negro slave revolt was taking shape in South Carolina.
Its leader was a remarkable free Negro, of great ability and
considerable intellect, named Denmark Vesey. Past middle
years, yet mentally very active and of great driving force,

Vesey lived in Charleston, where he worked for wages as a free artisan. Late in 1821 he began to enlist conspirators for a plan he had been considering for a long time, a great uprising of slaves.

For his lieutenants Vesey chose only Negroes who were literate, among them Mingo Harth and Peter Poyas, two men of fine intelligence, and Gullah, a huge, cruel and bloodthirsty black, reputedly a sorcerer. Vesey was a master of several languages, both spoken and written. He owned many books and read many more. He used the Bible to prove to his followers that God had ordained slaves to be freed of their bondage. He instilled into his trusted lieutenants the necessity of quoting from Scripture to the common uneducated blacks. He also discussed the rights of man, any man, with his aids in secular terms. Working swiftly and so quietly that for many months no white nor black not in the plot suspected what was afoot, Vesey and his able helpers organized between seven thousand and nine thousand men and women, all slaves, into a well disciplined band of conspirators.

Few or no domestic slaves were admitted, for Vesey distrusted them. Many of the plotters were craftsmen of one kind and another. In a little, 250 pikeheads and bayonets had been fashioned on the anvils of great planters, and more than three hundred great daggers and swords made. Several Negro barbers spent their spare hours making wigs and false whiskers with which to disguise the identities of the better-known slaves.*

Vesey seems to have thought of almost everything. In Charleston he detailed men to spy out every store and house containing arms and ammunition. Others made arrangements to steal horses and bring the rural plotters quickly into Charleston. And in the city itself Vesey's men surveyed the stables and took note of the number of animals that could easily be appropriated.

---

* Although at this period no white American wore hair on his face, many of the older blacks were bearded.

Late in April of 1822 Vesey thought the conspiracy well enough organized to set the date. He chose the second Sunday in July, and the word went out along the grapevine to the plantation slaves. A Sunday was picked because it had long been the custom of many plantation slaves to go into town on that day.

The plan had been carefully worked out. It involved simultaneous attacks on the city of Charleston from five different points, and a mounted force was to patrol the streets. All was going famously when the seemingly inevitable informer turned up. This informer did not know the huge extent of the conspiracy, but he did know that something was doing. Late in May Peter Poyas and Mingo Harth, two of Vesey's best men, were arrested. Mingo and Peter, however, would not "talk," and conducted themselves "with so much coolness and composure" that they were freed, although spies were set to watch them. In this emergency, Vesey decided to set the date for the uprising ahead one month. He sent out the word. But before the day arrived, another slave turned informer, and the conspiracy was broken by the arrest of all of the leaders. Thirty-seven of them, including Vesey, were hanged between June 18 and August 9.

Although Denmark Vesey's revolt was crushed before white blood was shed, it was of great importance to history. It so frightened South Carolinians and other Southern whites that they at once put into effect the repressive legislation that held until the end of the Civil War. Within a year after the exposure of Vesey's conspiracy, laws were passed forbidding the hiring out of slaves, and providing that every free Negro over fifteen years of age was to have a guardian responsible for his behavior. The congregating of slaves was forbidden. And to curb the possibilities made apparent by Vesey's use of the printed word, the instruction of Negroes in reading and writing was made a crime.

Another effect of Vesey's conspiracy was to focus attention on the possibility that all Negro slaves were not necessarily content with their lot. Northern papers began to wonder aloud, often hypocritically but nevertheless to some effect, if slavery was really such a boon to the nation as had long been supposed; and Southern editors and clergymen started to erect their defense of the institution.

The Vesey plot also touched off a long series of slave revolts, including Nat Turner's well known and bloody affair, which lasted until almost the end of the Civil War. But in 1822 the time was poor for a prophet like Ashmun, who had a plan to do away with slavery and with what today we call the Race Problem. Nor were the people ready to accept the ultimate implications of the warning Denmark Vesey had given them. From approximately this point onward, Northerners were to become progressively more irritating to the South. Yet there was one Northerner of the period, and a Massachusetts Yankee at that, who was working hard and against great odds to bestow a wonderful boon and comfort to his countrymen of the South. He was Frederic Tudor of Boston and Saugus, and his great contribution to civilization in warm climes was ice.

Most Americans, if they think on the matter at all, think of ice as a God-given benefaction, much in the same category as sunlight and water. Yet the use of ice in the warmer parts of the world is comparatively new, and this information has been so carefully kept from Americans, both North and South, that many a novelist has committed anachronisms that have not yet been detected.

The mint julep, more than any other drink, unquestionably personifies the South. Many a fiction laid in the South of the first and second decades of the nineteenth century has those gallant "Cavaliers" sitting on broad porches while they assimilate frosty mint juleps. A mint drink they may have had, but a julep never, not in those days. There was no ice in the South for this most Southern of drinks until the Ice King, as Tudor liked to be called, delivered his first cargoes to Charleston and New Orleans in 1820 and 1821 respectively. Tudor did more than to supply ice for juleps; he *invented* the ice business.

Cutting and storing ice was not a new idea to the Yankees of cold New England in 1806, when Tudor had his great dream. For perhaps thirty years a few of them had made a practice of cutting a small quantity and storing it in their cellars. The same was true of New Yorkers. But there had never been an ice business, not even in New England. Nobody sold ice. Hence, when Tudor proposed to ship ice to hot and far-off places he was considered little less than mad.

Frederic Tudor was born in 1783 of a prominent Boston family. He did not, like his brothers, attend Harvard, which he considered to be "a place for loafers, like all colleges." At thirteen he went to work in a Boston shipping office. Eight years later, after a voyage through the West Indies, he conceived his great idea, a tremendous piece of imagination for the time: He would cut the thick ice on a pond owned by his father in Saugus, a few miles northeast of Boston, and ship it in cakes to Martinique and other hot islands in the Caribbean.

Tudor was a strong-willed youth, otherwise he could never have carried out what almost everyone then considered a fantastic idea. But he was a true fanatic to whom the misfortunes and public ridicule that dog the steps of all great innovators were merely a challenge. With barely sufficient cash to pay for cutting the ice in the winter of 1805–06 and to charter a ship, Tudor sent two men in advance to the Port of St. Pierre on Martinique to prepare for his arrival there with the ice. In March of 1806 Tudor himself arrived in the brig *Favorite*, her hold packed with 130 tons of cold blue cakes, only to discover that his advance men had done nothing, in fact were not even present.

Tudor knew that ice was only a vague rumor to the natives of Martinique; they would have to be educated to its use. And now with a cargo of it at the dock, and the sun beating down, he knew he must move swiftly or lose the entire cargo to the heat. Always a man of quick decision and action, the young Yankee sought out the proprietor of the Tivoli Gardens, an eating and drinking place, and proposed to him to freeze "ice creams" for sale over the counter. The skeptical proprietor had never seen any ice or ice cream.

Ice cream as we know it today was probably the result of an evolutionary process during some five centuries. Water ices, what we call sherbet, appear to have been made in France and Italy for the nobility with snow fetched from the high Alps. The Emperor Nero is said to have enjoyed this dish. Marco Polo, the first great drummer, tasted frozen milk ices in Asia. Charles I of England imported a French chef to make ice cream. And a product very much like our own ice cream today was introduced into the United States before the end of the eighteenth century. On June 8, 1786, a Mr. Hall of 76 Chatham street, New York City, advertised some for sale as a novelty. Dolly Madison was the first First Lady to serve ice cream in the President's Palace.

But neither ice nor ice cream had ever been seen in the West Indies, and Tudor had to use all of his powers of persuasion to get the Tivoli Gardens man into a receptive mood. Tudor prevailed, freezing the mixtures himself, and on the first night "more than $300 worth of ice creams" were sold at the Tivoli to astonished and deliriously happy customers.

The proprietor also was happy—and no longer skeptical. "He became as humble as a mushroom," Tudor quaintly remarked. The local newspaper hailed "this remarkable epoch in the history of luxury and enterprise which began March 6 [1806] when ice creams were eaten here probably for the first time since the settlement of this country, lying fourteen degrees north of the equator." It was an event of the first importance, but for Tudor a costly one. What he termed the "decay" of the ice had been so great that he incurred a loss of almost $3,500. It served to teach him that he must find some better way of packing ice in the ship than in the hay

he had used in this first cargo; and also that he must establish some sort of warehouses at his ports of call. He returned
to Boston.

Long delay loomed. First came Jefferson's embargo on
American shipping. For three years young Tudor managed
his father's farm in Saugus, and experimented with model
icehouses, trying out various methods of insulation. Then, in
1810, he went to Cuba and by the sheer force of his dynamic
nature—and no bribes—prevailed on the Spanish colonial
government to grant him a monopoly in ice for six years.

Back again in Boston, he borrowed money to buy a ship
and to prepare lumber and timbers for what was to be the
first real icehouse ever built. The War of 1812 intervened,
preventing his return to Cuba. When he failed to meet interest payments on his loan, he was lodged in Cambridge jail.
Later he gained his release by pawning a fine watch. In 1815,
"pursued by sheriffs to the very wharf," Tudor got away
with his cargo of lumber and in Havana, Cuba, proceeded to
build the first house ever designed to preserve a large quantity of ice above ground. He finished it in time to house his
first cargo.

Sales in Havana started slowly but picked up as soon as
Tudor induced coffeehouses and bars to go into the business
of selling iced drinks and ice cream. "Drink, Spaniards," he
wrote in his Ice House Diary, his constant companion, "drink
and be cool, that I, who have suffered so much in the cause,
may be able to go home and keep myself warm." While the
happy Spaniards and natives were drinking their first cold
beverages and eating their first ice cream, Tudor was taking
stock of the performance of his first icehouse.

This building had been ingeniously constructed, with a
double partition and dead space between the walls, and its
heavy plank floor guttered to admit narrow troughs, like
eaves spouts, which caught the water from the "decaying"
ice and conveyed it to a barrel outside. Watch in hand,
Tudor stood at the barrel, timed the flow and weighed it.

The runoff at first was fifty-six pounds of water an hour. Discouraging. Tudor added a deeper bank of hay over the top layer of ice. The runoff dropped to thirty-odd pounds. He piled earth up around the building. At last he reduced the flow to a mere eighteen pounds an hour, which he considered to be the minimum.

The Havana cargo paid out prettily. Leaving an agent in the Cuban city, Tudor went on to Martinique, where he got a ten-year monopoly from the French government. He built an icehouse at St. Pierre, and left an agent there. Back again in Massachusetts he began to get cutting rights in the many ponds around Boston, including the soon-to-be-celebrated Walden. He erected storage houses by the ponds. He got another vessel. He wanted better insulation. He had tried rice chaff, wheat, tan bark, coal dust, and pulverized cork. None was good enough. Then in a moment of brilliant inspiration he hit upon one of the most obvious materials in all New England—pine sawdust. Now he had it. Pine sawdust worked famously, and the first cargoes packed in this aromatic refuse of Yankee mills carried the ice through the hot Caribbean with little loss due to evaporation. Tudor was elated.

The man was a dynamo of ideas and action, ruthless, too, the kind of businessman who for better or worse drove the United States into a frenzy of development such as no country before had known. He devised an airtight hatch for his ships. He contracted for sawdust with every mill around Boston. He invaded the South, putting up an icehouse and landing a cargo at Charleston in 1820, in New Orleans a year later. He invented what he called a Refrigerating Jar, a sort of primeval thermos container. He told his agents how to get business. "It may require years," he said, "to build up a big business. We must force our plan beyond the natural course of things." He told his agents to give the refrigerating jars free to such barkeepers as would agree to sell cold drinks at the same price as warm drinks. If the jar were not sufficient inducement, then the agent was to supply free ice for a period, perhaps even for a year. But the barkeeper must agree unconditionally to scll the iced drinks as cheaply as the warm. Tudor was later to formulate many more high-pressure methods to expand the use of ice, but now he turned his attention to the technology of production.

Among Tudor's options for cutting ice was Fresh Pond in Cambridge. Owner of Fresh Pond Hotel was Jacob Wyeth, whose son Nathaniel had some novel ideas about harvesting ice. In what was a most fortunate moment for Tudor, he hired young Wyeth in 1824 as superintendent of cutting operations. With a drive equal to that of his employer and an ingenuity almost illimitable, Nat Wyeth quickly revolutionized the methods of harvesting. He devised special saws, one operated by horse power. He invented special tools, such as tongs and pickaroons. He made a great auger to bore through a field of ice that had water on top, and thus to drain it. He adopted the curved slip and endless chain used in sawmills—making a moving belt line from pond to warehouse. Under impetus of Wyeth's mechanical genius and Tudor's salesmanship in foreign parts, the ice shipped by Tudor rose from 4,000 tons in 1826 to 12,000 tons in 1836, to 65,000 tons in 1846.

Tudor took care of promotion. He ordered his agents to aid in establishment of ice cream manufactures and vending places. Doctors and nurses were told of the great thaumaturgic properties of ice packs, and of cooling drinks. He wrote and broadcast handbills describing how food could be preserved with ice. And wherever it had been introduced or was introduced by Tudor agents, the use of carbonated water was urged. Iced, of course.

The first glass of carbonated water of historical record was made in 1767 by Joseph Priestley, the celebrated English Unitarian divine who also discovered oxygen. This soda water, as Americans today know it, was first bottled and sold as the Nephite Julep by Townsend Speakman, a Philadelphia druggist, in 1805. Speakman's contribution to America's appetite for soft drinks was the addition of fruit flavors to the plain carbonated water. Soda pop was the result. Then, about 1832, John Matthews, a brass founder of Massachusetts, invented the soda fountain, by which soda water could be automatically made and dispensed. It was soon discovered, by nobody but Frederic Tudor, that these fountain drinks were much improved when the mixing materials were iced. Tudor and his agents, you may be sure, saw that they were iced.*

Tudor was the first to send northern fruits to the tropics; he packed rows of big Baldwin apples into his ice-laden ships, and sold them at fantastically high prices. He also attempted to bring tropical fruits to the United States, packed in hay and ice, but the ship was set afire, apparently by spontaneous combustion, and he gave up the idea. But it was sound. Tudor wrote a letter in which he foresaw a huge business in bringing tropical fruits to the United States.

Tudor had had his troubles, but now new ones all but overwhelmed him. His Havana agent renewed the ice-monopoly agreement with the Spanish government, but in the agent's name. For the next ten years Tudor fought a court battle to regain what was rightfully his, and he won, but in the meantime he received no return from his Cuban investment. Then, in 1834, Tudor invested approximately $150,000, giving mortgages on his properties, in a gigantic speculation in coffee which failed miserably. Tudor was thrown into jail for debt.

---

* In time soda water and ice cream became excellent new menaces for the more excitable clergy. In the author's native town, of Newport, Vermont, as late as 1890, a powerful sermon was preached against "sucking soda" and eating ice cream in drugstores on the Sabbath; and in certain Midwest towns laws were passed against the abomination, and the selling of soda water on Sunday was prohibited. Druggists quickly devised the practice of selling, on Sundays, ice cream with syrups added. This sodaless soda was called a Sunday Soda, and presently became popular on weekdays as well. Out of respect to the cloth some cynical druggist changed the spelling to "sundae."

Tudor met the disaster with characteristic directness. Turn me loose, he told his creditors, turn me loose and I will repay you all my obligations. I cannot pay them if I remain in this jail. They did turn him loose, and fourteen years later he had paid off every cent, principal and interest, a total of $280,154.59. His recovery from the coffee disaster and his winning of complete economic independence in 1849 were due to Tudor's invasion of the East Indies and his roughshod and efficient manner of handling a rising competition.

Other Yankees, who had first ridiculed Tudor, were quick to catch on; they saw the Tudor fleet growing, his business creeping around the world. They began to bid up the cutting rights on the handiest ponds. Perhaps a score of them started ice exporting businesses. Tudor beat them down, holding most of his ponds. Nor did he stop with ponds. Before his competitors could think of it, up the Merrimack Tudor went, up the Androscoggin, up the Kennebec, and soon hundreds of farm boys in those regions were spending their winters cutting river ice for the Ice King. He met all competition head-on, and slugging. He would sell a whole cargo of ice at a loss to undercut one of the unspeakable copy-cats who had set up in the business. He set up a blacklist, and would employ no cutters or teamsters who were so ungrateful as to work for a competing concern. At one time in the 1840's he had at least fifteen competitors. One or two seem to have survived the decade, but they were in the London trade.

Tudor seems never to have considered the British Isles, but in the hot parts of the world the Ice King was supreme. In the 1830's he invaded India. On the day he learned that one of his cargoes had arrived at Calcutta, after being at sea four months and crossing the equator twice and was found to have lost little in transit due to melting, Tudor was proud enough to burst. This first cargo of ice to far-off India was an adventure that appealed to American businessmen, and

Tudor, the madman, became a respected and romantic figure of commerce. The first Calcutta cargo paid off handsomely, and so did later ones, there and in Madras and Bombay. Ice was a marvel to the Indians. Tudor's skipper, Captain Little-field, related how at first many of the indignant natives wanted their money back after leaving their purchases in the sun for a few moments. Others attempted to keep the ice by immersing it in water. A few careful souls even salted the product; and when the ice promptly disappeared, they thought the stuff was magic. One Parsee asked Captain Lit-tlefield if this strange material grew on trees, or was mined. But gradually the use of ice became understood and a habit, all to the glory and income of the Ice King—incidentally the only title Tudor ever wanted.

When Frederic Tudor was sixty-five years old, in 1849, he was unquestionably the Ice King of the world. In that year he shipped 150,000 tons—to the East and West Indies, to South America, to San Francisco, to Persia. In London, Edward Everett of Boston met the ambassador of Persia, who told the American that the greatest benefit his country had known in recent times was the introduction of ice from Boston. After many years of tribulations Tudor had given ice to the world, and had become wealthy and respected. At the age of fifty he had married a nineteen-year-old girl and fathered six children.

As old age came upon him Tudor grew a distinguished white beard to match his snow-white head of hair. He was a short man and slight, never weighing above 135 pounds; yet he was a natural leader and commander, and he maintained an almost military discipline among his employees. To the last he wore a blue frock coat with great brass buttons. His motto, written in his own hand in his *Ice House Diary*, tells something of his character: "He who gives back at the first repulse and without striking a second blow despairs of suc-cess, has never been, is not, and never will be a hero in war, love, or business."

Out of long habit the old man never failed to watch the weather closely in winter. "The frost covers the windows," he wrote in his Diary, "the wheels creak, the boys run, winter rules, and $50,000 worth of Ice floats for me on Fresh Pond." (That he always wrote "Ice" with a capital letter may indicate something.) Once an unseasonable thaw drove the old man frantic. As the eaves continued to drip, he tore out of his house in Boston, bought or rented a vast quantity of sailcloth, and had it hurried to one of his ponds and spread on poles like a tent, to keep the sun from getting at the ice.

Four years before his death in 1864, at eighty, the Ice King had the satisfaction of seeing his ships carrying his ice to fifty-three ports scattered all over the world. In 1860 he sent out 363 cargoes. And in that year "feeling the Ice business becoming a wild beast in its demands" on his strength, he turned management of his company over to a son. The Tudor Ice Company flourished for another quarter of a century, or until natural ice began to give way before the inroads of the artificially made product.

The genius of Frederic Tudor certainly influenced the habits of millions of people in all of the warmer civilized portions of the world. One might name, without much trouble, a score of American ambassadors whose combined influence on history was less than that of Tudor's.

While Frederic Tudor was inventing a business and a habit, Henry Miller Shreve, who seldom if ever has been admitted into history books, was becoming America's great builder of waterways. A hero in his day, and now long forgotten except by specialists, Shreve was easily the great river-tamer and civilizer of all time. Born in New Jersey, young Shreve became a fur-and-lead trader on the Mississippi. In 1814 he bought a share in one of the first steamboats on that river. In this vessel he ran supplies past the British batteries to supply Andrew Jackson's army at New Orleans, and himself helped to man a cannon during the battle. A few months later he successfully took a steamboat up the Ohio to Louisville, the first to accomplish that trip. Next he devised in his *Washington* a wholly new type of vessel, the shallow-draught stern-wheeler, first of the line that was to become famous on American rivers. He built others of the same type, and his success soon brought him into conflict with the monopoly granted to Robert Fulton, the inventor, and his partners by the Territory of New Orleans. Shreve won the suit, a most important one, for it opened the big river to free competition.

In 1827 Shreve was appointed superintendent of western river improvements, and no man better lived up to a title. In that day the Mississippi was for some 1,200 miles a water-jungle of snags and half-submerged forests. Small boats could thread the maze with difficulty, and steamboats of any size could make no headway at all. Now, what with the battle of New Orleans and the Louisiana Purchase, the Father of Waters was an American stream from its source to the Gulf. It was a highly important stream. Shreve was asked to make it navigable.

Setting up at New Albany, Indiana, on the Ohio, Shreve designed and built two huge snag boats, the like of which had never before been seen. He named them the *Heliopolis* and the *Archimedes*. Each vessel was in reality two boats, built side by side and held together by powerful beams. The foremost beam had a rammer on it, a sort of huge cowcatcher. All parts of the boats were made of the stoutest material, and the engines were said to be the most powerful ever put into a river craft. Late in 1829, Captain Shreve stoked up the boilers and set forth on a two-year cruise that was unique in history.

The snag boats, it was soon apparent, were the answer to the problem. Their mode of operation was to rush full-steam-ahead into an obstruction, then back off, and slam it again. No tree grew in or on the river that could withstand more than a few of these battering attacks. Soon as a tree was loose, a gin pole with tackle and machinery hauled up the broken snag, dropped it on deck, and there it was bucked into fuel to feed the mighty appetite of Shreve's big boilers. The whole process was the work of a mechanical genius. Within a short time, the two snag boats had "rendered three hundred miles of river as harmless as a millpond." And by the end of 1830, some twelve hundred miles of the Mississippi and its tributaries had been cleared of the waterlogged forests. Not until then did steamboating on the Mississippi come into its own.

Shreve's greatest feat, however, was still to come. This was the clearing of the Great Raft, as it was known in awe, from the Red River of the South. This "raft," which extended for 165 continuous miles from Loggy Bayou to Carolina Bluffs, was a mass of jumbled timbers, often twenty-five feet deep, and frequently forming a solid bridge from bank to bank. Since 1806, when a government party explored the Red and was amazed at the formation of the Great Raft, there had been talk of removing it. In 1824, it seemed urgent to have a military garrison on the upper Red River against the Texas border, where all sorts of trouble was brewing. Fort Towson was built five hundred miles above the head of the Great Raft, but government men said nothing, absolutely nothing, could be done about the raft itself. There God had put it, and there it must stay. So, supplies for the soldiers at the outpost had to be sent by long detour, by lakes, bayous and swamps. At low water even the detour was impossible.

Indians said that the raft had been growing for more moons than the oldest man could recall. It had blocked the river, causing it to overflow and submerge many Indian villages. The Big Medicine gods had been propitiated, in vain. A third government party took one look at the raft and said it was hopeless. And for more than a year the isolated outpost at Fort Towson got along as best it could, without any new supplies.

Then, in 1833, Shreve got a chance to tackle the Great Raft with his dreadnaughts. Moving the *Archimedes* into the Red River on April 11, he started battering. By the end of June, seventy miles of the raft had been cleared. Then sudden illness hit most of Shreve's crew, the appropriation for the work gave out simultaneously, and there was no money to pay off. Shreve went down-river to get things fixed up again. He also built a new snagger, the *Eradicator*, and with this ram added to his old fleet he went at the raft again.

It was nerve-racking work—ram, back, ram, back, a life of jars and jolts. None of the crews liked it, and they were often wanting to quit. Shreve was a born leader. He harangued his men, he threatened, bullied, praised. He laughed at the pests of mosquitoes, and told his men that the best way was to absorb sufficient poison from the pests to become immune. He joked at the abominable food supplies. And he kept those snub-nosed, double-jointed floating rams at work. After almost six years, or in March of 1838, the first commercial boat passed through the entire section of river that had been the Great Raft, and the greatest job of river clearing of all time had been completed. "The amount expended," said Shreve in his report, "has been $311,000." One doubts that the government ever got so much for its outlay of cash, for by the time Shreve put his snag boats away, the Ohio, the Mississippi, the Red, and a score of smaller streams were busy thoroughfares of traffic. It is fitting that Shreve's headquarters camp during the Great Raft days, then known as Bennett's Bluff, later honored his name by adopting the style of Shreveport.

There is one more man who belongs to this period. While Shreve was battering away at the countless snags of the rivers, a contemporary pioneer was running head-on into something more adamant than sunken trees. Abner Kneeland of Boston had attacked the *mores* and folkways of all Christian peoples: He had come out publicly for control of conception. In 1832 he published, under his own imprint, a small pamphlet entitled *The Fruits of Philosophy; or, The Private Companion of Young Married People.* This work did have something to say about the prevention of conception, and was the first such treatise published in the United States. It had been written by a friend of Kneeland's, Dr. Charles Knowlton, who advocated his suggestions on social, medical and economic grounds.

As is usually if not always the case in things of this kind, Kneeland was not indicted and arrested for publishing Knowlton's treatise. Instead, he was attacked through indirection, being charged—of all things—with publication in his paper, the freethinking *Boston Investigator*, of a certain profane, impious, and scandalous libel of and concerning God.

For the next five years Kneeland's case was never out of the public eye. Convicted at the first trial, he appealed, and at the next two trials the juries disagreed. It was to be noted in all of the trials that the prosecutors stressed the fact that the accused favored the abomination of physiological checks on conception, rather than the specific charges on which Kneeland had been brought into court. Finally, Kneeland was convicted and spent sixty days in jail, where he watched workmen erecting Bunker Hill monument on the heights above the prison while he composed articles on the hypocrisy of putting up monuments to Liberty in a country where freedom of speech was denied.

But Kneeland had fought a telling fight. Due to the enormous publicity of the trials, *The Fruits of Philosophy* went through edition after edition; and Dr. Knowlton himself was fined at Taunton, and in Cambridge, seat of Harvard college, was sentenced to three months in the workhouse. Virtually all of Boston's intellectuals signed a petition for Kneeland's release, and Theodore Parker wrote that "Abner will come out as beer from a bottle, all foaming, and will make other foam."

Parker was right. Abner came out of the jug swinging both arms. *The Fruits of Philosophy* quickly reached a circulation of a quarter of a million copies and at last reached England. Here it was Exhibit A in the famous test case of *The Queen* v. *Charles Bradlaugh & Annie Besant,* which created a ruckus that for a time seemed to threaten the very foundations of empire. It was won by the defendants, and is still considered the great milestone in the still continuing history of the dissemination of knowledge about a rather important subject.

Neither Doctor Knowlton nor Abner Kneeland, however, lived to witness the ultimate triumph of their contribution to knowledge and free speech. Knowlton died in 1850. In 1839, fed up with Boston, Kneeland and a group known as the First Society of Free Enquirers, set out for Iowa, where they founded a colony. No colony, probably, could have survived "Salubria," which was the name selected for the experiment. Silver-haired now, with kindly blue eyes, and "great purity and gentleness of character," Kneeland became a sort of patriarch of American Freethinkers. He taught school for a few years, and died, still in Salubria, in his seventy-first year. The battle he and Dr. Knowlton began still goes on.

Abner Kneeland was as typical of the cranks of the era as Tudor was of the businessmen and Shreve of the spearheading pioneers. Kneeland was one of the earliest of the cranks and reformers and experimenters of one sort and another who were in practice during the first half of the nineteenth century. They wandered over the Republic, keen-eyed for things they thought needed doing. Courageous, determined and often of one-track minds, they advocated both plain idiocies and sound reforms, and they brought to their work a burning fanaticism that often made them barely tolerated, at best unwelcome. The total over-all effect of their work gave Americans a new conception of what life could and should be, and it had a great deal of influence in shaping the Republic and the character of its people.

CHAPTER VII

The Ferments of Monomania

IT IS all very well to say that climate and geography and economic forces made the United States what it is today, but such a mechanistic philosophy of history does not take into consideration the power of the individual to hasten, to slow, or to direct and change to some extent the current of the great forces ebbing and flowing around him. I believe, for instance, that if Dorothea Lynde Dix had not been born when she was, the care of the insane in the United States might well have been delayed another half century. And I am convinced that old Robert Gibbon Johnson, by publicly eating a ripe tomato on the courthouse steps in Salem, New Jersey, in 1820—an age when tomatoes were considered as poisonous as arsenic—put that vegetable, or fruit, in the way of becoming a primary food in the United States. And all the way from mind to belly other single-track individualists, several of them to be described only as fanatics or monomaniacs, contributed to shaping the American nation and character. The yeast of our nineteenth century monomanias was indeed great in its fermenting powers.

Perhaps the least known of these worthy single-trackers is he whose end-product is paradoxically the best known and whose modest marker in Sleepy Hollow Cemetery at Concord, Massachusetts, bears the cryptic and bitter legend "He sowed, others reaped." Here lies Ephraim Bull, originator of the Concord grape, America's first great contribution to horticulture. A notable eccentric in a day of much eccen-

129

tricity, Bull learned the goldbeater's trade, which supported his fanatical hobby of experimenting with grapevines. These he raised and tended in his little garden on Fayette Street in Boston, until his hobby outgrew his premises. He moved to Concord, where he could have room to carry on experiments with an extraordinarily early-ripening specimen of *Vitis labrusca*, as learned men call the wild northern fox grape. Here for eleven years Bull planted, selected and cared for seedlings of this specimen, working to produce an immutable variety of grape that would be large, sweet, and early enough to elude the often early New England frosts.

A true monomaniac, and apparently a bore to almost everybody except Louis Agassiz, the naturalist, and Nathaniel Hawthorne, both of whom liked him, Bull raised 22,000 seedlings—of which he found only twenty-one worthy of preservation. But these were very good indeed. He seems to have exhibited his Concord grape, as he now named it, first in 1853, at Massachusetts Horticultural Hall. Its superiority over all competing varieties soon became apparent, and for one season, and one only, Bull received $5 a vine, bringing him in a total of $3,200. Then, however, commercial nurseries which had bought his vines for propagation put the new variety on sale, and Bull received little if any further income from his many years of devoted work. He turned into an embittered old man, given to raving about the curse of commercial nurseries. The accusing "He sowed, others reaped," cut into the stone that marks his grave, indicates how Ephraim Bull felt about things.

The Concord grape went across the continent in covered wagons, it went south on flatboats, and north into the upper reaches of New England and on into Canada. Within a decade it was the best known grape in America, and it is perhaps the most distinctly American contribution to horticulture we have. Unfortunately, grape juice of the unfermented variety, usually associated with the Concord grape, became a symbol of the Prohibitionists; but Ephraim Bull was not responsible.

Robert Gibbon Johnson of Salem County, New Jersey, did not contribute anything new to horticulture, but he—and he almost alone—put the tomato safely in the niche it now occupies as that of America's foremost canned fruit, or vegetable. Until well after 1820 the tomato, which is a native of South America, was an exotic curiosity in the United States, where it was called a love apple and used as an ornamental shrub. It was considered poisonous to eat.

Johnson, a wealthy citizen and a traveled man, had learned to eat tomatoes and found them good. He wanted to share his discovery, so, to push his hobby—which became as fanatical with him as the Concord grape did with Bull—he founded a number of county fairs in New Jersey, offering prizes for the finest tomatoes and other fruits and vegetables.

But as an edible the tomato made no progress at all until that momentous day in 1820 when old Johnson stood on the courthouse steps in Salem and announced in stentorian tones that he would there and then eat one of the lethal things. This he did with dripping relish, while the gaping crowd waited to see him writhe, then fall frothing to the ground. From this day the tomato started its useful career.* In tin cans it went to the ever-changing frontier, keeping scurvy from prospectors and miners, from lumberjacks and cowboys, the latter of whom were said to have learned to read from the labels. Canned tomatoes, more than any other dish, had a great and happy effect on the health of the spearheading men and women of the American frontier.

Sending culture to the back country was the desire of another monomaniac of the period. He was Josiah Holbrook of Derby, Connecticut, who was fired with a great enthu-

---

* James Stevens, the author, who worked many years in railroad construction camps, avers that canned tomatoes were of great aid in the work, serving as prime sobering-up antidotes on Monday mornings to the hard-drinking gangs. This thesis, with considerable support, will appear in Mr. Stevens's next book.

siasm for natural science by his study under the remarkable Benjamin Silliman, Senior, at Yale. In 1819 Holbrook founded an industrial school on his father's farm with the idea of combining manual training and farm work with knowledge drawn from books. The school failed, and so did an agricultural seminary that Holbrook established.

Going on the road as an itinerant lecturer on scientific and agricultural subjects, Holbrook got to thinking of "an association of adults for mutual education." This flowered in 1826 at Millbury, Massachusetts, as Millbury Lyceum Number 1, Branch of the American Lyceum, the first of several thousands of such groups that were to flourish until the end of the century. The Millbury Lyceum was an immediate success, and now Holbrook traveled the country over, founding more lyceums wherever he went. He talked eminent men into touring this first lecture circuit, and he must have been of great persuasiveness, for then or later he prevailed on Emerson, Horace Mann, Louis Agassiz and Professor Silliman himself to put up with the horrors of travel of the time, in order to bring culture to their back-countrymen. Holbrook also persuaded Dan'l Webster to tour the lyceums, and he booked Dr. Holmes, Henry Ward Beecher, Charles Sumner and other eminents.

In the 1830's and 1840's, it was a notable thing that the citizens of St. Johnsbury, Vermont, of Beloit, Wisconsin, of Boonesville, Kentucky, and Athens, Georgia, could look upon in the flesh and hear the great men of the day, and some of the merely well known men. And everywhere they went, both Holbrook and his lyceum lecturers encouraged the establishment of libraries and museums and the better training of teachers. By mid-century the American Lyceum was easily the great disseminator of knowledge in the country. The Chautauqua, remembered by a later generation, was a sort of stepchild of the Lyceum. The Chautauqua offered no such strong meat as the Lyceum, but went in for bell ringers, jubilee singers, preachers, William Jennings Bryan, and assorted stuffed shirts.

On the subject of education Holbrook was a monomaniac. Not content with the American Lyceum as it was, he went to Berea, Ohio, in 1837, to found a Lyceum Village. This was apparently to be a sort of fountain to supply lyceums, complete with lecturers, in all parts of the United States and of the world. A major part of the capital for establishing Lyceum Village was supplied by John Baldwin who, like Holbrook, was the possessor of a one-track mind. Baldwin's monomania was higher education for women, and it had stemmed from Baldwin's own mother, who had tried to enroll at Yale College and was refused entry.

Neither Baldwin nor Holbrook appears to have been a very good businessman. Whatever Lyceum Village was supposed to be, or to do, it failed in 1842 and became bankrupt. Holbrook returned east to continue promotion of lyceums. Baldwin, his farm and gristmill and sawmill mortgaged to the eaves, and the mortgages long past due, was in dreadful straits.

John Baldwin was a God-fearing man of the old school. He had come into the wilderness of Ohio shouting that all should repent, for the Kingdom of Heaven was at hand. His food and raiment, said one who knew him, were as plain as the biblical John's camel's hair and the locusts and wild honey. He always appeared like some humble pilgrim from a far country, one with a great mission in his mind and heart. Baldwin's mission was to found a great school of higher education for women. Men were also to be admitted, on the same basis as women.

With the dream of Lyceum Village gone glimmering, and his property sunk in mortgages, Baldwin took to praying every day. For his prayers he went alone to a hemlock grove on his farm, and there he "covenanted with God not to spend a quarter of a dollar in any useless way, but to give all except a bare support toward any cause God might direct, if He would only show me the way out of my troubles." God listened, and obviously accepted the covenant. On the thirtieth day of prayer, as Baldwin was returning home from the hemlock grove, he noted a ledge of peculiar rock he had not seen before, although he had passed it many times. He picked up a piece of this stone. "I examined its texture and quality of grit," he said later, "I took from my pocket my knife and in a few moments found that it would put a keen edge on steel. This, I said to myself, will make superior grindstones, this is my deliverance; and before the sun was down I had by means of an old ax and some primitive tools, shaped a grindstone in my cellar. I·hung it and found that it was most excellent grit to sharpen tools."

In this event was the founding of the great Berea grindstone industry, which in time sent out hundreds of thousands of stones to sharpen the scythes of untold prairie farmers, of countless axes of Lakes States lumberjacks, of the kitchen and butchering tools of all the Midwest, and beyond.

Close on the heels of his discovery, Baldwin wanted a lathe for fashioning stones. Making a model of wood, he shouldered it and one moonlit night, bareheaded and barefooted as was his wont, he toted it to Cleveland, fourteen miles distant, to have the design duplicated in metal. The lathe was successful.

Quick riches rolled in on Baldwin, but never for a moment did he forget his covenant with Jehovah. Not a penny did he or his family spend for anything above plain food and plain clothing. The rest of the fortune from grindstones went into education in the form of co-educational colleges at Berea, in Kansas, Louisiana, and India. Thousands of country boys and girls of the past three or four generations owe what higher education they have to old John Baldwin and his grindstones, plus the fact that Baldwin's mother could not be admitted to Yale. Baldwin was a good example of a one-track mind in action.

Another zealot of the period, one who had greater influence than either Baldwin or Holbrook, was Samuel Gridley Howe, who might be better remembered if his wife, who was Julia Ward, had not written *The Battle Hymn of the Republic* and thus made him, for all purposes of publicity, merely Mrs. Howe's husband. But all blind persons know who Samuel Howe was. In 1831 he opened, in his father's home in Boston, the first school for the blind in the United States. Howe was the kind of man who, to comprehend the situation of his six pupils, went about the schoolroom blindfolded. With little precedent to guide him, he devised methods of teaching the blind to read by means of embossed letters, which were known as Howe Type.

Howe's greatest obstacle was the quite general attitude of the public that nothing whatever could be done to make the blind economically and socially independent. Nothing had ever been done to train them, or even to give them the least encouragement. By holding public exhibitions of the pupils he had trained, Howe quickly changed all this. The public came and was amazed to see the blind *reading with their fingers*. It was startling, unheard-of; and so powerfully did it excite the imagination of the public that Howe was never afterward to want funds for his work. He was given the mansion of the wealthy Perkins family in Boston, which he turned into the Perkins Institution for the Blind. He raised money for the embossing of books. He found positions in business and professional life that could be filled by the blind, then trained pupils to fill them. In a few brief years he changed the thinking of and about the blind from a feeling of hopelessness to one of great promise.

For forty-four years Howe directed this school. He also visited seventeen states in behalf of the founding of similar schools. Taking the deaf-blind child, Laura Bridgman, under his personal care, he taught her to communicate with others and made her what Helen Keller became to a later generation. Becoming interested in a blind child who was also mentally retarded, Howe went on to originate the methods of treatment and education of those unfortunates often called idiots which are in use today. It is doubtful that any other man of the nineteenth century had so great an influence as Howe on the blind and mentally backward in the United States.

There was one woman, however, whose influence in a related field could match that of Samuel Howe. She was Dorothea Lynde Dix. On a Sabbath day in March of 1841, this shy, slight spinster of Boston's bluest blood, sickly and almost forty years of age, taught a Sunday school class in the House of Correction at East Cambridge, Massachusetts, and went home that night so shocked and terrified at what she had seen that she could not sleep.

What had shocked Miss Dix was the truly ghastly condition of four insane persons confined in the East Cambridge jail. Their cell was dark, airless, unheated. The walls shimmered with frost. The place was filthy, unfit for pigs.

This first experience with the plight of America's insane of the period changed Dorothea Dix's whole life and gave it a purpose. She became a fanatic. This ill, slim woman with the burning blue eyes and the low, sweet voice, this fanatic touched with genius, arose next morning with a determination that never faltered.

She set out, immediately and almost single-handedly, to attack the prejudices and superstitions of her time. She set out to win a monumental fight to have the mentally ill considered as human beings and not as sub-humans to be kept in filthy cages, often in chains, and beaten with rods to quiet their cries.

Miss Dix did not discover her genius until that Sunday in 1841. Born in Hampden, Maine, in 1802, young Dorothea became tired of stitching and distributing the pamphlets which her father, a wandering religious fanatic, thought would change the world. At ten she left home of her own

accord, ran away, and went to live with her grandfather, the
well known Dr. Elijah Dix in Boston. At fourteen she began
teaching school, and was still an unmarried schoolmarm
when she saw the pitiful creatures slowly freezing to death
in the East Cambridge jail. She learned through inquiry
that conditions of the insane in Cambridge were considered
perfectly all right.

Nor was this a cynical attitude of some especially hard-
hearted jailer. It was the common attitude of the time. In
1841 the medieval conception of insanity as a possession by
devils had changed to one just as cruel—namely, that the
insane had been born depraved, there was nothing to be
done about it, and the best way was to treat them as so many
dangerous animals.

To appreciate the task facing Miss Dix it is necessary to
remember that in 1841 there was scarcely an institution in
the United States that could be termed an insane asylum.
Close confinement, usually with chains or manacles, was the
only measure considered, so both the mildly and the violently
insane were put into jails, almshouses and prisons, where they
were without exception housed in the worst quarters.

Worse, many a warden and attendant made a private income from charging visitors from ten to twenty-five cents to
visit the "crazy house." It was thought good sport indeed
to watch the fantastic gestures of the unfortunates, to listen
to their ravings and to goad them to fury by questions, or
by prodding them with sticks.

Such was the state of civilization regarding treatment of
the insane in the United States, little more than a century
ago.

Dorothea Dix presently developed a drive that lasted for
forty years and was furious in its intensity. The first thing
she did was to bring public attention to bear on the insane
in Cambridge, and only after a stout battle was a stove installed there and some attempt at sanitation made. Then,
so far as the general public was aware, Miss Dix dropped

out of sight. This was a relief to most public officials and prominent citizens; they had roundly condemned her for her "unwomanly conduct" in matters which could better be left to men. It was an attitude she had to contend with for many years. Woman's place, said nearly all men and women too, was in the home.

Out of the spotlight after the Cambridge affair, Miss Dix was busy. Quietly, unobtrusively, but with notebook in hand, the middle-aged woman began a two-year investigation of the hellholes in which the insane were kept in towns and cities throughout Massachusetts. She found a great deal to report, but she reported nothing at all until her dossier was filled and overflowing with as shocking and damning a mass of evidence as was ever collected. Then she wrote, at white heat but with calm good judgment, her famous Memorial to the Commonwealth of Massachusetts, a document that should rank with the Emancipation Proclamation.

"I shall be obliged to speak," wrote Miss Dix, "with great plainness, and to reveal many things revolting to the taste, and from which woman's nature shrinks with peculiar sensitiveness. I proceed, gentlemen, briefly to call your attention to the present state of insane persons within this Commonwealth, in cages, closets, cellars, stalls, pens—chained naked, beaten with rods and lashed into obedience."

Miss Dix managed to convey to the gentlemen of the Commonwealth a very real and horrible sense of what she had seen. With simple direct prose, cool yet bitterly effective, she related the dreadful practices going on in what the United States, and especially Massachusetts, thought was the most progressive and enlightened state in the Union, as undoubtedly it then was.

She did not dwell on generalities. Miss Dix named the places and the victims. At the almshouse in Danvers she found a young woman confined alone in a tiny outbuilding. "There she stood, clinging to or beating the bars of her caged apartment, the contracted size of which afforded only space for increasing accumulation of filth—a foul spectacle, gentlemen. There she stood," cried Miss Dix, and the legislators squirmed, "with naked arms, disheveled hair, the unwashed frame invested with fragments of unclean garments, the air so offensive that it was not possible to remain beyond a few moments . . ."

With this grim picture before the uncomfortable solons, Miss Dix went on to tell of more, and worse. At Newton she had found a woman chained to a wall, living in what amounted to being a toilet. At Groton she had discovered a youth, heavy irons around his neck, who was chained to the wall with six feet of great steel links. Miss Dix described these and scores of others, piling horror upon horror with her direct prose, now detached, now burning with the fire of intense indignation.

It was the greatest sensation produced in the Massachusetts legislature since 1775. Nor was it in vain. With a speed hardly ever given to legislative assemblies, that of the old Bay State at once provided for rooms—and good rooms—for 200 insane patients at Worcester hospital. This was the immediate result, the forerunner of many measures taken by the state in subsequent years.

Miss Dix never stopped. Although her sudden and dramatic entrance into public affairs was still widely resented by solid, old-fashioned males, she received encouragement, both financial and otherwise, from Bostonians of her own Beacon Hill class.

As soon as she had turned Massachusetts officialdom topsy-turvy, she went to Rhode Island and started methodically to work as before. The report she finally presented was even more searing than that on Massachusetts. Indeed, no such recapitulation of horrors had been written or read before.

At Little Compton, Miss Dix had found one Abraham Simmons confined in a cell seven feet square, all of stone, even to the floor. It was double-walled, the keeper casually admitted, so he would not hear Simmons's "piercing screams."

There was no light, no aperture for air. When Miss Dix visited the hole, the walls were covered thick with frost. The man was chained by one leg. The keeper's wife told Miss Dix, laughingly, that in winter they often "raked out as much as a bushel of frost at a time," but that Simmons had "never showed any signs of freezing." The poor man had been confined in this den for "above three years."

Miss Dix prepared a special article on Simmons. It was a sardonic piece, mordantly entitled "Astonishing Tenacity of Life," which she had published in the Providence *Journal*. Beginning her indictment as though it were an article of scientific interest, she presently described the plight of Simmons and studded the description with barbs. She supposed, she said, that Rhode Islanders considered themselves Christians; but she doubted gravely whether they could address themselves to the God of the unhappy Abraham Simmons, there in his ghastly den.

Abraham Simmons immediately became a martyr, known throughout the United States. Rhode Island hurriedly followed Massachusetts in providing care for its insane wards.

Maine came next, and then the untiring woman invaded New Jersey and the West and South. For twenty years, or until the outbreak of the Civil War, she traveled by stage, steamboat and horseback, and sometimes in primordial railroad trains, throughout the Union, investigating, reporting, making friends among the wealthy and influential in order to have their aid in founding hospitals and asylums.

Once she was nearly drowned in a stage fording a river. Again, in Michigan, her stage was held up by bandits. She remonstrated with one of the robbers, telling him how foolish he was. He looked at the slim, white-haired woman. "My God! I know that voice," he exclaimed. It turned out he had heard Miss Dix speak in the insane ward of a Philadelphia jail. The robbers returned the loot.

The courage of Dorothea Dix was without bounds. Into a New Jersey dungeon she went to talk to an alleged maniac who was chained by both arms and both legs and kept in darkness. The keeper said the man was extremely dangerous to approach, and warned Miss Dix that he would tear her limb from limb, were she to get within reach. She went directly up to the poor fellow, spoke to him, called him by his name. He stared for a moment, then broke down and wept.

The chains of this desolate man were removed. Miss Dix had him put into a clean bed in a pleasant room. After two months he was so far recovered that he performed useful work around the hospital. Time and again Miss Dix went into filthy dungeons and cages, all alone, and talked to the victims of man's stupidity; and she showed what decent treatment and medical attention could do for the allegedly hopeless cases, those who were said to live in a shadow world of their own conjuring.

In three years this lone woman, beset by lung trouble, traveled better than ten thousand miles and visited eighteen penitentiaries, three hundred jails, and more than five hundred almshouses and other institutions where the insane were kept. New asylums sprang up in her wake, all staffed by doctors—not sadistic thugs—who believed that something could be done for mental cases, as Miss Dix made her way throughout the country, as she badgered and charmed and praised and blamed and pleaded with the legislatures of New Jersey, Illinois, Kentucky, Tennessee, Mississippi, Louisiana, Alabama, the Carolinas and Maryland. Wherever she went, the plight of the mentally ill was vastly improved.

With her own native land now alive to the great curative powers of humane treatment for unfortunates, Miss Dix sailed for England and the Continent. There she investigated conditions, found them extremely bad, and was responsible for founding large hospitals for the insane on the Isle of Jersey and in Rome. At last the movement of culture (in its best sense) was moving from West to East.

Miss Dix returned to the United States at the outbreak of the Civil War, and three hours after the 6th Massachusetts regiment was fired upon in Baltimore, on its way to the fighting front, Miss Dix was on a train bound for Washington to offer her services as nurse. A bit later Surgeon General William Hammond appointed her Superintendent of Women Nurses for the Union Army, the first such in American history. For the next four years she served her country ably and courageously.

In her sixties when peace returned, Miss Dix went back to her work for the insane; she did not stop until death overtook her at eighty.

That she is so almost completely unknown today is due in part to Miss Dix herself. She never permitted any personal interviews or what would today be called publicity. She would allow no asylum to be named for her. The only portrait of her that I recall hangs in Harvard Memorial Hall, in Cambridge, not far from the place where in 1841 she first learned of the condition of the insane. She was likely the most distinguished, and certainly is now the most forgotten, woman that America has produced in three hundred years and more. It seems a pity that of fifty graduate students of a large Western university, not one had heard of Dorothea Dix; and two of them identified her as a newspaper columnist devoted to the heartaches of morons.

What Miss Dix did for the insane and Dr. Howe for the blind, Thomas H. Gallaudet did for the deaf—or the deaf-and-dumb, as they used to be known. This son of a Philadelphia merchant became acquainted with a deaf-mute, Alice Cogswell, to whom he taught the names of various objects. He then went abroad to study methods of educating the deaf, and returned to found the first free school for the deaf in America, at Hartford. He also had part in founding similar schools elsewhere in the United States, and two of his sons continued their father's work. For exactly one hundred years, from 1817 to 1917, one or more Gallaudets were devoting their energies to improving the lot of the deaf.

In view of the state of the world in 1945 and the efforts being made to bring some sort of civilization into international affairs, it is perhaps not meaningless to recall that a farmer and rural teacher who was also a clergyman, by name Noah Worcester, proposed a league of nations and a world court—in the year 1814. Calling himself the Friend of Peace, this New Hampshire man, ready with an international system and looking ahead a century and more, wrote and paid for the publication of the first classic of peace literature. Worcester called his book *The Solemn Review of the Custom of War, showing that war is the effect of popular delusion, and Proposing a Remedy*.

Worcester had seen war at first hand, as a fifer boy at Bunker Hill and Bennington, and he thought that war was both idiotic and unchristian. For a quarter of a century he ruminated on war, its causes and effects, and a possible remedy; then he wrote his proposals in the *Solemn Review*, which made quite a stir. Worcester recommended nothing more nor less than a confederacy of all the nations of the world, together with a high court of justice for settling international disputes.

Though he became a monomaniac on the subject, Worcester was far from naïve. He did not expect a heathenish and savage world to accept common sense very readily, and he devoted his later years to educating at least a part of the world for his proposed reform. This he did through the Massachusetts Peace Society, which he helped to organize, and its periodical, *Friend of Peace*, which he edited. The years crept on, and though the old fire still burned brightly in him, Worcester felt his physical powers waning and welcomed the help of an influential recruit whom his *Solemn Review* had converted to the league of nations idea. This was William Ladd, born in New Hampshire, but a man of the world, wealthy and with connections among the powerful.

Ladd carried on where Worcester left off, traveling widely in the United States. Within five years he had founded a national group, the American Peace Society. The society offered prizes for the best essays on the subject of a congress of nations to prevent war. These were published and distributed widely both in America and in Europe. With many other influential persons, Ralph Waldo Emerson became interested and wrote on the subject. Emerson called war an "epidemic insanity," perhaps as good a description as has yet been penned. Judge Thomas Grimké of South Carolina, and his remarkable son and daughters—Thomas, Angelina and Sarah—carried the banner in the Southern states and also invaded the North. The society put pressure on the legislatures of all the states to urge upon Congress some sort of international arbitration system, and in 1841 the first International Peace Congress was held in London.

Now appeared Elihu Burritt, the Learned Blacksmith of New Britain, Connecticut, a man of unusual intellect who had spent many years at forge and anvil and while so engaged spouted the Hebrew he had learned by candlelight the night before, or the French, or the Danish, or the Syriac, or perhaps ruminated aloud as he digested Cuvier's *Theory of the Earth*. Nor was it a mere smattering of knowledge; when Burritt learned anything he learned it from the roots up. In 1843 he was asked to give a lecture in Boston on natural science. Shy and awkward, with great hands, Burritt possessed a tanned, lined face, with fine mouth and eyes and forehead, which seem to have interested people at once and to have compelled their sympathy. He lectured extremely well, and the American Peace Society enlisted his support. He already had read Worcester's great work on the subject, and now Burritt took hold famously, and the society took on new life.

Burritt edited the society's periodical, but he did not think it enough. He wrote and sent out thousands of small leaflets which he called "Olive Leaves." He published a small and auxiliary paper, *Bond of Brotherhood*, which he distributed in railroad cars and canalboats. And he lectured, both at home and abroad, and had a strong hand in bringing about four international peace conferences between 1848 and 1852. These were bad times for any sort of peace conferences; seemingly, all times are bad times in which to discuss international sanity. Yet over and over since then, the world has been obliged to consider some system different from that which it has known since time began. The ideas proposed in 1814 by Noah Worcester, and which Ladd and Burritt and others championed, compose a far from dead subject one hundred and thirty years after. Except for new terminology, and that only in part new, Worcester and Ladd and the stout Learned Blacksmith would have felt perfectly at home, and no doubt very happy, could they have walked into the great world peace conference held in San Francisco in 1945, to discuss leagues of nations, world courts, and the like. In their day they were at best tolerated as eccentrics.

There was one eccentric, possibly a fanatic, of the nineteenth century who may have had no great influence on the United States, yet he was a man to be reckoned with in any discussion of the Bill of Rights. In our own day, when the State everywhere crowds the Man, and the trend is toward regimentation, it is well to recall the greatest individualist of his day. He was Joseph Palmer, of Fitchburg and Harvard (town, not college) Massachusetts, now forgotten, and this is bad forgetting, for Palmer was of a race of men that is now all but extinct, and his story, I think, is as heartwarming as it is improbable.

Palmer first came to national attention because he was the victim of one of the strangest persecutions in history. Neither race nor religion had a part in it. It was brought about because Joe Palmer liked to wear a beard, one of the most magnificent growths ever seen in the United States, a regular he-beard of Old Testament size; and what made this beard particularly heinous was that it was almost if not quite the only beard east of the Rocky Mountains, and possibly beyond.

One lone set of whiskers amid millions of smooth-shaven faces is something to contemplate, and Palmer paid dearly for his eccentricity. He was born almost a century too late and seventy-five years too soon to wear whiskers with impunity. He was forty-two years old in 1830, when he moved from his near-by farm into the hustling village of Fitchburg. He came of sturdy old Yankee stock. His father had served in the Revolution, and Joe himself had carried a musket in 1812. He was married and had one son, Thomas.

When the beard first made its appearance is not of record, but Palmer was wearing it when he came to Fitchburg, and here, because of it, he immediately became the butt of cruel jokes and derision and, in time, the victim of downright persecution. But before relating the violence caused by Palmer's famous beard, it is imperative, if one is to comprehend the proceedings at all, to trace briefly the history of whiskers in America up to the time of the Palmer beard.

This continent was explored by men of many nationalities, most of them wearing whiskers. About Ericsson and Columbus and Amerigo Vespucci we are uncertain, since there are no authenticated contemporary portraits of them. But after them came a host of beards. Cortes, Ponce de Leon, Cartier, Champlain, Drake, Raleigh, Captain John Smith, De Soto—all these worthies sported whiskers of varying length and style.

Then came the Pilgrims and the Puritans, bearded almost to a man when they arrived at The Rock and elsewhere. But the beards of these first settlers did not endure. American whiskers were gradually reduced in size until they were scarcely more than mild goatees, and soon disappeared entirely. By 1720 at latest, American colonists were wholly free of facial hair. Try to find a Copley portrait, or a Ralph Earle, with a whisker in it. And the fighting men of the

Revolution were beardless. Not a mustache nor a suspicion of a mutton chop appeared on the faces of Washington, Gates, Greene, Knox. Even old John Stark and Israel Putnam were smooth-shaven. So was the backwoods general, Ethan Allen. It was the same with the other Patriots, and with the British also—Cornwallis, the Howes, Burgoyne. No signer of the Declaration had either beard or mustache.

And so it continued down the years. No President before Lincoln had whiskers (although Van Buren affected for a time a bit of sideburn fringe). Until 1858 the cartoonists' conception of Uncle Sam—their own creature—was of a tall and lanky yet smooth-shaven man. The chinpiece had not appeared. All in all, Americans did not go hairy until the Civil War was under way.

Thus when Joe Palmer came to town wearing a beard in 1830, whiskers had been virtually non-existent for at least a hundred years. In spite of his hirsute oddity, Palmer was an honest kindly man of many intellectual interests. He was also quite immovable in the matter of principle, which in his case included the right to wear a full and flowing beard.

Everywhere he went small boys threw stones and shouted "Old Jew Palmer!" and made life miserable for his son Tom. Women sniffed and crossed to the other side of the street when they saw him coming. The windows of his modest home were broken by unknown rowdies. Grown men jeered him openly. The Reverend George Trask, local pastor, took Palmer to task for his eccentricity; but Palmer replied with exact Scriptural reasons, nay, commands, for beard-wearing. He apparently knew every whisker reference in the Bible. Old Doctor Williams told Palmer to his face that he "should be prosecuted for wearing such a monstrosity." And when Palmer went to Boston to attend literary and reform meetings, of which he was very fond, huge crowds followed him the length of Tremont street, jeering. He was present at the celebrated Chardon Street Convention in 1840, and one has no difficulty locating him in Emerson's amusing comment on that gathering:

If the assembly was disorderly, it was picturesque. Madmen, mad-women, men with beards, Dunkers, Muggletonians, Groaners, Agrarians, Seventh-Day Baptists, Quakers, Abolitionists, Calvinists, Unitarians, and Philosophers—all came successively to the top, and seized their moment, if not their hour, wherein to chide, or pray, or preach, or protest.*

By the time of this convention, Joe Palmer had become a national character, made so by two events that happened in quick succession in his own town of Fitchburg.

In spite of the snubs of the congregation, Palmer never missed a church service, but one Sunday he quite justifiably lost his usually serene temper. It was a communion Sunday in 1830. Palmer knelt with the rest, only to be publicly humiliated when the officiating clergyman ignored him, "passed him by with the communion bread and wine." Palmer was cut to the quick. He arose and strode to the communion table. He lifted the cup to his lips and took a mighty swig. Then: "I love my Jesus," he shouted in a voice loud with hurt and anger, "as well, and better, than any of you!" Then he went home.

A few days later, as he was coming out of the Fitchburg House, he was seized by four men who were armed with shears, brush, soap, and razor. They told him it was the sentiment of the town that the beard should come off, and they proposed to do the job there and then. When Palmer started to struggle, the four men threw him violently to the ground, seriously injuring his back. But he had just begun to fight. As they were about to apply the shears, Palmer managed to get a jackknife out of his pocket. He laid about him wildly, cutting two of his assailants in their legs, not seriously but

* *Works*, X:32.

sufficiently to discourage any barber work. When Palmer stood up, hurt and bleeding, his gorgeous beard was intact.

Presently he was arrested, charged "with an unprovoked assault." Fined by Justice Brigham, he refused to pay the nominal fine. Matter of principle, he said. He was put in the county jail at Worcester and there he remained for more than a year, part of the time in solitary confinement. Even here he had to fight with the fury of a determined virgin, for Jailer Bellows came with several men with the idea of removing the now famous beard. Palmer threw himself at them as fiercely as a bear protecting its young, and to such effect that the jailer and his men retreated without a hair. Palmer also successfully defended the beard against two attempts by prisoners, who vowed to shave it off.

In the jail Palmer wrote letters which he managed to smuggle out a window to his son, who took them to the Worcester *Spy*. They were published and soon were being widely copied by other newspapers. In his letters the bearded prisoner stated that he was in jail not for assault, but because he chose to wear whiskers—which was unquestionably the case. He complained about the food and of the quarters, but worse, said he, was the lack of any religious life behind the bars. All heathens, the jailers.

People all over Massachusetts were soon reading these letters. They began to talk and to reflect: Was it not inherent in the Constitution that a man could wear, on his back or on his face, what he pleased? Were there any state laws or town ordinances against the wearing of beards? What had been ridicule or indifference to Palmer's plight now turned to sympathy. It was not long before the sheriff came to realize he had a Tartar and quite possibly a martyr on his hands. He went to Palmer and suggested that he run along home and forget it—the fine and everything. No, said Joe, a thousand times No. Matter of principle. The jailer urged him to leave. His aged mother wrote him to come home.

Nothing could move him who was now widely known as The Bearded Prisoner of Worcester.

Day after day he sat in his limbo, keeping an elaborate and pathetic journal of his persecutions. And time after time he told the officers and the thoroughly worried magistrates that they had put him there and they should have to take him out. "I won't walk a single step toward freedom," he roared through the bars. Nor did he. He sat there in a chair like a whiskered Buddha until the desperate sheriff and jailers picked him up in his chair and carried him to the street.

Never again was violence attempted on Joe Palmer's beard, which by the time of his release, or rather his eviction, from jail, was a beard famous as far away as New York and Philadelphia. Free now, he soon became a minor figure in New England's intellectual ferment. A hater of slavery, he went to Boston often for the meetings of Parker and Garrison, contributing both time and money to the rising movement for Abolition. He met Emerson, Thoreau, Alcott, Channing, and these men found him an odd but stanch character, the possessor of much good sense. He loathed liquor as he did slavery, and was active at temperance meetings. He visited the communities at Brook Farm and Hopedale, but he could not accept their devout belief in co-operation.

When Bronson Alcott and family, with Charles Lane and a few others, bought a farm in Harvard town, near Fitchburg, named it Fruitlands and attempted to found something they called the Con-Sociate Family, Joe Palmer was interested. He donated to the colony a lot of fine old furniture and up-to-date farm implements. When he saw that Alcott's idiotic ideas about farming were going to bring famine to the group, he brought his own team and plow and turned up the soil. He was, in fact, the only sensible male connected with that wondrous experiment.*

---

* In Louisa May Alcott's *Transcendental Wild Oats*, Joseph Palmer appears as "Moses White."

Fruitlands had the distinction of being the worst-managed and shortest-lived of all American co-operative colonies. When the half-starved Alcotts and the others moved away, Joe Palmer bought the farm and moved there with his wife and family. Here for more than twenty years he carried on a strange sort of community of his own devising. He was widely known now, and never lacked for company. Emerson and Thoreau visited him, and so did every reformer who passed through or operated in New England. The merely curious came to see the famous beard. The Palmers always kept a pot of baked beans on the stove, plenty of bread and butter in the butt'ry. All were welcome to come and to stay, so long as they had no trace of liquor about them.

In place of persecution, Palmer now found himself something of a hero, which was only fitting. The years crept on, and with them the great beard grew even more prodigiously, spreading like a willow. A photograph taken at about this time shows a growth that would make Walt Whitman a beardless youth in comparison. And at last, many years before he died, the whiskers, you might say, of all America came into fullest glory. This Second Coming of the beard was sudden, an almost instantaneous growth that covered the face of the male United States.

One cannot know with certainty the reason for this sudden era of whiskers; it can only be recorded. Lincoln when elected was smooth-shaven, but when inaugurated wore a beard. Grant, the lieutenant, had worn a tiny mustache; Grant, the general, a full beard. Robert E. Lee went smooth of face to war, and was presently full-bearded. In 1860 Jefferson Davis was clean of chin. He was soon wearing whiskers longer than Lincoln's. Nearly all of the generals of the Civil War, on both sides, were peering out of whiskers by 1862, and so were their men. Stonewall Jackson grew a tremendous beard. Beauregard had a beard, a sort of imperial, and mustache; and Custer wore a similar combination.

And General Ambrose E. Burnside, a real dandy, gave his name to a special type of whiskers.

The baseball players of the Sixties and Seventies, as depicted by the careful Currier & Ives, had whiskers. Bankers grew a style of their own. Razors went into the discard, and vendors of quack beard-growers swarmed into the new market. The proper gift to a male was an elegant mustache cup. Manufacturers of soap, patent medicines and cough drops—notably cough drops—came out with one or more bearded faces on their labels. Whiskers, through some odd turn of the folkways, were now a sign of solid worth, a badge of integrity and character in every line of endeavor. If the poor barbers thought the end of things was at hand, it is not difficult to understand why.

As for old Joe Palmer, he was immensely happy, a true prophet who had lived to see his justification and his glory. Few prophets have been so fortunate. All over America, Joe Palmer knew, were now full beards, Van Dykes, goatees, galways, dundrearys, mutton-chops, burnsides, fringe beards (like Horace Greeley's), and millions of stupendous mustaches of the over-Niagara type. Aye, the hairy prophet had come into his own. Yet Palmer was no man to gloat. Only once does he seem to have remarked on the greatly changed styles of men's faces. That was when he met the same Reverend Trask who had so churlishly upbraided him many years before for wearing his beard. Trask himself was now wearing a luxuriant growth. Meeting him on a Fitchburg street, Palmer stroked his own beard and remarked: "Knowest thou that thy Redeemer liveth?"

Joe Palmer died in 1875, when beards were at their fullest, and was thus spared the dreadful sight of their withering and final disappearance.* He died, indeed, at exactly the right

---

* The tragic whisker debacle of the last quarter of the nineteenth century has been expertly charted by Mr. Lewis Gannett, who used his Alma Mater, Harvard, to trace the decline of hair. The classes of the 1860's were hairy as goats. The class of 1870 had four beards. Two years later

time, and he took some pains to make certain, no matter what styles frivolous men might adopt, that he was not wholly forgotten. In the old cemetery in North Leominster, not far from Fitchburg, is his monument, a rugged oblong stone as tall as a man; and on its front is an excellent medallion carving of Joe Palmer's head, with its noble beard flowing and rippling in white marble. Below the head appears a simple legend: "Persecuted for Wearing the Beard." I like to believe that Palmer's steadfast example has put heart into many a weak or faltering man.

---

beards were going out, mustaches coming in. The class of 1900 was the first without a beard, and the last Harvard football mustache appeared in 1901, the last baseball mustache in 1905. No President of the United States since Taft (1909–1913) has worn hair on his face.

CHAPTER VIII

A Cloud on the Wind

THE astounding progress in material things made in the United States during fifty years after 1800 amazed and often irritated foreign visitors, especially the unique English snob tourist, and it made Americans cocky. Orators pointed to the ever-lengthening railroads and highways and canals and vowed that they were binding the people into a mighty whole, a nation united and indivisible. Yet, after about 1840, even the most stupid orators must have known better. They must have known, if they reflected at all, that the young and yeasty United States was splitting apart in the middle.

Slavery had been tried in the Northern colonies as early as the seventeenth century, but it fitted neither the climate nor the geography. Hence it had been permitted to lapse; and once the practice became obsolete, the North began passing laws against it. No harm in that; prohibition of slavery was as painless and as meaningless as the Maine law that protected beavers after the beavers all had disappeared. Yet anti-slavery laws in the North did do one important thing: they gave Yankees a glowing sense of Christian superiority over the South; and the fact that Yankee textile barons were creating a slavery in many respects less humane than chattel slavery made no difference, because it was ignored.

But the Yankee state laws did not interfere with what a Yankee captain carried in the hold of his ship—or not very much. Nor did the federal laws against importation of slaves

—not for a long time. Out of Portland, Portsmouth, Marblehead, Salem, Boston and Newport went Yankee ships for
Africa, while their often pious captains salved their consciences, if need were, by reading the Bible: *Both thy bond-
men and thy bondmaids, which thou shalt have, shall be of
the heathen.* . . . It was all clear and right enough.

They sailed to Africa, loaded their black ivory, then away
to the West Indies or the Southern states, to deliver cargo
and to take aboard another, this time of blackstrap molasses
for the busy rum factories of Medford and Newburyport and
Salem. In time, true enough, it came to be a risky business—
the slave part of it—because of hijackers and revenue men,
but it paid enormously in dividends and it never ceased so
long as there was a market.

But there were men, both North and South, who said publicly that slavery was morally wrong and should be stopped.
This was long before Harriet Beecher was out of pigtails,
for contrary to general belief—at least in my childhood—
her book did not "start the Civil War." It is quite likely
that Sir Walter Scott, a Highland novelist, had more to do
with that than did Mrs. H. B. Stowe.

Jehudi Ashmun, as related, was one of the earliest prophets
of troublous times a-coming—one of the earliest, that is,
who had what he thought was a remedy, a prevention, for
the trouble. Had America listened to him, and acted on his
suggestions, there might have been no four years of murderous insanity. Nor was Ashmun entirely a lone voice in his
day. Before Ashmun John Woolman, a quiet Quaker, had
sensed something of what was ahead. As early as 1746 he
visited Virginia to observe slavery at first hand. He found,
he wrote, the dark gloominess of a sable cloud hanging over
the land, and the consequences were certain to be grievous to
posterity. It would rain blood, that cloud. Woolman called
at plantation after plantation, always traveling on foot, trying in his gentle way to rouse the sleepy consciences of the
planters. Because it was closely allied with the slave trade,

Woolman forswore the use of sugar, and he brought every argument he could devise against the use of slaves.*

Another Quaker, Anthony Benezet, went beyond Woolman. He not only damned slavery but had a plan for emancipation. To no perceptible avail, although it is certain that Benezet's writings had great influence on John Wesley and in fact on all Methodism. When the old century was ending, however, Bishop Francis Asbury could see little progress. Methodists, Baptists, Presbyterians, all in the highest flights of rapturous piety, still maintained and defended slavery.

Not all the South was for it. Those noted commanders in the Confederate army, Joseph E. Johnston, A. P. Hill and Fitzhugh Lee, never owned a slave. James G. Birney, Alabama planter, freed his slaves and fled to Ohio, just ahead of a mob, where he became one of the most potent antislavery leaders. Edward Coles of Virginia moved to Illinois with his slaves, emancipated them there, bought them land and provided them with cabins. The Grimké sisters, Sarah and Angelina, of a wealthy South Carolina family already mentioned in connection with the American Peace Society, came North and took up the cause of abolition, being most effective in their lectures. In Saint Clairsville, Ohio, as early as 1815, Benjamin Lundy, a native of New Jersey and of Quaker descent, organized the Union Humane Society, perhaps the first anti-slavery group in the country. Lundy went on to found and edit *The Genius of Universal Emancipation* and to organize anti-slavery groups, even in the South. It is significant of the early abolition movement that of the one hundred thirty societies founded before 1827—mostly by Lundy—no less than one hundred were in the South.

Wherever he went, Lundy carried what printers call a shirt-tail full of type, and wherever he stopped for a few

---

* At a much later period, abolitionists in the North urged a boycott on imported sugar and called upon the farmers of Ohio, New York and New England to increase their output of maple sugar.

days, another issue of *The Genius* appeared. The periodical seems to have been published at least two or three times in each of a dozen or more states. Lundy was different from most abolitionists; he cared not how the Negro was freed so long as it was brought about.

But time could not wait long. A rising wind was bringing the cloud swiftly on. The first of the many great revolts of the slaves, that led by Denmark Vesey, came to put wide cracks into the belief that slaves were really just happy children, glad to live in bondage. The North, perhaps, had been more given to this belief than had the South. The North contained much and powerful pro-slavery sentiment. It was in Alton, Illinois, where Elijah Lovejoy, editor of a paper advocating not abolition but gradual emancipation, was murdered by a mob. Boston was far from safe, and William Lloyd Garrison, editor of *The Liberator*, barely escaped mobsters bent on strangling him with a length of rope.

While the agitators for abolition kept a constant drumming in the ears of the North, a few fanatical believers in direct action got under way. These men were known as the Slave Stealers. One of the first was the Reverend Charles Turner Torrey, late of Scituate, Massachusetts, who moved to Baltimore, ostensibly to start a business but really to aid the escape of slaves in Maryland and Virginia. Torrey was believed to have sent more than four hundred blacks to freedom before he was arrested and charged with slave stealing. Convicted, he was sent to prison, where his mind gave way and he died. His body was taken to Boston and a monstrous propaganda funeral was held in "honor of this martyr to the anti-slavery Cause."

Although Martyr Torrey's death and carefully staged funeral stirred Yankees to new heights of abolition feeling, it was the happy conjunction of Jonathan Walker, a shipwright, and John G. Whittier, a poet, that conspired to make the most effective, because it was the most maddening, atrocity story of the entire era.

Jonathan Walker, a native of Massachusetts, worked as a shipwright, then became skipper of a merchant vessel. He was soon captured off the Florida coast while taking seven runaway slaves to liberty in the West Indies. He was put into jail at Pensacola, and kept for many months, meanwhile wearing leg irons that were all but buried out of sight in his flesh by the time he was brought to trial. The jury found him guilty with great speed, and "awarded him to be branded on the right hand with the letters SS." Which meant Slave Stealer.

Walker was first put into a pillory, where townsmen and townswomen were permitted to pelt him with bad eggs and filth. Then he was taken into the courtroom to be branded. As an officer started to tie Walker's right hand to a railing, the prisoner spoke up. "There is no need of tying it," he said, "for I will hold it steady." The hand was tied, nevertheless, and then the red-hot iron was applied. "It made a splattering noise," related the stout-hearted Walker, "like a handful of salt on a fire, as the skin seared and gave way to the iron." This splattering noise was presently to be heard in a million homes and schools in the North, and the brander's iron was to sear a million minds.

After being branded Walker returned to New England, where news of his experience had preceded him. Abolitionist friends took him to meet a tall swarthy man with piercing dark eyes who used the *thee* and *thou* of Quaker speech. Whittier was a Quaker and a hot abolitionist. The poet found Walker a simple, honest, God-fearing man who felt that stealing and freeing slaves was the work of the Lord. They talked long, then the poet went away to write at white heat what became by far his most moving and effective verses against slavery. This was "The Branded Hand." From 1845, when it appeared, to the end of the war, the poem was the most declaimed, in schools and homes and from lecture platforms, of any; and many a late convert to abolitionism, both male and female, confessed that it was the story of Jonathan

Walker as told in smoldering lines by Whittier that acted for them like a fire bell in the night, awakening them before the great dark cloud was split by the thunder of Sumter.

Another bell, clear and loud and eloquent, was pealed by the brown hand of Frederick Douglass, the escaped slave, now nearly as forgotten as Walker and "The Branded Hand." Born into slavery in Maryland, this intelligent and forceful Negro ran away to find harbor in New Bedford, Massachusetts, and was soon attending meetings of the anti-slavery society there. Taking the platform himself, he was an immediate sensation. Of commanding appearance, well over six feet, with a strong face and leonine head, he quickly developed into a speaker who could convince almost any audience. But his row was not easy. He was mobbed more than once, beaten, snubbed, then became a hero of the Cause without peer; and his great, rich voice and fine appearance were of immense effect in changing the pro-slavery thinking in the North.*

The furious Garrison, the vitriolic Theodore Parker, Wendell Phillips. these and other lesser voices, all were now pounding away at the South. In the Senate, Charles Sumner of the Bay State was abusing the South and Southerners in the most intemperate language he could muster, and Sumner's poisonous vocabulary had few equals. And for the best part of thirty years, or from about 1830 onward, Congress could accomplish almost nothing without consideration of its effect on the growing tension between the North and the South. Much of its energies, in fact, had to be devoted solely to the fight to "keep the balance" of Slave and Free states.

The battle in Congress resulted in resounding "compromises" that settled nothing. In 1820 the Missouri Compromise dedicated the major portion of Louisiana Territory

* Douglass aided in recruiting the celebrated colored regiments of Massachusetts. He was twice married, his second wife being white. "My first wife," said this mulatto, "was the color of my mother. My second wife the color of my father."

to freedom, the smaller portion being left to slavery. The Compromise of 1850 abolished slavery in the District of Columbia—all of seventy square miles—but made it much easier for masters to secure return of slaves who had run away to the North. The appeasers and pussyfooters of 1850 also provided that any territories that might come into the Union later could do so with or without slavery, as their constitutions might provide at the time of admission. Four years later, by the Kansas and Nebraska Act, the Compromise of 1820 was abrogated, and the whole of the vast interior of the continent, which had been dedicated to freedom in 1820, was thrown open to slavery if and when the settlers and squatters so desired. This reopened the question, which had long been regarded as closed, and set the scene for Bloody Kansas. The open question was answered, in favor of slavery, in 1857, when the Supreme Court of the United States held in the case of one Dred Scott that the Missouri Compromise really had been null and void from the day it was passed, and that Congress had no powers whatever to exclude slavery from the territories.

But who was Dred Scott? In twenty-eight books on American history, ranging in date from 1881 to 1939, and picked at random, Dred Scott is merely a name in a law case, described in the gibberish of lawyers as *Dred Scott* v. *Sanford, 19 Howard 393*. Five generations of American school children have been made to parrot Scott's name, and if any of them ever learned who Scott was, then they did so by free research of their own. None of their books, if any of their teachers, could have told them.

The unsung and unknown hero of this famous case was not Scott, anyway, but Henry Taylor Blow, of Virginia and Missouri. We shall get to him presently, for he should be in all accounts of the period. As for Dred Scott, he was born a slave in 1795 in Southampton County, Virginia, on the pleasant plantation of Captain Peter Blow, who in 1827 removed with his family and slaves to St. Louis. On Captain

Blow's death Scott was assigned to his daughter. In 1833 Scott was purchased by John Emerson, surgeon in the Army, and accompanied him as man-servant to various Army posts in Illinois and Wisconsin Territory. While in Illinois Scott married Harriet, a slave woman who had been purchased by his master.

Dred Scott was a particularly stupid Negro, shiftless, and reliable only at widely spaced and not to be guessed moments. In 1838, apparently fed up with Scott, Surgeon Emerson left him to shift for himself in St. Louis, and he became man-servant to Colonel Henry Bainbridge at Jefferson Barracks. But Emerson was still Scott's legal master, and when Emerson died, Scott was assigned to Mrs. Emerson, the widow. Mrs. Emerson had seen only too much of Scott. She hired him out at wages to various families in St. Louis, none of whom would keep him for long. He could not be depended upon even for the simplest tasks, and soon he was wholly without employment and with no means to support himself and family. Scott now appealed to the son of his original master.

Henry Blow was a generous and public-spirited man. He had made a fortune from Missouri lead mines, gave liberally of his money to the city's efforts along educational, cultural and charitable lines, and was considered, one judges rightly, one of the finest men in St. Louis. In spite of the place of his birth, Blow was much in favor of emancipation and was doing all he could to oppose extension of slavery to new states and territories. He had gone so far as to favor publicly, and that in Missouri, the immediate and uncompensated emancipation of slaves in that state.

Well, here was the worthless Dred Scott on his hands—not legally so, for Mrs. Emerson was Scott's owner and the responsible party. But Blow was a man who felt that he was morally in duty bound to take care of his father's old slave. He supported the Scott ménage and at the same time instituted and financed a suit in the state courts to secure freedom for the Scotts. The contention here was that a slave who had lived in free territory, such as Illinois and Wisconsin, automatically became free on his return to a slave state. This contention hardly makes sense, and it did not make good law in Missouri. In 1852, after the case had haunted the Missouri courts for seven years, it was adversely decided and quaintly filed away as *Scott, a Man of Color*, v. *Emerson, 15 Mo. 576.* And there it might have remained till Kingdom Come, except for Henry Blow.

Blow was disappointed but he wasn't done. He arranged to have the case taken to the United States Supreme Court. For jurisdictional purposes, Dred Scott was sold in a fictitious transaction to his master's brother, John F. A. Sanford, who lived in New York. The courts ground their lumbering way. In the meantime, Dred Scott, who could neither read nor write, was performing janitor duties and running errands in St. Louis. He had not the least idea of what the noise was all about, but he thoroughly enjoyed and made the most of the steadily mounting notoriety coming to him. He liked to talk about it, especially to mouth a few horrendous and satisfying legal terms he had picked up as the pawn in what was on the way to being America's law case of the century.

At last, in 1857, the United States Supreme Court, by one of its five-to-four decisions, drearily said that Dred Scott was still indeed a slave. His status, remarked the august body, was determined by the courts of Missouri, which had decided he was not free. Not being a citizen of Missouri, within the meaning of the Constitution, he was not entitled, as such, to sue in the federal courts. Next case . . .

Henry Blow was beaten, but he did not sour. By another fictitious sale, hastened unquestionably by the ironic fact that his last owner, the Widow Emerson, had just been married again, this time to the Honorable Calvin Clifford Chaffee, red-hot abolitionist from Massachusetts, Dred Scott was transferred to Henry Blow, who thereupon emancipated

NATHANIEL BOWDITCH, THE GENIUS OF
SALEM, MASSACHUSETTS

ELKANAH WATSON

JEHUDI ASHMUN

SAMUEL COLT, ESQ.

NOAH WEBSTER

ELIHU BURRITT

DOROTHEA DIX

SAMUEL GRIDLEY HOWE

LAURA BRIDGMAN

In full beard.

His stone tells the story.

JOSEPH PALMER MADE THE BILL OF RIGHTS MEAN SOMETHING.

Scott and his family. Scott had but a year to live. He enjoyed it hugely, as the lazy porter at Barnum's Hotel in St. Louis, where he was an object of the greatest interest. Dred Scott's name was on its way to a secure place in American history. Incidentally, Henry Blow, stanch to the last, paid Scott's funeral expenses.

With the adverse decision in the Dred Scott affair, which nullified and threw overboard the Missouri Compromise, the deepening shadow now had reached out over the great plains, across the Rockies, on into California and the Oregon country.

The great puzzle to the North, the unintelligible mystery, was the paradox of the South's thinking in regard to slavery. Here was a great region which became steadily more attached to slavery as the attacks on it increased. This might have been explained by simple psychology, had the South been a country of millions of slave owners. But the South was no such thing. In 1860, slightly over one in four Southerners was directly or indirectly connected with slaveholding. There were but 384,000 slaveholders among more than 8,000,000 Southern whites, and of these only 225,000 had as many as twenty slaves each.* The great majority of white Southerners, the so-called poor whites and the yeomen alike, far from having what could be called a stake in slavery, were under severe handicap because of it. Yet they stood shoulder to shoulder with the great planters when the Peculiar Institution was attacked. The reasons for this paradoxical attitude probably stemmed from the romantic fiction the South had been building up about itself since the Revolution, or thereabout.

The South's fancy legend began with the patently erroneous belief that all of the South's early settlers were aristocratic Cavaliers from England, wealthy bluebloods who had

---

* The United States Eighth Census.

been driven from their magnificent homes by the lowbrow
Cromwell and had taken refuge in the pleasant Southern
colonies of America. Here, so the legend continued, these
noble Cavaliers had fashioned for themselves a world both
singularly polished and mellow, dominated by the upper-case
twins of Honor and Chivalry, and supported by the labor of
the black slave.

This fancy belief, as historians have been increasingly able
to prove, bore little relation to reality. The South's first
white settlers of English stock were very much the same as
those who settled at Plymouth and Salem and Boston, which
is to say, they were made up of free tradesmen, or yeomen,
and indentured servants, most of whom left England in an
effort to better their lot. There were also a number of cargoes
made up chiefly of convicts, who might be merely debtors
or political prisoners, or could be cutthroats and prosti-
utes.

The main differences between New England and, say,
Virginia came about because of climate. The one was harsh,
the soil none too good; the other was balmy, the soil of the
best. New England's unit of settlement was the community,
or town. That of Virginia, the farm or plantation. Neither
New England's climate nor its soil lent itself easily to slave
labor. Virginia's did, for agriculture was its means of living, or it was until the soil finally wore out—and then Virginia went in for the breeding of slaves.

A Yankee farmer worked like a demon, and so did all of
his family. Either that, or they starved. A Virginian directed
his army, or his squad, of slaves, in their labor. Somehow,
the Yankee, both farmer and townsman, found time to do a
good deal of reading, and when he read it was often a solid
fare of sermons which reminded him, if he needed reminding,
of his compact with God and how God had chosen him and
him alone to take His Word throughout America. When the
Virginian read, he read Sir Walter Scott, who not only loved
Cavaliers but made a whacking good living from them. The

Virginian's way of life drew him to Scott's cardboard ro-
mances, just as his way of life also precluded any great intellectual curiosity.

The curious Yankee, Eli Whitney, teaching school in the
South and feeling sympathy for the hard-working slaves,
devised a machine to relieve much of the hardest labor in
cleaning cotton—and thus saddled slavery more firmly on
the South than ever. The cotton gin greatly lowered the cost
of producing cotton, and released the plantations from the
narrow coastline strip in which they had been confined and
spread them into the vast and theretofore despised interior.
Cotton beat back the wilderness, cut the forests, and set
slaves to plowing and planting all the way to the Mississippi
and beyond.

Eli Whitney, Yankee of emancipation leanings, spread the
cotton kingdom and slavery to all parts of the South within
one generation.

The birth rate of slaves, high though it was, could not
keep up with the swift expansion of cotton lands, so other
Yankees stepped in with their ships to supply new stock from
Africa. Thus the ramifications of slavery soon ran from
Austin, Texas, to Bangor, Maine.

Plantations left the great mass of Southern whites to become small independent farmers, if they were able, or to sink
into the role of the tenant-farmer, tilling the soil for another.
Some farmers, in fact a good many of them, rose through
the years to take their places in the planter class. More became share-croppers. Such was the economic split occasioned
by slavery in the South.

Yet, just because the small farmer and the hillbilly share-
cropper were economically and socially outside the pale of
the planter class, they did not develop what Marxians term
class consciousness. Hardly. They were still white and free,
and they had the black man to look down upon. Slavery conferred on the poor-white the feeling of superiority, the bond
that bound the non-planters to the planters. They were all

brothers, these white men. They were all free. They were, so help them God, in spite of any indications to the contrary, independent. This was tremendously important, as W. J. Cash has pointed out.* Slavery, said Cash, exempted the poor-white "from all direct exploitation, specifically waived all claim to his labor, and left his independence totally unimpaired." Thus, so long as slavery prevailed, he might rest in his place forever, secure in the knowledge that his estate in this respect would never grow worse—after his fashion as free an agent as the greatest planter in the country.

The ego-warming distinction between white and black was ever present. It elevated the poor-white Southerner, to his thinking, to the level of a member of the dominant or planter class. No matter that the blacks in the big plantation houses might sneer at the poor-white, come what might, he would always be a white man. And faced with that capacious distinction, as Cash summed it up, all other distinctions were foreshortened, dwarfed, and all but obliterated.

Also important was the fact that although he might seem outside the main stream of Southern culture, the common white took his attitudes from the planters. Even he read Sir Walter and he, too, became a descendant of the gallant Cavaliers. He liked to race horses, the nearest thing to the medieval tournaments of Scott's novels; he enjoyed gargantuan drams of raw whisky; he hunted the possum and the fox; and he liked to let go wild yells. His attention to courtesy was great, and he liked a flourish with it. And he followed the planter in building up the South's greatest fictional creation—that of Pure Southern Womanhood.

Hence, during the forty years or so in which the North's attacks on slavery steadily grew in size and rancor, the poor-whites closed ranks with the planters and presented a united front of such solidity and perseverance that the North could not understand, any more than it does today, how it was accomplished. It was to be a front that held astonishingly

---

* In his *The Mind of the South* (New York, 1943), an extremely able and balanced work.

well through four years of bitter war and privation, a front that constantly amazed all the world—except the South.

As the North's attacks increased, Southern orators arose to attack the boorish, calculating, indecent and obscene Yankee, and incidentally to defend slavery. The art of oratory has always been held in high esteem in the South, which has produced fire-eaters and mob-masters without peer. William Yancey and Barnwell Rhett were two of the ablest, but there were hundreds more spellbinders, few of them of the planter class, who put the South's legend about itself into beautiful words. The Southern orator gave his audience to understand that any Southerner could whip a dozen Yankees, hands down; he did more than to infer that the Yankee was only a money-grubbing monster, a white slave to the dollar, but a fiend incarnate who intended to turn all the Negroes loose on the South. Then, what would become of Pure Southern Womanhood?

These men, these orators, were not mountebanks. They were honest men, who believed what they spouted to be Gospel. This oratorical arena, wherein one great Southern champion confronted all the imps of hell of the North, and slew them with words, butchered them with phrases and consigned them to the Pit, was the splendid theater of Southern politics. Here under the torches, men listened to the magic flow and watched the noble gesturing, which swept away the loneliness of the forks of the creek, of the canebrakes, and brought them together as brothers, filled them with the contagious power of the mob, fetched them all up out of the muck, and placed even the meanest of them smack in the center of the South's gorgeous legend of itself. They were, one and all, white men, descendants of men in plumed hats who had ridden white chargers and defended Pure Womanhood in Cavalier castles from the barbarians.

It was all wonderful, but the sole real interest ever involved was that of the great planters.

Aiding the secular orators were the parsons, who told their flocks that the God of the South was a tribal god—Jehovah,

certainly, but the Jehovah of the Old Testament, He of
battles and a flaming sword. The God of the Yankees, however, so the parsons said, was Antichrist, at last loosed from
Gehenna. Hear the Reverend J. H. Thornwell on the matter
as it looked to him in 1850, one year before he became president of the College of South Carolina. "The parties of this
conflict," roared Dr. Thornwell, "are not merely abolitionists and slaveholders—they are atheists, socialists, com-
munists, red republicans, jacobins on the one side, and the
friends of order and regulated freedom on the other. In one
word, the world is the battleground—Christianity and
atheism the combatants; and the progress of humanity is
at stake."

The South's parsons left no doubt in the minds of their
flocks.

The parsons also brought Christian dialectics into the
business. They proved by the Bible that slavery had been
ordained by God, and cited countless passages to show that
slavery was the natural condition of the poor black man. At
this point the planters picked up the idea and carried it
along to aid in conjuring up the Big Heart of the South.
This Big Heart, said the planters—and they believed it—
was the only reason the planters held to slavery at all. In
his natural state the black man had been a pagan, an out-
cast. Slavery made of him a Christian, much to God's happiness. Slavery would get him into heaven, much to his own
happiness. It was only because of his sense of Christian
duty and his love for the Negro that the planter condoned
slavery.

Almost everyone who has read history in a more than casual manner knows that when the great figure of God appears
in a controversy, the shooting cannot be far off. It was so
with the slavery controversy. But in 1857 there was to be
one last great verbal blast against the South, the mogul of
all blasts, and it was loosed by a Southerner of the planter
class, Hinton Helper.

By all odds the most completely forgotten figure of all the great figures of the anti-slavery days is that of Hinton Rowan Helper, a true Southern gentleman of the old school, complete with frock coat, boiled white shirt, string tie, and goatee. Tall, spare, soft-voiced, he was of distinguished appearance, an embodiment of all the graces of the Old South. That is, except for his ideas about slavery. Helper has seldom got a line in the history books. He deserves more recognition.

No one, so far as the record shows, was ever hanged for owning a copy of Mrs. Stowe's *Uncle Tom's Cabin,* or even arrested. Such was not the case with *The Impending Crisis,* the 413 pages of carefully prepared and concentrated dynamite that Helper wrote and published in 1857. Men *were* hanged for possessing this book. Many more men were mobbed; and the legislatures of the South, characteristically, passed laws specifically forbidding its sale, purchase, and possession. It was also the book that blew the Congress of the United States to pieces.

There isn't a bloodhound in Helper's book. In it no sadistic Legree beat and tortured slaves. What made it particularly infuriating to the people of the South was that the author attacked their culture, and that he was one of them, a member of the slave-owning class. He knew, did Helper, as Mrs. Stowe did not, what he was talking about.

Born in 1829 and reared on a North Carolina farm that was worked by his father's slaves, Helper was graduated from Mocksville Academy, worked briefly in a store, and in 1850 took ship around the Horn for California, where the gold excitement was great. He remained in California three years, returning East in 1855 to write a book about the wonders of the Gold State.

Since early boyhood Helper had been reflecting on the effects of slavery. He had seen it in practice at his own home. He thought it economically unsound, and the more he saw of it the more certain he was that it ought to cease. The

moral aspects of slavery interested him not at all. He looked
on the Negro at best as a sub-species of humanity, incapable
of being civilized. And now, after his travels in the West
and North, he came to believe that the South, which he
dearly loved, was being left behind in a social and economic
desert. He was constantly amazed, he related, at what he
termed the progress of the rest of the United States as compared with what he termed the decay of the South.

Helper decided to write a book of warning to his fellow
Southerners. For the next two years and more he traveled
about the country, gathering his materials, and writing. He
completed the manuscript in 1857, in Baltimore, and first
attempted to have it published there. The printer refused,
and cited a Maryland law, passed in 1831, that forbade the
printing of anything that "had a tendency to excite discontent amongst people of color." Helper was as disgusted as
he was disappointed. Packing the bulky manuscript into his
valise, he went to New York.

Here he ran into more discouragement. Harper's read the
script, and politely said they did not care to publish it. It
was the same at Appleton's, at Scribner's, and a few other
established houses. Weeks passed while the tall, courteous
young man with the misleading drawl tramped the streets
and waited in editorial offices. Finally he approached a firm
of combined publishers and book agents, one of those concerns that would publish any old book they thought their
door-knocking salesmen could peddle. The firm was Burdick
Brothers, 8 Spruce Street, New York, and they were men
who tried to play safe. They told Helper they would publish
his book if he would guarantee them the cost of paper and
printing. This was really "vanity" publishing, but Helper
did not know it and it probably would have made no difference with him: He had a Message. He agreed to the one-
sided proposal of Burdick Brothers, and the book appeared
late in 1857.

For the next several years Burdick Brothers had time for

little else than the printing of successive editions of Helper's book, the complete title of which was *The Impending Crisis of the South: How to Meet It,* by Hinton Rowan Helper of North Carolina. Incidentally, it is interesting to note that the first edition was dedicated to three men—Henry M. Willis of California, formerly of Maryland; Woodford C. Holman of Oregon, formerly of Kentucky; and Matthew K. Smith of Washington Territory, formerly of Virginia. Also, went the legend on the title page, "to the Non-Slaveholding Whites of the South, generally, Whether at Home or Abroad, This Work is Most Cordially Dedicated by their Sincere Friend and Fellow Citizen The Author."

In his Preface the author trusts that his friends and fellow citizens of the South will read the book. "Nay," says he, "proud as any Southerner though I am, I entreat, I beg of them to do so." He goes on to hope that the book will be received as offered, in a reasonable and friendly spirit, and that they who read "will reflect upon it as an honorable and faithful endeavor to treat a subject of enormous import, without rancor or prejudice, by one who naturally comes within the pale of their own sympathies."

One wonders if the author really was so naïve as to believe for a moment that his vitriolic attack on everything the South prided itself in would be received in "a reasonable and friendly spirit." I think Helper was naïve to that extent. Men consumed by one idea get that way. They see their own plans and suggestions as the only ones possible, the only ones containing reason. Not for a moment does the genuine fanatic reflect that all men are not as he is. The desired goal is there, straight ahead. The clear way is outlined, lighted. Nothing, nothing at all remains, but to follow it.

The Impending Crisis made an immediate noise, throughout the country, and in Congress. It created a sensation, so contemporaries have written, far greater than that which *Uncle Tom's Cabin* produced. The North started buying the book faster than the amazed Burdick Brothers could print it. The South did not read many books, other than the Waverley Novels, but the immediate national rumpus kicked up by Helper's work caused Southern merchants to ask their Northern supply houses to include, secretly, a few copies in each shipment of goods. It got around. Southern legislatures met, once the contents of the book became known— often in specially called sessions—to pass special acts forbidding its sale and possession.

The Reverend Daniel Worth, of an old and eminent North Carolina family, was found to have a copy. Neither the cloth nor his family could protect him. He was arrested, tried, and found guilty. The entire state was aroused by the trial, and the excitement spread. The Reverend Mr. Worth appealed—and escaped to the North while out on bail. His attorneys had advised him to get out while he could, for they were certain the conviction would be affirmed; and that even if it were not, North Carolina would not hold him alive, anyway.

In Arkansas, three men were hanged by mobs for owning copies of the book. So far as I can learn no such punitive action was taken against Mrs. Stowe's novel. And in all or nearly all of the slave states men were mobbed and beaten for having Helper's book in their homes. It is doubtful that very many of those to whom the book was dedicated—the non-slaveholding whites of the South—ever read the book, but the South's social and political and church leaders certainly did.

The biggest sensation was in Congress. In what was possibly an unguarded moment, the Honorable John Sherman gave the book his endorsement. This was followed by an uproar second only to that of the earlier Sumner-Brooks affair, and was responsible for Sherman's defeat as speaker of the House in 1859. This event, together with much bitter newspaper comment, plus the hangings, mobbings, arrests, and trials in the South, sent the book's sales soaring wildly.

It sold 100,000 copies in its first year, which was a stupendous pile of books in those days, and in 1859 it was "digested" (seems they had digests even then), but with the
particularly maddening portions of the text left untouched,
and put out as a campaign document by the Republican
party. Millions of copies of this booklet were distributed.
How many copies of the book, in both forms, were sold, is
not known, but one anonymous contemporary writer said
that the volume "went through 140 printings."

Just what was in it, in this book, that angered the South
as nothing had angered it before, or has since? A careful
reading of the fat, closely printed work gives the probable
answer. It was not the Introduction, with its looking down
the nose at Mrs. Stowe: "Yankee wives have written the most
popular anti-slavery literature of the day. Against this I
have nothing to say; it is well enough for women to give the
fictions of slavery; men should give the facts."

Neither could it have been the sixteen pages of solid statistics which the author marshals to support his thesis. These
show the comparison between North and South in such matters as Exports, Imports, Manufactures, Miles of Canals
and Railroads, Patents Issued, Schools, and so forth, including Public Libraries, of which the slave states had 595 containing 649,477 volumes, and the free states 14,911 containing 3,888,234 volumes. Nor could it have been Helper's disposal of the old canard, much in favor in the South, that
white men could not labor beneath the Southern sun. One
doubts, too, that Helper's massing of Precepts & Sayings of
the Old and New Testaments to prove slavery morally wrong
troubled the Southern planters, or other of his readers. With
the identical sources Southern preachers were proving that
God liked slavery in the South very much.

The text begins to warm up when it gets to Cotton. Helper
sets out to show that Cotton is far from king, and that it is
steadily losing ground in importance. "The lowly hay is
king," says he, "and it is time you came to know it." Cotton

raised by slave labor is uneconomic, says the author. So is anything else. "Indeed, the unprofitableness of slavery is a monstrous evil, when considered in all its being. . . ."

And presently the author gets down to his really insulting pages, pages studded with blistering invective that Charles Sumner must have envied, with withering strictures on the subject, not of slavery but of what passed current for civilization in the South. "Slaveholders," he says, "are too lazy and ignorant to write. Southern divines give us elaborate Bible arguments; Southern novelists bore us ad infini tum with pictures of the beatitudes of plantation life; Southern verse-wrights drone out their dactyls or grow ventricious with their turgid heroes, all in defense of slavery."

All pap, says the author; pap produced by a region that "is fast sinking into a state of comparative imbecility and obscurity." Garrison wrote no more maddening lines than those. And there were more, and worse. Helper discovers a South filled with degenerate oafs, with "illiterate chevaliers of bowie-knives and pistols." The South can never have a literature of its own, or an art, or science, or even manufacture, so long as it supports slavery. "Priest, politician, novelist, bardling" of the slave states, they all spend their time "ringing the changes upon the 'biblical Institution,' and then have their books printed on Northern paper, with Northern types, by Northern artisans, stitched, bound and made ready for the market by Northern industry." How, says he, in the name of common sense, can Southerners fail to see "an overwhelming refutation of their miserable sophisms in behalf of a system against which humanity protests?" This is the only place in the book where the author mentions humanity. Perhaps Helper used the word as a sop to Northern abolitionists, whom Helper considered sentimentalists of the worst sort. His whole work is predicated on the thesis that slavery is economically impossible.

Helper constantly addresses the non-slaveholding whites. Their freedom, he says, is only nominal, and their "unparalleled illiteracy and degradation is purposely and fiendishly perpetuated" upon them by the oligarchism of the slave-holders. "How little the poor white trash, the great majority of the Southern people, know of real conditions of the country . . . it is sadly astonishing."

After composing all of the insults to the South he can think of, the author comes to his remedy for slavery. It must be in taxes and boycotts (this word was not then in use) so stringent that they will make slavery immediately impossible. Then, more taxes to be used to transport the Negroes back to Africa and set them up as a nation—the idea that Jehudi Ashmun lived and died for. Every last Negro, free and slave, must be shipped out of the country, and at once. (Liberia was ready.)

With his remedy propounded, Helper finally lays down the law and issues a direct challenge to the oligarchs:

And now, sirs, we have thus laid down our ultimatum. What are you going to do about it? Something dreadful, as a matter of course. Perhaps you will dissolve the Union *again*. Do it, if you dare!

He closes the book on an ominous note, soon to echo from the guns at Sumter. Says his last sentence: "IF . . . the oligarchs do not quietly submit to the will of a constitutional majority of the people, as expressed by the ballot box, the first battle between freedom and slavery will be fought at home—and may God defend the right."

Southern attacks on the book were many and bitter, but none of them appear to have attempted to refute any of Helper's thesis, which was pounded home on page after page with maddening comparison of statistics. Southerners simply abused the author as few men have been abused, and he became "the best known and worst hated man in America."

Helper's later life was anticlimax. Appointed consul at Buenos Aires, he served until 1866, when he returned to the

United States and in quick succession wrote three books on "the Negro Question" which were little more than unbalanced denunciation of the black race as a menace to the North and South. He said flatly that he wanted "to write the Negro out of America . . . out of existence." To the end of his long life he loathed Negroes and would never, if he could help it, stay where they were employed.

With money from his book royalties, Helper proceeded now to become a monomaniac on the subject of building a railroad from Hudson's Bay to Patagonia, and to this plan he devoted the rest of his days. His last years were spent in poverty. Robert Lincoln O'Brien, who knew Helper, recalled him as at least six feet tall, very thin, with a short, straggling gray beard. "I never saw him in anything but a long black Prince Albert coat," says Mr. O'Brien,* "presumably because such an article once acquired lasts forever. In the tail pocket of this coat the old man always carried two or more boxes of Smith Brothers' cough drops. No other brand, just Smith Brothers. These he consumed regularly himself, and he urged them upon anyone, friend or stranger, who had a cold or merely coughed.

"Mr. Helper's mind was perfectly clear when I knew him. He could still berate John Sherman for cowardice in trying to squeak out of responsibility for recommending Helper's book. He liked to tell, too, how impressed he had been when as a young man from the country he came to Washington and saw the National Hotel, four stories high. He walked all around it several times, gaping, he said, in astonishment that any building could be so large and so magnificent. He was very much against the Negro to the last. He told me that he could not work with Garrison and the abolitionists because they thought the Negro too good to be a slave, while Helper did not think the Negro good enough to be around on any terms.

---

* In letters to the author, 1944–45.

"Speaking of his famous book, Helper related that one Southern planter read it and was so indignant he threw it into the fire; and when he came back to his plantation after Appomattox, to find everything gone, his sons killed, he moaned that all his undoing had been because of his treatment of the Helper book which had been telling the truth, only that he was unwilling to receive it.

"The old man grew shabbier and shabbier. He lived in a very cheap hotel, probably a flophouse, in the Capitol Hill section, and there one night in 1909 he committed suicide, by shooting, I believe."

It seems odd that Helper is so forgotten. But anyone who takes the trouble to read *The Impending Crisis* will know that Mrs. Stowe was not alone in writing influential books. And Mrs. Stowe's pen, as she so often and gracefully admitted, was guided by God. The only aid Helper had with *his* book was "A Compendium of the United States Census of 1850," which, incidentally and most ironically, was compiled by J. D. B. De Bow, a native of nowhere but Charleston, South Carolina, close by Fort Sumter. And when Helper was done with his book, it raised immeasurably more wind to speed the dark cloud that had been gathering for thirty years and more.

CHAPTER IX

Not Battle Fronts Alone

EVENTS far behind the fighting lines affect the outcome of war far more often than one would believe from reading general histories, which assess the struggle in terms of men killed and ground taken or lost. And most history books seldom mention any soldier of less than corps-commander rank. I left school, as did many another, in the belief, logical in view of the teaching, that the entire Civil War was directed by no more than four men—Generals Grant and Sherman on one side, Generals Lee and Stonewall Jackson on the other.

The reason for this simplification is understandable, but it does leave out many a good and important story. Wars are neither won nor lost on the conventional battle fronts alone.

It is seldom pointed out, for instance, that except for an event in New York City, in July of 1863, the battle of Gettysburg, instead of being a mere turning point in the tide of war, might well have been the last or next-to-last battle of the entire war, with the North victorious. The event that precluded this possibility was the great draft riot in New York. The riot, in turn, was the product of an imbecilic and utterly unfair method of conscription for the Union army.

On July 2, 1862, Lincoln had called upon the states to raise three hundred thousand men. The states, even by drafts from their own militia, produced only 88,000 soldiers, all organized into new regiments and enlisted for nine months. Congress well knew the obvious remedy for this impossible condition, but did nothing about it, preferring to talk on about the noble sons of the North who would spring to arms. Congress could not bear to think seriously of conscription.

The winter of 1862–63 brought more reverses to the Union armies. The Rebels were driving into Northern territory. At last in March of the latter year, Congress passed what it called the United States Conscription Act. It amounted to being a travesty on the action really needed. All men between the ages of twenty and forty-five were declared liable for service, and had to register. As man were needed, the number to be raised was divided among the states in proportion to their populations. No attempt was made to first draft the younger men and bachelors. Instead of exempting heads of families with several dependents, cash payment was made the basis of exemption. A man, no matter his status, could commute service in a particular draft by payment of $300; or evade service for the duration of war by procuring a substitute to enlist for three years. It did not matter that the substitute died the next day after enlisting, or if he deserted, as thousands of substitutes did. The whole system was extremely unfair to the poor.

This was the condition of things when the first drawings for the draft were made in July of 1863. New York had a large population of Irish-Americans who, ever hostile to Negroes, had been greatly stirred and alarmed by Lincoln's Emancipation Proclamation. They feared the black man as a competitor in the labor markets. They were stirred again by the shipment into New York of several hundred Negroes for use in breaking a longshore strike. Now came the draft, July 13.

For the next four days New York saw mob rule such as no other American city has seen, before or since. Some 20,000 rioters took over the town entire and showed what they thought of the draft, of Emancipation, of law and order. They tore up railroad tracks, cut down telephone poles, and wrecked telegraph offices. Three thousand of them stormed the Union Steam Works arsenal, drove off the guards and workmen, helped themselves to carbines and ammunition, then fired the building and ranged everywhere in the city, shooting indiscriminately. Another mob, estimated at 5,000, attacked the Colored Orphans Home at Fifth Avenue and Forty-third street, and burned it to the ground—but not until they had amused themselves throwing pickaninnies out of the windows.

Negroes swung from lampposts the length of Clarkson Street, with fires burning beneath them. The Draft Enrollment offices were wrecked and fired. Stores and homes were sacked. The Eleventh Regiment turned out with howitzers and blew canister and grapeshot into the mobs, but the troops, outnumbered fifty to one, were set upon and slugged, and some of them were shot. Thirteen regiments of regular troops were hurriedly detached from General Meade's army at Gettysburg and sent to the city by express trains over tracks cleared for the purpose. They arrived just in time to prevent destruction of the *Tribune* building. And they had to fight and fight again, for the mobs threw up breastworks all along Ninth Avenue and resisted to their last cartridge and brickbat. At the end of the fourth day, while smoke hung in a gloom over most of Manhattan, something like order was gradually restored by Meade's regiments. The dead in the riots numbered some fifteen hundred—a greater loss of life by far than any one of a number of formal and celebrated battles of the war.

Not only did Meade lose thirteen regiments to put down the Manhattan rioters; his forces were further depleted by the dispatch of other units to prevent similar riots in other Northern cities. Thus was George Gordon Meade robbed of an opportunity to follow up his victory at Gettysburg by driving full force against the retreating Lee and his terribly hurt army. Meade was bitterly criticized by the armchair warriors of Washington—who should have been thanking their stars that Meade and his men had prevented, at Gettysburg, the almost certain capture of the capital.

New York's draft riots have been credited by a few historians as a Confederate victory, which they assuredly were.

One of the North's great unsung victories was in the making on the day that Charles Francis Adams was appointed minister to Great Britain. This son of John Quincy Adams waged and won a battle that called for courage of the highest sort, as well as a cool and keen head. Adams had all the qualifications. He arrived in London in May of 1861, just in time to learn from the British newspapers that England had recognized the Confederacy as a belligerent. So had France. Nor was Adams long in learning that the British ruling classes were almost without exception in sympathy with the South.

Although the lords and ladies of England had often remarked on the barbarity of the United States in adhering to slavery, long since outlawed in the Empire, they scoffed at the idea that there was any moral purpose involved in the Civil War. In a little, too, as the great cotton spinning mills of England ran out of their raw product, the protest against the North's blockade of Southern ports became loud and powerful. Agents of the Confederacy working in London had fine connections, and they used them to good advantage to embarrass Adams at every turn.

Snubbed by nearly all of England's high officials, snubbed socially, too, and virtually isolated in the English capital, Adams nevertheless kept his temper. One of the coolest men imaginable, he needed all of his aplomb in these times; but he never truckled to the empty snobs who took pains to insult him, and conducted himself with a cool reserve that could match that of the greatest lord.

The Confederacy had placed orders in British shipyards for fighting vessels, among them two ironclads of the ram type, so greatly improved in destructiveness that no ship of the Northern navy could afford to meet them. While these were building, in the face of international law to the con-

trary, Adams with great skill and force set about to prevent
their delivery. For many months he brought argument and
pressure to bear on Lord John Russell, foreign secretary,
and used every scrap of favorable news, such as the fall of
Vicksburg, to convince Russell that the South could not
possibly win. Adams also had to combat the influence of the
Emperor Napoleon of France, who wanted England and
Russia to join him to intervene on the side of the South in
the war. Napoleon had designs on Mexico.

The business of the two ironclad rams went on, and as
time passed Adams took an increasingly firmer stand, telling
Russell that if the rams were permitted to sail, the United
States intended at all hazards to protect its commerce. This
was stiff talk, and Adams followed it up, in September of
1863, when the rams were finished and ready to leave port,
by a dispatch to Russell that gave the Englishman pause.
Should the rams depart, wrote Adams, "It would be super-
fluous in me to point out to your lordship that this is war."
Three days later Russell notified Adams that the departure
of the rams had been prohibited by official orders. It was a
great victory for the North.

With Adams winning out in the matter of the ironclads,
the efforts of Confederate agents in England virtually came
to an end; and Adams retained his strong position to the end
of the war. Not alone, of course, but more than any other
man, Charles Francis Adams was responsible for keeping
Great Britain, and hence France, from recognizing the Confederacy as an independent nation and from intervening, as
they more than once were on the verge of doing, in the war
between the states.

One of the great traditions of the war between the states
is that of the Confederate raiders, the horse captains and
their men—leaders like Stuart, Mosby, Morgan, Forrest and
Quantrell. They were fearless men, for the most part gallant
as well, and a large library could be formed of the books

about them. Into that library, too, should go a volume containing the story of another Confederate raider, Lieutenant Bennett H. Young, as yet unknown to virtually all Southerners and to all Northerners except for a few retentive souls in Vermont. Lieutenant Young was a raider to ride and raid with any of them. His was the raid that sent a shiver throughout all the North, and his was the raid that had repercussions as far away as Queen Victoria's court in London. Let me sing of Lieutenant Young and his epic:

Promptly at half-past three on a fine October afternoon in 1864, the biggest story of his life broke right under the nose of the editor of the *Daily Messenger* in St. Albans, Vermont, fifteen miles from the Canadian border. The minute it broke he knew it was one whale of a big story, for Main Street was full of noise, bullets sang dreadfully through his windows, and a man stumbled into his sanctum streaming blood all over the floor.

Even then the editor simply could not have realized how truly big the story was, for he had no way of knowing that the Civil War was at that moment having its northernmost battle on the elm-shaded streets of the editor's home town, six hundred miles from the capital of the Confederacy.

The St. Albans raid had its inception in a special order, dated June 16, 1864, at Richmond, Virginia, and signed by James A. Seddon, secretary of war of the Confederate States of America. The order was vague. It authorized Lieutenant Bennett H. Young to "organize for special service a company not to exceed twenty in number from those who belong to the service and are at this time beyond the Confederate states."

Lieutenant Young had just returned to Richmond after escaping from the Federal military prison pen at Camp Douglas, near Chicago. He had been one of Morgan's hard-riding raiders since the day he left school at Center College, Danville, Kentucky, to fight for the South, and had been

captured in 1863. For a time he had been held at Camp
Chase, Ohio, then at Camp Douglas. Now in Richmond he
told Rebel officers that a few determined men might stage
mass escapes of Southern prisoners held in many of the
poorly guarded Northern prison camps.

The idea sounded good to the brass-hats, hence the special
order to Young. Verbally he was instructed to pick his men
from Southern prisoners who had escaped into Canada—
hundreds had fled there—and to organize attacks and uprisings in such prison camps as he thought easiest to crack.
Young was twenty-one years old, and, as events were to
prove, of the greatest courage.

The Canada of 1864 was trying officially to sit on the
fence, so far as the American war was concerned, but the
Dominion was infested with a considerable number of Confederate agents, as well as with the many escaped Southern
prisoners of war. Most of the agents had money to spend.
With their courtly manners and much entertainment, they
managed to work up a good deal of sentiment for the South.

Lieutenant Young had his pick of the expatriate rebs.
He selected his twenty with care, mostly ex-cavalry men,
some who like Young had served with Morgan's Horse. They
had to be good men, crammed with courage, but cool-headed.
Young chose well, it turned out.

For a time Young worked on a plan to attack Johnson's
Island, in Sandusky Bay, Ohio, where a large Federal prison
camp was situated; but either through loose talk on the part
of somebody who knew about the plot but was not in it, or
because of the alertness of the Federal secret service agents,
word of the scheme leaked out and it had to be aban-
doned.

Either Young or his superiors now figured on a raid on
Yankee cities close to the Canadian border. It was thought
that such raids would demoralize communities far behind the
lines of war. A raid here, a town burned there, these might
worry Yankee generals into thinking that the South had

mobilized a large force in Canada; and that Yankee troops, then pressing the South so hard, would be deflected to protect the International boundary.

So, on Saturday, October 15, four personable but quiet young men registered at the American House on the main street of St. Albans, Vermont. Traders from Montreal, they said, over to do a little buying. Strangely enough, no one seems to have remarked their accent of speech, which surely could never have been mistaken for either British or French. The young men strolled casually around town, going into stores and banks, but attracted little attention. They seemed, perhaps, a bit shy of the townspeople, the which in Vermont, however, was considered nothing eccentric or suspicious.

On Saturday night perhaps six or eight more strangers checked in at the American House, separately. On Sunday four or five other travelers arrived and took lodgings at a boarding house near the center of town. A number of new faces appeared at services in the Congregational church that evening.

Yankee life in a Vermont village continued as usual throughout Monday and Tuesday, and Wednesday morning. St. Albans was a busy trading center, with three banks and a score of stores and business establishments, and on Wednesday the hitching racks on the main street presented about the average number of wagons and buggies.

At exactly half-past three in the afternoon the raiding parties struck simultaneously all over town. The event had been wonderfully well timed and coordinated.

Albert Sowles, cashier of the First National Bank, was alone in his place of business except for old General John Nason, a military relic eighty years old, who sat reading a copy of the Springfield *Republican* which told, that day, of Vermont troops fighting against the Rebels at far-off Cedar Creek—way down somewhere in that bloody land beyond Mason and Dixon's Line. As the bank clock struck the half-hour Cashier Sowles looked up to see three men in greatcoats entering the bank. They drew large revolvers as they advanced. General Nason was absorbed in his paper.

"We are Confederate soldiers," one of the men announced briskly, to the incredulous cashier. "We've come to give you a taste of General Sherman's idea of war." While the speaker kept Sowles covered, the other two men ran around the counter and into the vault. Working swiftly but making no false motions, they tossed bonds, greenbacks and various kinds of state and town currency to the value of $58,000 into haversacks which they had secreted under their greatcoats.

At this moment the aged General Nason looked up from his paper to contribute the only bit of humor, unconscious or otherwise, recorded that day. "Who are these gentlemen," he cackled. "Seems to me they are rather rude in their behavior."

Just as the three raiders had filled their sacks with money and were about to leave, William H. Blaisdell, St. Albans merchant, came into the bank. He took in the scene at a glance and went into action, grabbing the nearest robber and throwing him to the floor. They rolled over and Blaisdell looked up and into the tunnel-like mouth of a revolver.

No shots were fired in the bank. "We're not killers," said one of the raiders. "We aren't robbers. This money is for the Confederacy." Which sounds like a non sequitur. Still incapable of believing that the Civil War had come to Vermont, the cashier, the merchant and the old soldier were marched across the street to the village green, where a number of citizens were already under guard of more armed strangers in greatcoats.

At half-past three other events were taking place in the St. Albans Bank, farther down the main street. At that hour three armed strangers walked in to find Cyrus Bishop, assistant cashier, and Martin Seymour, clerk, busy at their counters. Bishop looked up to see the big revolvers, then made a leap and a bound which took him into the directors' room.

He slammed the door shut. While two of the raiders covered Seymour, the third man went after Bishop, kicking in the door, and bringing the assistant cashier out at point of gun. Bishop was then forced to open the big safe. At that moment the bank's front door opened and in walked a Mr. Breck of the local firm of Breck & Wetherbee, come with $400 in currency in one hand to make a deposit. "Right over here, mister," commanded one of the raiders, waving his gun. "I am taking all the deposits today." He reached out and snatched the money from the astonished Mr. Breck.

Still working fast and with remarkable coolness, the robbers collected currency totaling $73,522, and stuffed it into the bags they wore under their coats. While this was going forward one of the strangers typically gave a brief dissertation on the justness of the South's great Cause. He wagged his big revolver at his prisoners and had them repeat after him what he said was the "Confederate oath of loyalty." It doubtless sounded a bit comical in the accents of the Green Mountains. After this horseplay the raiders herded the three men into the bank directors' room, locked the door, and departed.

Much the same sort of thing, at half-past three, was going on in the Franklin County Bank, also on the main street. Marcus Beardsley, cashier, was settling an account for some wood-sawing with one Jackson Clark when the raiders, four in number, entered and waved their guns. They quickly gathered some $70,000 in greenbacks and various kinds of currency, put the two men into the vaults, and turned the bolts.

Everything was beautifully timed by the raiders. Half-past three was the hour when things began to happen at the fine livery stable operated by William & E. D. Fuller. Half a dozen strangers—some thought they had counted ten—appeared at the stable door, each armed with a gun. They told the hostler to bring all the horses out of the stalls, and to be quick about it. They meanwhile grabbed what bridles and the few saddles they could lay hands on. As the horses were backed out of the stalls, the raiders bridled them, and mounted.

Now came E. D. Fuller himself, one of the stable's proprietors, on the dead run. He had heard the commotion from across the street. "Put back them hosses," he shouted, and he plowed head-on for the group of armed men. One of the mounted raiders rode to meet Fuller. "Get out of here, God damn you, or I'll blow me a hole through you," he ordered.

Now, what was it in the soul of a livery-stable keeper that made him determined to resist, to fight these armed strangers who were stealing his horses? Was it a quality inherent in livery-stable keepers? Three sets of bankers had let three sets of raiders clean out their vaults, and raised not an arm to resist. But it was not to be thus with the fine Morgan horses in the Fuller stable. On the threat to blow a hole through him, E. D. Fuller disappeared for a moment, but returned to the scene almost instantly, now armed with a monstrous Colt revolver. Taking his stand in front of the nearby shoe shop of Bildad Paul, Fuller coolly up with his gun and pulled the trigger. He pulled it again and again, but nothing happened. Only miserable clicks answered his finger. To his dying day E. D. Fuller cursed the gun that wasn't loaded.

By this time thirty or forty citizens were being held under guard on the village green by armed men on horseback. The raid had been a fearful surprise, and for a few minutes all St. Albans was paralyzed. Motionless, speechless, the cluster of citizens stood there on the pretty common, utterly dazed that the war, which they had thought was being fought in Virginia and other heathen parts, had come upon them with the speed of lightning. It looked, indeed, as if the raiders would make a perfect getaway, so precise had been their timing, and so great the terror of the townsfolk.

Coming down the street at this moment was Captain George P. Conger, of the First Vermont Cavalry, home on leave from the wars. Lieutenant Bennett Young, chief of the raiding party, was in the street directing his men. The raiders were about to leave St. Albans. Noting the uniformed Conger and sensing in him a potential troublemaker, Young took him into custody at once and put him on the green under guard with the other citizens.

Captain Conger was prisoner for only a moment. Making a brave dash for the American House that faced the green, he disappeared into the hotel amid a shower of bullets that shattered windows and chipped bricks. Coming out at the back side of the hotel, Conger ran down Lake Street, sounding the alarm, yelling for all to get weapons and attack the robbers on the green.

Things now began to happen rather fast. Revolvers, shotguns, even muskets of the War of 1812 came out of shed chambers and out of closets and from above fireplace mantels as the embattled townsmen rallied to Captain Conger's alarm. Conger himself managed to lay hands on a rifle. He came around one end of the American House and opened fire on Lieutenant Young, who returned it with his revolver. Other citizens were converging on the green. Firing became general. Windows around the square belched smoke and dull-red flame. A raider was seen to lurch on his horse, then to steady himself. E. J. Morrison, prominent citizen, grunted horribly, clutched at his stomach, then stumbled into the *Daily Messenger* office, streaming blood. Printers picked him up and carried him out, under fire, to Dutcher & Sons pharmacy, where first aid was rendered.

Collins H. Huntington, citizen, came toward the green, firing. A shot from one of the raiders laid him in the street; and at almost the same time another raider bullet struck Citizen Lorenzo Bingham. Bullets tore through the doorway of the *Messenger* office, and the editor now fled to secure a gun. The front of Miss Beattie's women's shop was peppered and pockmarked. The windows of A. H. Munyon's store tinkled and crashed. Little Johnny Branch, town boy aged twelve, saw that the air over the village green was heavy with the smoke of black powder.*

Lieutenant Young was commanding the raid in a fashion that would have pleased his old chief, General John Hunt Morgan. His every move displayed good judgment. And now, when all of his men had reported on the green, he gave the order to ride. With bullets whining all around them they galloped north and so out of town. Canada was their goal, at least twenty miles by road. In their haversacks they carried slightly more than $200,000.

Captain Conger, the Vermont cavalryman on leave, took command of the local forces. Gathering perhaps a dozen men who had both arms and horses, he led the pursuit, being trailed by other townsmen as fast as they could secure horses. Conger's troop had good mounts, and they rode in a chase that would have made perfect cinema. At the village of Sheldon they rode thundering across a bridge in flames, fired by the raiders a few moments before. The raiders had also set fire to a house and barn close to the road.

The raiders did not pause at the customs and immigration stations at the border. They tore into Canada. Nor did Conger let international law stand in his way. He and his men crossed the line at a gallop, and near the hamlet called Slab City, on the Canadian side, they pressed the fleeing raiders so closely that several leaped from their mounts and ran into the woods. The others continued on toward Montreal.

Back in St. Albans new panic had broken out. Incendiary fires, started by some kind of devilish chemicals secretly left by the raiders, flared up in the American House, in a busi-

---

* John Branch, last eyewitness of the raid, told the author in 1939 that the St. Albans village green looked for a moment, to his youthful eyes, as he imagined the battlefields of Antietam and Cold Harbor to be. Mr. Branch also remarked on the fact that on the same day as the raid, General Phil Sheridan was making his famous ride from Winchester, in an action in which Vermont troops figured.

ness block, in several stores. The fire laddies turned out and were busy for some time, and the more excitable citizens thought that the town was doomed.

Rumors flew around that the raid was merely an advance party for a mighty Confederate army that had been secretly organized in Canada and was moving on Vermont from the north. Telegrams went to the secretary of war in Washington and to Vermont's governor at Montpelier, asking for immediate military aid to repel the coming host of Rebels.

As for the battle of St. Albans, the casualties were few. In the village three citizens had been hit; one, Morrison, fatally. It was learned later that four of the raiders had been wounded, one of whom died.

A company of soldiers soon arrived from Burlington. St. Albans citizens, as well as people of other border towns in Vermont—Richford, Newport, Derby—formed companies of home guards who patroled for several weeks. But no further raids occurred.

The St. Albans raid brought international complications. Yankees, including the doughty Captain Conger, had crossed the border, had arrested ten of the raiders and made an attempt to take them back to St. Albans. Canadian authorities prevented this, and put the alleged robbers or raiders or whatever they were into protective custody at Montreal. Of the booty, $86,000 was taken from the raiders by Canadian officials and later returned to St. Albans.

Now began a court battle, attended by monumental publicity, to extradite the "villainous robbers, arsonists and murderers," as St. Albans and other Yankee newspapers described the raiders. The New York *Tribune* thundered for their release to Vermont authorities. All over the North the press took up the cry. In the midst of it Lieutenant Young wrote a humorous letter to the St. Albans *Messenger*, and inclosed three dollars for a subscription, giving his address as "Montreal Jail." Another raider wrote a long letter to Landlord Skinner of the American House, St. Albans, inclosing "my check for five dollars in payment for my room, which I neglected to settle for because of the bustle and excitement which accompanied my business in your fair city." This lad must have enjoyed his stop in St. Albans a great deal, for he asked the landlord to give his warmest regards to the fascinating "young lady who occupied the room adjacent to mine."

Northern papers continued to cry aloud for the blood of Lieutenant Young and his hard-raiding men. They called on the British Crown to see that justice was done. Canadian authorities of course realized that if the raiders were returned to Vermont they were assured of a speedy drumhead court-martial and a good hanging. After a long time, and two trials, the fourteen apprehended raiders were discharged on the ground that they were belligerents of a foreign nation at war. The court, as related, returned $86,000 of the booty found on the captured men. What became of the rest of the swag is not at this date clear, but much of it was doubtless used for or by the Confederacy; and in April of 1865, the Canadian Parliament appropriated $70,000 in gold which was turned over to the St. Albans banks.

Lieutenant Young got safely back to his homeland, but the end of the war found him a marked man. His fame or notoriety was so great that he was, like Confederate Secretary of War Breckinridge and certain other Rebels, excluded from President Johnson's amnesty proclamation. This, in the South, was a very great honor, especially for a young lieutenant. For a time it also worked a hardship on Young. He went to live abroad until 1868, then returned to his native Kentucky to practice law in Louisville and to die in 1919, aged seventy-six years.

A melancholy footnote to the St. Albans raid concerns poetry. It has been mentioned that the raid occurred on the same day that General Phil Sheridan rode a horse twenty miles from Winchester, Virginia, straight into immortality, to sound effects by Thomas Buchanan Read, a Philadelphia

painter who also wrote verse. Read's stirring lines saved
Sheridan from the oblivion that has overtaken most Civil
War figures, no matter how gallant and able. If any Confederate soldier deserved a rousing good poem, it was Lieutenant Bennett Young, he who took the war into the farthest
reaches of Yankeeland and conducted the most northerly
battle in the struggle between the states.

Lieutenant Young was a typical product of his time and
place. All Southerners considered cavalry the greatest and
most honorable arm of the service. They were horsemen.
Cavalry was their orthodox style of making war. The unorthodox man of the Civil War, the man who envisioned what
war was to become in future years, was just as courageous as
Lieutenant Young—and he is just as forgotten today. He
was Thaddeus Sobieski Coulincourt Lowe, and mark him
well. He was a man slightly in advance of his time, yet he
influenced it, and his influence was powerful in bringing
about a striking change in the business of military reconnaissance.

Lowe, a product of New Hampshire, was twenty-six years
old in 1858, when he made his first ascent in a balloon. His
interest at this time was in science, not the military art; he
wanted to know something about currents in the upper air,
in what has since become known as the stratosphere. After
several ascents he gained the interest of Professor Joseph
Henry of the Smithsonian Institution, who gave him some
instruments, and Lowe himself invented a device for getting
latitude and longitude quickly and without a horizon. Then,
at a time that could hardly have been more ill chosen, he
crawled into his balloon at Cincinnati on April 20, 1861,
and nine hours later landed near Pea Ridge, on the border
of the Carolinas, probably the worst spot in the world, just
then, for a man with a broad "A."

A damyankee dropping out of the clouds on Carolina one
week after Sumter could be but one thing—a spy. Lowe was

arrested, and came near to being hanged then and there from a handy telegraph pole. Hanged he would have been, in spite of his protestations that he was a scientist endeavoring to learn about the vast currents that wafted far above the sacred soil of the South, had it not been for a gentleman present, a Southerner, who had witnessed Lowe make an ascent from Charleston the year before, and vouched for him as a pure scientist. Lowe was released, and returned North.

With the war well under way, and going none too successfully for the North, Lowe turned his thinking to the possible use of balloons as an aid to the Union armies. He devised a captive balloon, in which he made several ascents from the Mall in Washington. President Lincoln and Secretary Cameron were impressed, but General Winfield Scott, now aging, showed no interest, not even when Lowe took aloft one of the new magnetic telegraph machines and sent a message to the White House. "The city," he tapped out to the President, "with its girdle of encampments, presents a superb scene." This was a novel, not to say a startling event, and Lowe was told to go ahead with his strange ideas. Soon he was sailing over Virginia, at the stupendous height of five hundred feet, and sending down messages that he could see scattered camps of the Confederates and a great cloud of dust around Fairfax Courthouse.

This was getting somewhere. Lowe was made chief of a newly formed aeronautic section of the army. He took the first aerial photographs the country had seen, snapped from his balloon. This was a marvelous thing at the time, and the current crop of excitable war correspondents went whole-hog for Professor Lowe, as he was christened, and his new method of reconnaissance. These writers said that Lowe's new weapon would soon put a stop to the war; Southern troops could not move without Union knowledge; Northern generals could plan and map their campaigns from the air; it was likely that a balloon corps would attack the South and

lay it in ruins. It all read like the claims of air-power en-
thusiasts eighty years later.

Professor Lowe himself made no wild claims. He believed
simply that aerial observation could be a great aid to ground
troops. And so it proved to be. From the beginning of the
war to the battle of Gettysburg Lowe constantly went aloft
in balloons and directed their use by others. Union generals,
inept and otherwise, found Professor Lowe of the greatest
help; and the Confederate Jubal Early, one of the faster
moving commanders of the war, often cursed Lowe and his
observation balloons for spying out his most carefully con-
cealed movements of troops.

With the end of the war Lowe dropped his interest in
aeronautical affairs, yet he was still of an inventive and
curious mind. In 1868 he made the first artificial ice in the
United States for commercial purposes. He should be remembered, however, as the daddy of the observation balloon.
He brought a new weapon into warfare.

Until the Civil War little or no organized effort had ever
been made to ameliorate the harsh conditions under which
soldiers lived, and suffered. That struggle was hardly under
way when it became apparent that the antiquated medical
department of the United States Army had broken down in
the face of tremendous casualties, plus thousands of sick
soldiers. Public-spirited citizens, cognizant of the work of
Florence Nightingale and the British Sanitary Commission
in the recent Crimean war, organized a similar group which
was made an auxiliary of the Army Medical Corps.

To raise money for its activities Sanitary Fairs were held
in the larger cities. Mary Livermore, a reformer who had
been devoting her energies to Temperance, dropped the
white ribbon and became the main dynamo of the United
States Sanitary Commission. At last women were to play an
important part in American wars. A few hours after the
3th Massachusetts Regiment was fired on in Baltimore on

its way to the front in April of 1861, Dorothea Dix was heading for Washington to offer her services to Surgeon General William Hammond, who appointed her superintendent of women nurses. On her heels came Dr. Mary Walker, dressed in trousers and otherwise garbed as a man, to perform so gallantly under fire as a surgeon that Congress awarded her a special bronze medal. There came Clara Barton, too, who did not belong to any group but did wonders in collecting and distributing material comforts for sick and wounded soldiers, and served at the front as well. (After the war Miss Barton devoted four years to directing a search for missing men.)

Down from Boston in the first van came the tall spinster Louisa May Alcott, ill and weary from supporting Transcendentalism but with enough fire and energy and softness left to make her a fine nurse in the Union hospital at Georgetown until her own health broke. Yes, the women were at last going to the wars. Out in Illinois Mary Ann Bickerdyke, forty-four years old, raised five hundred dollars from her fellow townsmen of Galesburg, and away she went. She was a large woman, with "a comely weatherbeaten face and flashing blue eyes." Before the wars she had been a "botanic physician," treating all and sundry with herbs, but not with charms, for Mary Ann was a devout Christian who had no time for magic.

The status of Mary Bickerdyke was never clear. General Grant found her capable and courageous, and gave her a pass that let her go where she would at the front. She went everywhere. General Sherman, when an officer asked him about the woman, said he did not know her status but that she ranked *him*. She went where the guns boomed and the smoke hung heavy in the air. Under the guns of Fort Donelson she worked furiously to save the wounded. Always careless in her dress, she had somehow got into a Confederate coat. "May I inquire, madam," said a suspicious Union surgeon, "under whose authority you are operating?" Mary

Ann had a tart tongue at times. "My authority, sir," she snapped, "comes from God Almighty. Have you any authority that ranks that?" Possibly Mary Ann had read Ethan Allen.

Old fogies of both sexes privately and sometimes publicly deplored the fact that frail, fragile woman was being exposed to the vulgarities and horrors of hospital and battlefield. The idea of women at the fighting front was so new and startling that at first only those with great moral as well as physical courage dared to offer themselves as nurses; but in time the old Tory line was breached, and long before the war's end female nurses, although in the minority, were commonplace. Even in the South, where little organization of the kind was attempted, Sally Thompkins and like women served as did their sisters in the North. Looking back on the period, it would seem that the service of women nurses in the Civil War was the first great impetus given to what for many years was to be known as the female suffrage movement.

And during the great tragedy of the war the United States Congress passed one piece of legislation that was to have a profound effect on the country, both North and South, both at once and until the present day. This was the Homestead Act of 1862, one of the most important steps taken by a United States official body since the Declaration of Independence. President Lincoln signed it and gave it his blessing, and although its effects soon became apparent, he did not live to know its vast influence on the country.

CHAPTER X

Bury the Dead

EXCEPT for the South, the years immediately following the Civil War were filled with an intense throbbing and movement which had begun in the 1840's and continued even throughout the great struggle. With the coming of formal peace, and public comprehension of the Homestead Act, it seemed that most or much of America could not trouble with much else than to fill the smaller voids between the Appalachians and the Mississippi and the great voids beyond the big river; to net these voids with railroads, to tame the savage forests and the great plains, and to build cities amid the stumps and on the irrigated deserts.

While the South fought back at its carpetbagger persecutors and brooded on its fate, the North forgot the war between the states—that is, except for the Bloody Shirt politicians and other professional old soldiers, all of whom used the war for ulterior purposes for everything from a seat in the senate to a handout at the door:

> "I was with Grant"—the stranger said;
> Said the farmer, "Say no more,
> But rest thee here at my cottage porch,
> For thy feet are weary and sore."
>
> "I was with Grant"—the stranger said;
> Said the farmer, "Nay, no more—
> I prithee sit at my frugal board,
> And eat of my humble store." *

---

* From "The Aged Stranger," a poem by Bret Harte which satirized the professional old-soldier motif in American life after the Civil War. After

The North did not brood over the war. Instead, it went into a frenzy of expansion and exploitation. "Let the dead Past bury its dead," wrote a poet in Cambridge on the Charles, "act—act in the living Present." Although Longfellow's lines referred to a different occasion, they fitted perfectly the mood of the North. Men were leaving the dead past to bury its dead, and were acting for all they were worth in the present. Especially in the West—and the West now began at Buffalo—were men acting in the present. Western agriculture was growing swiftly into an immensity of plowed land. Great industries were building in Eastern and Midwestern centers, and these stopped and held many a new immigrant from Europe; but more of the newcomers struck for the open spaces of the West, and to their number were added hordes of native Americans who had become discontented on the Atlantic seaboard.

It required railroads to carry the great migration that was in the making. True, the Erie Canal and ships on the Great Lakes had started untold thousands on their way to the first frontier; and quite a number by 1850 already had reached the Pacific shore, either by way of the Horn or of the Isthmus, or by covered wagon across the plains. Yet it was not until the bands of steel were laid that the tempo of westward movement reached its peak.

The coming of the railroads was swift, too swift indeed for their own good. Consider, for instance, what faced a traveler, or even a piece of freight, going from New York to Chicago in 1853. The traveler boarded a train in New York for Albany. At Albany he changed cars, and waited hours for a train for Buffalo. At Buffalo he changed cars and waited for a train to take him the few miles to State Line, where he changed cars for the run to Erie. At Erie

---

the farmer has expended all his hospitality on the aged stranger whom he takes to be a worthy veteran, the stranger at last manages to complete his sentence: "I was with Grant—in Illinois—some three years before the war." The farmer then proceeds to beat up the aged stranger.

he changed. At Cleveland he changed, this time crossing the river there in a scow to another station, where he got a train that landed him in Toledo. Here he changed once more— and this time went to Chicago. That added up to six changes of cars on the run. Several of these changes were due, it is important to know, because railroads operated on different widths of track.

It probably did not call for pure genius to understand that a single gauge for all railroads would be a fine thing for all concerned. In any case this idea was being put into execution late in 1853. And now one gets a fair sample of the obstruction which most progressive changes are certain to meet, if the changes impinge on the economic interests of any group. What became known as the Erie War is worth citing.

At Erie, Pennsylvania, citizens did not welcome the proposed change. The tracks that led into Erie from the East were broad-gauge; the tracks that left Erie for the West were standard-gauge. All travelers between New York and Chicago, or between Buffalo and Chicago, had to change cars at Erie. They not only had to change cars, but they had to wait for hours, often overnight, and thus did the eating houses and hotels and bars and other places of transient commerce do very well by the floating population. When, in spite of spirited protests by interested citizens, work actually began to coordinate the tracks, the interested citizens declared war.

The first attempts to halt progress in Erie were made in the courts, where the pie-and-sandwich men and beer sellers fought to prevent the railroad from making necessary alterations within the city limits. The efforts failed, and the bohunk laborers of the accursed railroad started ripping up the old tracks and laying the new gauge. Seeing ghastly visions of an Erie where trains stopped only long enough for water for the locomotive, an Erie merely stared at by faces from within the coaches, Erie's sandwich-and-pie merchants took direct action.

On December 7, 1853, a cannon was fired in Erie. A huge mob thereupon formed, by previous agreement. They drove off the railroad laborers, ripped up the new tracks, and stole the shovels and picks. The more frenzied members of the mob then proceeded to the railroad bridge that came into town, and destroyed it. At near-by Harbor Creek another mob tore up the new tracks. It was reported that even the mayor of Erie and the county sheriff were acting as leaders of the destructive mobs. Declaring a state of martial law, the governor of Pennsylvania sent militia, but the militia boys fraternized with the rioters and even helped them to tear up more of the new and damnable tracks. Back in New York Horace Greeley berated Erie and its direct-actionists. "Let Erie," he wrote, "be avoided by all travelers until grass shall grow in her streets, and till her pie-men in despair shall move away to some other city." The rumpus continued well into the next year, when the railroads prevailed and Erie folks decided they would have to get along as best they could under the single-gauge track conditions.

A few years after the Erie War a passenger might travel from New York to Chicago without change. The Erie War, indeed, had marked a great step in American railroading. Henceforth the cars on nearly but not quite every American line were interchangeable with cars of another line, obviously a fine thing for everybody except perhaps the pie merchants of Erie. It was an impetus to the lines that were pushing back into the thick woods of the Lake States, out onto the plains and across the Bad Lands, and in 1869 a man could cross the continent on rails. It was wonderful. Everywhere the network of steel was spreading, thickening. In 1870–71, no less than 1,835 miles of new rails were laid in Illinois alone; and other rails had reached into farthest Wisconsin.

The story of the building of American railroads is a great one, and it has been told with spirit and admiration. Yet the men most responsible for filling the coaches of the new railroads with passengers are almost unknown. They were the emigration agents who spread the American Fever throughout Europe. Their influence on America was immense, perhaps as great as or even greater than that of any other group of men one could name, offhand or after consideration.

The instigators of emigration to the United States from Europe were not all official nor even paid agents. These unofficial and unpaid agents carried on their work because they saw in America an opportunity that was denied their countrymen at home. One of the most influential of this sort was the Scandinavian novelist, Fredrika Bremer, who toured the United States and found most of it good, especially the region around the Great Lakes. She grew lyrical about Minnesota, and thought it could become a glorious New Scandinavia. Here, she said, would the Swede find again his clear, romantic lakes, the plains of Scandia rich in corn, and the valleys of Norland. The Danes might here pasture their flocks and herds and lay out their farms on less misty coasts than those of Denmark. Miss Bremer thought that the Minnesota climate, the situation, the character of the scenery all would agree with her people better than that of any other of the United States.

After Miss Bremer came the celebrated Jenny Lind, to sing for $1,000 a concert under the none-too-modest aegis of Phineas Taylor Barnum. *Fröken* Lind returned to her homeland with a fortune made in the United States, and she spoke well of the new country. So did Ole Bull, the Barnum of the violin. Unpaid also as an emigration agent was Johan Reinert Reiersen, perhaps the most effective of them all through his book *The Pathfinder for Norwegian Emigrants in the United North American States and Texas*, published in 1844 after the author had toured all of the American West. Reiersen's *Pathfinder* quickly became the Bible of those Norwegians who had any idea of leaving their homes for the New World. The book was a classic of its genre. It was an astonishingly accurate study of conditions in the American midwest and in Texas, filled with wise comment on soils, waterways, and the probable courses of Western settlement. It took up the possibilities in various kinds of agriculture. It warned the stranger against slickers of all sorts, especially real estate men. It described the best and cheapest ways of getting to America, and then to the region desired.

Reiersen himself favored Texas, where he later founded a successful colony of Norwegians; and although the most of his countrymen sought other regions of the United States, his writings brought them to America by the many thousands —and to the good of every place where they settled. Always Reiersen told his old countrymen of his deep faith in the United States, whose institutions, he said again and again, "must necessarily conquer the entire civilized world."

Hans Mattson of Sweden was another notable spreader of the American Fever, and he was roundly damned for it at home. He first visited America in 1851, and two years after, not satisfied with the lands where Swedes had settled in Illinois, he went up the Mississippi to a spot near present Red Wing, Minnesota, where he founded the famous Vasa Settlement. No great speaker or writer, Mattson was nevertheless a born leader, a man to follow. Tall, huge, generous, and strictly honest in an occupation that was infested with charlatans, he was appointed official State Emigration Agent of Minnesota in 1866. He made a trip to Sweden; and wherever he stopped in his homeland, bands of his countrymen were soon packing their things to cross the Atlantic. Swedish newspapers attacked Mattson for depopulating his native country. Local politicians viewed him with alarm. Local pastors searched Holy Writ for arguments against leaving one's home.

Mattson kept on with his unholy work. During the sixties and seventies he acted as agent for the Northern Pacific

Railroad, for various land companies, and for the Canadian government. He seems never to have soared into the unrealities so common to exploitation of all kinds, but to have kept his enthusiasm for the United States and Canada on a sound basis. How many Swedes and other Scandinavians Mattson jogged out of their placid life is not to be estimated, but the number must have been very great. Let nobody say that the opportunities for advancement were the sole reason that Europeans by hundreds of thousands came to the United States in the 1860's, 1870's and 1880's. Those Europeans, many of them, might well have lived and died in their homelands had it not been for the inspiration and urging of men like Reiersen and Mattson. More than one American of Scandinavian descent has told me the same thing: that his father often blessed the name of Hans Mattson because Mattson had been the force that prompted him to leave Sweden.

The hundreds of thousands of settlers who flocked into the Lake States were very often struck by the sheer beauty of the place names they found ready—words like Algoma and Michigamme and Alpena and Tuscola. They are beautiful names. What man, or woman, with any trace of poetry in his soul would not be happy with Itasca or Iosco or Missaukee or Allegan? Yankee and European migrant alike found them pleasant to the ear, melodious and romantic, and gave praise to the native red men, whom they called great poets and believed responsible. They were right in thinking a man with music in his soul had named their lakes and bays and hills and plains and rivers, but he was a paleface and a genius. Henry Rowe Schoolcraft was the man.

Geologist, ethnologist, explorer and first-class American on all counts, Schoolcraft discovered the true source of the Mississippi in 1832 and named it Lake Itasca. Many a Minnesotan believes to this day that Itasca is pure Indian. It is, rather, pure Latin, as applied by the poetic yet scholarly Schoolcraft; and comes from *caput*, meaning source or head, and *veritans*, meaning true. Yet it has the sound of being what we think of as Indian.

As Indian agent at Sault Sainte Marie, and later as superintendent of Indians in the Territory, Schoolcraft ranged Michigan, Wisconsin and Minnesota, charting the streams and lakes, noting the minerals and soils, listing the birds and beasts. His first wife was an educated and brilliant quarter-blood Chippewa. Schoolcraft spoke the language like a red man, and his sympathies were with them, whom he studied constantly. Most white men had been content to know the Indian surface only. Not so with Schoolcraft. Out of his notes over a period of many years he published in 1839 his two volumes of *Algic Researches*, in which he describes with understanding and accuracy the mental characteristics, the history, manners and customs of the Eastern tribes, together with their great tales and legends. It was out of these *Algic Researches*, and with further aid from Schoolcraft, that Longfellow winnowed the story of Hiawatha. Together, Longfellow and Schoolcraft gave America its first great epic poem, properly enough about a native American.

Schoolcraft went on to compile, with government aid, six massive volumes on Indian tribes. Of more interest to the layman are the Schoolcraft place names. Itasca has been mentioned. Schoolcraft wanted to name what is now Lake Superior *Algoma*, a compound of Algonquin roots signifying Algonquin Sea. It failed, regrettably, yet Algoma remains on our maps, in places as widely separated as Wisconsin and Oregon. Schoolcraft often used Arabic, and from this language he combined *al*, meaning *the*, and *pinai*, *partridge*, to make *Alpena*, or "partridge country." Alpena is an honorable and cherished name in Michigan, and most Michiganders, even residents of Alpena City on Thunder Bay, will tell you that it is "an Indian word."

Latin, Arabic, English, Algonquin—Schoolcraft used them all, and well, in various combinations. You will still find his inventions on the maps as Arenac, Alcona, Oscoda, Tuscola, Illigan, Allegan, Leelanau, Colcaspi, and they are among the great glories of our land. 'Tis a pity that Schoolcraft did not travel longer and farther. He might have saved us from our one thousand Smith rivers, our five thousand Elk creeks, and our ten thousand Mud lakes. No giver of names to go on maps should be else but a poet, and Henry Schoolcraft was a poet.

What Schoolcraft did for the American language, another adopted son of Michigan did for material America. He was Charles T. Harvey, now forgotten, or rather never known to general history, where he has belonged for ninety years—has belonged as much as if not more than does George Washington Goethals, he who built the canal across Panama.

In 1852 Harvey was twenty-three years old, and in that year he came out to the new country of Michigan to sell weighing scales for the Fairbanks Company of St. Johnsbury, Vermont. At Sault Sainte Marie he came down with typhoid. While recovering he looked about him with a keen eye, while back of the eye was a brain of imagination.

Young Harvey saw a number of unrelated things which he put together in his mind. He saw rich piles of copper and of iron ores which were piling up around Lake Superior because the new and experimental mining concerns could find no way to get them down to the rising industrial centers of Ohio and Pennsylvania. What stopped traffic between Superior and the other Lakes was a solid mile of shallow water and swift tumbling rapids at the Soo, a fall of nineteen feet. Since the eighteenth century men had talked of building a canal here; and in 1798 men of the Northwest Company of fur traders had made a sort of ditch for their canoe fleets. But no one had attempted a real canal, much less a canal large enough to carry steamships around the rapids.

Harvey envisioned such a canal. He saw a thousand miles of fine waterway, merely by making one mile of good ditch at the Soo, a waterway from the western end of Lake Superior clear through to the Atlantic. Michigan wanted such a fine highway to the sea, but any canal must pass through federal land at Fort Brady, near Sault Sainte Marie village. The War Department had refused to consider such a thing.

Young Harvey returned to Vermont and imparted his idea and some of his fire to his employers, the Messrs. Fairbanks, as hard-headed a crowd of Yankees as could be found. They were interested in spite—or because—of the fact that the great Henry Clay had damned the Soo canal idea in Congress, terming it "a project beyond the remotest settlement of the United States, if not the moon." Clay did not get around so much as Charles Harvey did. The Fairbankses had powerful friends; and they themselves could in no manner be called weaklings. The matter of the canal went before Congress again, and this time construction was authorized. The Saint Mary's Falls Ship Canal Company was organized with Erastus Corning of Albany, New York, as president, and the following directors: Erastus Fairbanks; John V. L. Pruyn, chancellor of the University of the State of New York; John F. Seymour, Utica; John W. Brooks and John M. Forbes, both of Boston; and Harvey, who was made general agent and chief engineer of the company.

Congress finally voted a land grant to aid the construction. On June 1, 1853, when he was almost twenty-four years old, Harvey arrived at the Soo with a shipload of supplies and four hundred men he had inveigled into the adventure beyond the moon. "We will start digging here and now," he said, as he stepped hard on the top-side of a Number Two shovel to turn the first spade of earth.

Although the course was to be little more than a mile, the job was a titanic one in its day, for several reasons. Harvey's capitalist backers were all in New York or New England;

at least six weeks were required for an exchange of letters. The nearest telegraph station was in Detroit, 450 miles away. The nearest machine shop was on Saginaw Bay, half as far. Every stick of blasting powder must come from Delaware, a good thousand miles. Stone for the canal's sides had to be quarried near Malden, Ontario. And wrought iron by the hundred thousand pounds had to come from 'way down in Pennsylvania. It should be borne in mind that transportation in 1853 was rudimentary.

The region around the Soo was savage backwoods country. There was not sufficient labor at or anywhere near the Soo to operate more than a few wheelbarrows. The four hundred men Harvey had brought with him soon began to peter out. So, Harvey sent agents East to board ships from Europe before they could be docked in Boston and New York and grab off what immigrants they could. These determined and imaginative man-catchers told whopping big lies about opportunities for getting rich by digging the Soo canal, and they succeeded by various means in shanghaiing sufficient laborers to keep Harvey's force at around fifteen hundred men.

The job was less digging than blasting. All drilling was done by hand, and there was a monstrous pile of it to be done—done through rock that was flinty long before history began and was getting harder, so the drillers said, every day. And this job at the Soo called not only for muscle but also for resistance to the elements. During the short days of winter, a winter of close to five months' duration, there was a bare eight hours of sunlight much of the time. The thermometer commonly hovered around zero, or below, at midday, and took sudden drops to 35 degrees below zero.

But Harvey could match the winter; at the head of every runway for wheelbarrows—which were the main power in moving dirt—he stationed a man to watch the barrowmen and to rub promptly with snow the faces of those who gave sign of frostbite. He detailed crews of firemen to cut wood and keep great bonfires going, around which the laborers might thaw out a bit—so long as they were not too long at the business.

Incredible winds roared down off Superior, bringing blizzards to pile snow higher than the bunkhouse roofs, and sleet that stung like birdshot. Tools and equipment were buried again and again. Men at work suddenly grew dreamy, then fell from cold and had to be taken to the bonfires to be thawed out—which a few of them never did. Good cookhouse refrigeration was assured, and every cook in the outfit was provided with an ax. When he wanted more meat he went out into the shed and hacked it off the sides of beef that were frozen hard as plank.

Young Harvey was no desk engineer. He faced the winds and the cold and the snow, and drove his men to the limit. What hours he himself worked, no other man knew. He was up and about before the first cookhouse fire was lighted. And the working-stiffs told one another, wonderingly, of seeing Harvey, silhouetted against a high drift of snow, sighting his level by the light of Borealis itself. The Northern Lights blazed and crackled and dimmed, night after night, and the white pines along the right-of-way snapped and boomed from savage frost. Nothing could stop Harvey's driving frenzy. This was the way America was to be built. . . .

During the first winter word came to Harvey that some members of the company had become alarmed at the difficulties faced in building a canal in such a climate and in such a place. One of Harvey's trusted men on the job was John T. Whiting, an old-timer of the region. Harvey asked him to go East and put heart into those of his backers who were growing faint. Whiting set out on snowshoes and walked to Saginaw, then journeyed East by various methods as far as Syracuse, then on to Albany and St. Johnsbury, visiting members of the company, into whom he managed to instill some of the fire and the iron that Harvey was expending on the project. They dug into their pockets for more cash.

The winter wore itself out, but it had thinned the ranks of the crew. Harvey had to resort to his immigrant-catchers again, and he also set others of that gentry to operating in Eastern cities, picking up down-and-outers, who were shipped virtually under guard to the point of production.

The second winter was almost as bad as the first, but the work never ceased. Then, during the last few cruel months of the last spring and summer, an epidemic of cholera broke out in the camp. Men began to die at the rate of two a day, then four a day; and at last came a dreadful day when ten died. All of them were buried as discreetly as possible in the dark of the night, in an effort to keep the others, or most of them, from knowing that the disease was present in such deadly power. Harvey had to detail special trusted men to act as body-snatchers and undertakers, for more than two hundred died in all. The melancholy squads would wait until the crew had gone to work of a morning, then they would make the rounds of the bunks, collect the bodies, hide them, and at night bury them furtively here and there in the woods, where their skeletons have since frightened generations of prospecting boys. But not a single day's work was lost by the crew.

It was a hard and cruel two years of work and pain and death. Only one strike marked it. The grumbling of hard-driven workmen at last flared up one day in resentment over the harsh conditions; more pay was demanded. Harvey met them, as he did everything, head-on. He shut down all the cookhouses and placed tough men armed with double-barreled shotguns at their doors. No work, no grub. The men debated. A thousand of them threw down their picks and paraded. Harvey sent them word to parade and be damned—they would get nothing to eat until they worked. The strikers lost two meals, then returned to their drilling.

Harvey's driving fury continued until, on April 19, 1855, he opened the sluice gate to the cofferdam on the Lake Supe-

rior side, and let the cold waters of Gitche Gumee flow into
Lake Huron by way of the Soo canal. On June 18 the first
boat, the steamer *Illinois*, Captain Jack Wilson, west-bound,
was locked through without trouble. An event of greater importance and more indicative of the canal's place in our
history occurred on August 17. On that wonderful day the
brig *Columbia*, Judson Wells, master, with one hundred tons
of fine, black Marquette-range ore on her decks, passed eastward through the new Soo locks and canal on her way down
to the iron-making ports along Lake Erie. It was a historic
occasion of far greater meaning than anyone could have
dreamed, and it was not allowed to pass unnoticed. A blacksmith at Sault Sainte Marie fired an anvil cannon that shook
windows; and more than half of the males of the town were
reported to have got drunker than so many boiled owls.

When the Soo canal was dug, the iron-ore beds of the
Eastern United States, never very extensive, were nearly
played out; the United States was fourth, possibly only
fifth, among the iron-making countries of the world. Twenty-
five years later it was incomparably first. The Soo canal,
more than any other thing, was responsible. It was the big
factor in getting mountains of ore cheaply to the mills; the
device that permitted the United States to make, first, good
iron, then good steel, cheap enough to speed the building of
America at a dizzy pace.

The Soo is yet and by far the most important commercial
canal on earth. In peacetime its water-borne commerce ex-
ceeds that of the Suez and Panama canals combined, and
the Soo, it should be remembered, is open to commerce no
more than seven months a year. During World War II, the
Soo was likely the most important mile in all the United
States, for it is the mile that still connects—as no roads or
railroads could connect—the Menominee, the Marquette, the
Gogebic and the Mesabi ranges with Pittsburgh, an affinity
that created the guns and shells and armor plate used in all
of our wars since 1861.

The successful completion of the Soo canal was not the last of Charles Harvey's contributions to life in the United States; and the protean genius of the man is indicated in his next effort. In 1865 he settled in Tarrytown, New York, at a time when overcrowded Manhattan was agitating for adequate transportation. "Streetcars and omnibuses have their uses," Horace Greeley was complaining, "but we have reached the end of them. With such service it would not be decent to carry live hogs and hardly dead ones. . . . Give us a chance to breathe!" A New York City commission headed by Peter Cooper urged as the only possible remedy a practical rapid transit system, and advertised in the principal cities of the United States and Europe, inviting engineers to submit plans for a system suitable for use in New York. Harvey, the engineer of the back country, considered the subject and submitted a plan, which he called an "Elevated Railroad." From among scores of plans offered by leading engineers, Harvey's was accepted.

Taking direct charge of the project and exhibiting the same drive that had put through the Soo canal, Harvey built a trial half-mile section of elevated railroad on Greenwich Street. On a December day in 1867, attired in frock coat and silk hat, Harvey himself and alone piloted the first car, little more than an open platform on four wheels, over the rails, being pulled by a system of cables. By July of the following year the project was complete, and Governor Reuben E. Fenton was one of the astonished passengers to make the first official run. The West Side Elevated Railway was incorporated to extend the road along Ninth Avenue to Thirtieth Street.

Black Friday, September 24, 1869, sent banking houses crashing, and work on the West Side El was halted temporarily. But the idea was sound and the system workable, and the El prevailed. For the next forty years the first elevated railroad on earth provided Manhattan and surrounding communities with its chief mode of transportation. The

genius of Harvey operated equally well in both the great
city and the great open spaces. It is passing strange that the
man should remain unknown to all compilers of biographical
dictionaries and also to nearly all Americans.

The copper ores released from their limbo by the Soo
canal piled up fortunes for families in Boston and other
parts of New England. The iron ores made available through
the same source piled up fortunes for families in Cleveland,
Pittsburgh, New York and other cities. The building of the
Soo had by-products; the wages paid the canal laborers and
the miners seemed and indeed were fortunes compared to
what those Europeans had known in their own countries;
they wrote home to encourage their relatives and friends to
come to America. Every German and Irishman and Cousin
Jack and Scandinavian who worked with pick, ax or shovel,
and saved more money than he spent, was a great inducement
to his countrymen to leave their homes and cross the sea.

Swiftly and constantly the stream of immigrants from
the Old World and the emigrants from Eastern and Southern states filled up those great spaces which map-makers had
only recently designated as "Unknown" and "Prairie" and
"Great American Desert." Swift and constant was the
slaughter of the beaver, and the disappearance of the bison.
Sure and steady were the aggressive palefaces who en-
croached on the red men, breaking first one treaty, then
another, moving the Indians to reservations, then driving
them out to newer and worse reservations. And the red men
fought back. Led by able and spectacular chiefs like Sitting
Bull, or intelligent and quiet chiefs like the Nez Percé
Joseph, the Indians desperately tried to stem the flood. Blue-
coated soldiers killed them by hundreds. Red liquor slew
them by thousands. Government rations made them fawning
dependents, or moody outlaws given to sudden hideous attacks on homesteaders. Crushed by thoughtless cruelty one
year and softened the next by sentimental and wholly im-

practical "kindness," the poor red man's character became utterly confused. By the mid-eighties he had ceased to be much of a menace to settlers.

The next menace to the homesteaders was either overproduction or bad distribution or maybe railroads or perhaps simply middlemen and gamblers in grains. Some said one thing, some another. It mattered little, and it did nothing to alter the fact that ten-cent and twenty-cent wheat was no way for a farmer to get rich. In the 1870's the railroads seemed to many to be to blame for the farmers' plight, although "grasping local merchants" were rated not far behind as the menace. Whatever it was, farmers were being dispossessed at an alarming rate; other farmers were moving, while still solvent, into the towns and cities to work for wages. Everywhere the farmers cried for some sort of an organization that would better their lot by taming the railroads and the merchants, and the middlemen who bought their products. What was needed at this time was one of those most typical of all American products of the nineteenth century, a genuine fanatic with a purpose.

A budding fanatic was ready at hand. He was Oliver Hudson Kelley, born in Boston in 1826. After roving through Illinois and Iowa as newspaperman and telegrapher, he took a homestead in Minnesota in 1849. Highly intelligent, and a good writer, he had contributed a number of valuable articles to the reports of the United States Commissioner of Agriculture and had also made a trip through Minnesota to survey conditions for the Bureau of Agriculture. He turned in such an excellent report that the Bureau asked him to do it for the South.

These trips were made right after the end of the Civil War, and by the time Kelley had completed his surveys he had also conceived an idea. Farmers, he had found, had little social intercourse with each other. For the most part, either in the West or South, they and their families lived isolated lives. They took their stand on a farm and there they congealed, and often decayed. Kelley thought that a fraternal association would be welcome to them and a good thing for agriculture. Kelley also knew an employee of the Bureau of Agriculture named William Saunders, who had outlined on paper a kind of association for farmers, but had done nothing with it.

In 1867, along with Saunders and five others, Kelley organized the National Grange of the Patrons of Husbandry. He became secretary. A bit later he set out to convert the most individualistic group in America to his idea of an association. It was far from easy. The purpose of the Grange appeared to be somewhat vague. Most farmers thought they had no time for social doings of any sort. Many were actually hostile. But Kelley, though a downright fanatic on the subject in hand, was practical, and shrewd. He was filled with boundless enthusiasm, never dismayed, and he had the almost unknown quality—in a fanatic—of a sense of humor. The combination was unbeatable.

Traveling often on something less than a shoestring, Kelley swept through the Middle West, dispensing charters for local granges to pay his expenses. Michigan, Illinois, Wisconsin, Minnesota, Iowa, they fell one after the other to Kelley's charm and forceful argument. Working days like a demon, he spent his evenings writing letters, and articles for the agricultural press. He said little about the political possibilities of the Grange, but stressed the social and intellectual benefits of the order. There was also the mystery of the order, something along the line of the Odd Fellows, which appealed to many. But it is quite likely that the more intelligent farmers saw what might be accomplished politically by a solid front. Certainly such men as Ignatius Donnelly of Nininger, Minnesota, did, and Donnelly, one of the most engaging speakers and personalities in the country, lent his eloquence to the Grange.

Once he had organized the West, Kelley, a human engine as a friend described him, ranged into the South, and even there and in spite of his Yankee accent and manners, he founded grange after grange. By the middle of 1874 there were more than 20,000 locals of the order, with a total of at least one and one-half million members. The Granger movement was getting up steam. In thirty-two states legislatures were soon and almost simultaneously harassing the railroads with rate regulations. The Grangers did not formally sponsor these efforts, but they were the men behind them. And although the railroads fought back and usually managed to get the Granger laws repealed, or modified, the movement was of immense effect in leading up to the governmental regulation of tariffs that soon followed. The Grangers, in fact, were the first effective force in the United States to challenge the dominance of the railroads.

Many local and state granges turned their power against middlemen who bought and sold farm products. They also started co-operative buying groups for the purchase of agricultural machinery and other things needed by farmers. One of the proud boasts of the Grange was that women were admitted to full membership. The women proved as effective as the men, and often of greater stamina in the efforts for co-op buying and selling.

Most merchants, both country and city, were understandingly alarmed by the Grangers and fought them, but not so young Montgomery Ward, a New Jersey boy who had worked for Marshall Field in Chicago. Ward thought the Grange a fine thing. He had traveled as drygoods salesman in the rural sections of the Midwest. He knew something of the farmers' problems, and their hopes and desires. He knew that in all truth the farmer did get little from his produce and that he paid very high for what he bought of manufactured articles. In 1871 Ward had accumulated a little capital. Just as he was about to open what he called a mail-order house, for the purpose of selling for cash and direct to farmers, the great Chicago Fire wiped out all his assets. A year later, in 1872, he borrowed $800 from George R.

Thorne, and set up shop in an old livery stable on Kinzie Street in Chicago.

Ward paid no heed to city trade. He appealed to the farmers and his catalog, issued in 1872, said in bold print that Montgomery Ward & Company was founded "to meet the wants of the Patrons of Husbandry." In other words, he wanted the trade of the Grangers. He stressed the fact that he did not pay enormous rent, that he did not sell his goods to country merchants on six months' time, that he had no agents or middlemen of any sort, that he bought strictly for cash and was going to sell the same way.

The Grangers began immediately to patronize Montgomery Ward. Four years later the Ward catalog needed 150 close-printed pages to describe the Ward wares, and Montgomery Ward & Company was also selling grain for farmers at the startlingly modest commission of one cent a bushel. The company boasted that it had also saved consumers millions of dollars simply by forcing local merchants to sell *their* goods at fair prices.

The rest of the Montgomery Ward story is legend. Although it was not the first mail-order house in the country— that distinction probably belongs to Thompson of Connecticut—it was the first to appeal specifically to the rural trade on a large scale, and it started both a legend and a trend that was to continue down to the comparatively recent introduction of chain stores and co-operatives.

The first great drive of the Granger movement lasted only briefly, then it broke up into varied groups that changed their names, openly entered politics, and finally were swept into the Populist uprisings of the last decade of the century. Yet, the Patrons of Husbandry did not disappear. Their lodges have continued as social and intellectual meeting places for millions of farmers. Many a farmer and his wife have reason to know that the Granges have been perhaps the greatest single civilizing force in rural America of the past three-quarters of a century.

Socially, the farmers of the last quarter of the nineteenth century needed something like the Grange to brighten the ceaseless toil and endless isolation of the homesteads. It is significant that this was the identical period that rural and small-town America began dosing itself with an amazing variety and amount of patent medicines, a majority of which contained at least seventeen per cent alcohol. The subtly misnamed Temperance Movement had been making steady progress in rural districts for almost three decades. The frontier churches, usually Baptist and Methodist, were strongly against liquor, and they declared in camp meetings and roadside bethels that God was against it too.

So the classic demijohn of the American farmer, older than the nation by a hundred years, largely disappeared, and into this void streamed a river of proprietary medicines without parallel in history. The manufacturers of these concoctions knew what they were doing; they were filling a keen and continuous demand for something in lieu of the cup that cheers and is said to have the sting of an adder. But because alcohol had come at last under the tabu of the rural *mores*, the concoctions must appear in the guise of medicines. And so they did, and they doubtless helped many a farmer and his wife to face the extreme heat and cold, the grasshoppers and weevils, the floods and droughts, the mortgages and all-around bedevilment that seemed to dog the steps of rustic Americans.

The advertising that sent the rush of stomach-warming medicines down the throats of millions was about as subtle as the medicine radio advertising of more recent years. It first enumerated the boundless "symptoms" of ailments to which all flesh is heir. These symptoms had to be described in vivid language and to be so all-inclusive that a man must have been made of stone or wood to have missed having at least two or perhaps a dozen of them. Did the skin itch? Ah, my friend, that is the first feeble warning of the hell to follow quickly when dermatosis begins its deadly work. Were there spots before the eyes, did the memory grow weak, did the back ache, and was there, by any chance, a buzzing in the ears? God save us, Brother, lose no time! Send at once for a bottle of Jones's Electric Bitters, or Howe's Arabian Tonic.

No matter the ill, certain relief was available in a thousand compounds, usually liquid, usually containing allopathic doses of *spiritus frumenti*. The farmer, or his wife, took a tablespoon of Electric Bitters, as directed on the label; and presently a soothing sensation, a feeling of well-being—even of great and new strength if three tablespoons was the dose—pervaded the human frame, the stomach warmed, the arteries flowed faster, and any previous pain ceased or was notably dulled.

By the mid-1880's rural and small-town America was addicted to patent medicines. That this addiction may, as many medical men believe, have done material harm to the stomachs and constitutions of Grangers, is of little social import. The significant result of patent-medicine taking was that it speeded the so-called Temperance Movement (to be treated in a later chapter) which at the end of the second decade of the next century finally bloomed as national prohibition and fostered on the United States a coincident disrespect for law and a crime wave, from neither of which has the nation yet recovered.

Late in the century two men appeared in the Middle West to contribute more to rural America than any two men before or since. It is not too much to say that the efforts of William Dempster Hoard and Stephen Moulton Babcock changed the thinking of millions of farmers and brought into being the gigantic dairy industry as we know it today.

Hoard was a true fanatic. Born in New York State in 1836, he worked on farms and in what passed for dairies, and wherever he worked he insisted, as part of the contract, that he have time to spend at least an hour every day with the best farm books and periodicals he could find or subscribe to. In 1857 he went to Wisconsin, where he took a license to preach in the Methodist church. Becoming involved with an elder over a matter of doctrine, Hoard publicly burned his license and went to work in a logging camp. He served in the Union Army throughout the Civil War, then returned to Wisconsin to operate a farm along ideas he had accumulated, and to start a country newspaper which grew into *Hoard's Dairyman*, known today in all parts of the English-speaking world.

Hoard had long been a keen observer and critic of dairy practices, especially of breeding and feeding. He considered the practices to be abysmally ignorant. He had evolved a number of revolutionary ideas which he began to expound in his periodical. He stated that dairying was carried on in a wholly unscientific manner. It was a hit-or-miss business, he said, and usually miss. Little attention was paid to feeding. None at all to breeding. Hoard started in to change the thinking of every man who kept cows.

You don't hunt prairie chickens with a bulldog, Hoard shouted week after week in his paper, then why will you insist on dairying with beef cows? This was a simile any farmer could grasp, and Hoard laid it on, pounded it home, ringing the changes, using every analogy he could devise. He needed all the eloquent power of his pen, for farmers were hard to change. Sot. To their way of thinking, the old ways were the best ways. So, Hoard proceeded to demonstrate on his own farm what scientific breeding and feeding could do. Year upon year the Hoard herd of cows gave down with enormously increasing amounts of milk, and richer milk. Hoard beat the drum for the silo, then considered a wild aberration. He cried aloud for more alfalfa. He said that the wheat-weary soil of Wisconsin and other states would respond to grasses grown to feed cows.

Hoard first organized a county dairymen's association, then a state association. His paper gave aid to the forming of similar groups elsewhere. His editorials, couched in language suited perfectly to his public, constantly pounded home the idea that racehorses gain their speed from breeding and care; that dairy cows are made by breeding and feeding, and not just born that way. Hoard encouraged the making of cheese in Wisconsin and fought the railroads for cheaper freight rates for Western cheese to Eastern markets. He was largely responsible for the founding of the first dairy school in the United States, at the University of Wisconsin. *Hoard's Dairyman* became known as the Dairyman's Bible, and Hoard himself became the Jersey Cow Candidate for governor of Wisconsin, and was elected.

Coincident with much of Hoard's revolutionary work, and needed to bring that work to its fullest effectiveness, was the inventive genius of Stephen M. Babcock, another Yorker, born in 1843. Educated at Tufts College, Cornell, and Göttingen in Germany, Babcock specialized in chemistry. In 1887 Hoard and members of the Wisconsin Dairymen's Association asked Babcock if he could devise a practical test for measuring the butterfat content of milk. Such a test was needed for the reason made clear by a leading dairyman of the Wisconsin Association. "Why," asked he, "should I try to produce milk of a high standard to pool with that of poor quality, or to produce cream that has two or three times the money value of that of my neighbor's, then sell them for the same price my neighbor gets?"

Babcock moved to Madison and went to work. The dairymen saw a tall, lean man of great good humor and white beard, who always wore a cap and a black bow tie. He never seemed to be in much of a hurry; and, farmerlike, would stand and chat with friends and acquaintances. But he managed to put in long hours in the little shop set aside for him. The job, it turned out, required three years, and in 1890 Babcock issued perhaps the most celebrated monograph in the long history of cows and milk. This was Wisconsin Agricultural Station's *Bulletin No. 24*, in which Babcock described his newly invented testing machine.

Babcock's machine was as startling as Hoard's ideas had been, and it was simple. Any farm boy could operate it. It measured samples of cream in small bottles that were whirled around in the machine; and the results told quickly and accurately, from the viewpoint of butterfat, which cow of a herd was one to keep and to breed from, and which cow should be made into beef. Once a dairyman saw the Babcock tester in action, he recognized its possibilities as applied to his own herd. The elimination of low-butterfat cows began at once, and the consequent improvement of herds in the United States was manifest and heartening.

Babcock, had he wished, might have retained the patent on his revolutionary invention. He chose instead to give it to the public with no strings. Applied to Hoard's ideas of breeding for milk and high butterfat content, the Babcock tester went around the world; and it has been of immeasurable effect, especially in the United States, in putting and keeping the dairy industry on a scientific base. Although they have seldom if ever managed to get into our history books, Hoard and Babcock together have had an immense influence on life in the United States.

CHAPTER XI

Laissez Faire and Mr. Alger

WITH the Blue and the Gray dead safely buried, and the country building with a speed that amazed even the most depraved boosters, it was probably inevitable that Americans should go into a period of the grossest materialism. It was still a formative period in which the leaders of American thought and action might have directed things differently, and to the advantage of far greater numbers of Americans. A few did make the attempt, and they found themselves battering their heads futilely against a strong and massive wall.

This wall was composed of natural greed that was unfettered either by law or tradition, of cynicism that battened on greed, and of indifference, three quite human failings. All this made for an attitude of low morals in business and industry, and even lower morals, so it turned out, in government. Many writers have presumed to stand aghast at the mendacity of the United States federal administrations and most of the state governments from the end of the Civil War to the end of the century. It was the era of boodle, of Get It, of open and shameless corruption in public life. In business and industry it was the darkest jungle era of free cannibalism.

Neither historians nor laymen should have any sensible reason for being aghast at what went on. Morals and ethics are not immutable qualities of either Good or Bad, changeless as Time. There are *styles* in morals and ethics just as there are styles in clothing. The former change the more

223

slowly, but fluctuate they do, and the period after the Civil War saw a particular style of morals and ethics conquer the United States of America.

Business and industry had but recently come into American life on an important scale. There were no traditions, or at least no powerful traditions, to guide business and industrial leaders. They had never had a philosophy of their own. But now they were about to have one, and it was to dominate the United States for better than half a century. This philosophy was called by economists the doctrine of laissez faire, a French term that may freely be translated as "let things alone as they are," and cynically translated as a sort of semi-anarchy directed and dominated by the more aggressive members of society. What "laissez faire" came to mean in the United States was the non-interference of government with business—until and unless business requested it.

The administrations of U. S. Grant, and in lesser degree of those that followed for thirty years, were generally amenable to the precepts of laissez faire so long as they were paid—"got theirs" was the phrase—by the leading practitioners of business and industry. The idea, of course, was far from new—the idea of Commerce bribing Government. It had been practiced since the earliest history was written. Sometimes it was much in style, and barefaced. Other times it was against the prevailing *mores*, and furtive. At no time, in the Western world, perhaps, had it vaunted its presence as it did from Appomattox to the end of the century in the United States.

Legislatures, the Congress, cabinet members and high officials, they all played the game and were paid well in cash for their complaisance. They could not have done so had not the man in the street, the so-called common people, been willing, or at least indifferent. As for the leaders of business and industry, usually described as the corrupting influence, they were simply following the lines of least resistance and they patently found uncommonly willing corruptees in government places of high honor and great trust. Had the great and good divines of the period been in commerce at the time, I make bold to say that they too would have followed the lines of least resistance. No small few of the divines of the period found it most difficult, at first, to bring hallowed Christian ethics into some sort of workable compromise with the thundering facts of the economic order all around them. Because Christianity was Oriental and because the vast majority of Oriental peoples had little of material goods, the philosophy of the New Testament ran counter to what was actually happening in the United States. But most of the preachers were able, after deep communion with themselves and Holy Writ, to discover that, after all, bigger and better business did have the sanction of God, that high tariffs were made in heaven, and that labor unions and all reformers were products of Gehenna.

The era of barefaced boodle and corruption should not be considered, as it seems usually to be, as a time when *bad* men took advantage of *good* men and ground them down into the muck of the city slums and the mortgaged desolation of the farms. It should be considered as a gaudy three-ring circus, balloon ascension and jungle war combined, and enjoyed in literature as such. America had just been released from four years of bloody war right on the doorstep and in the front parlor. Now, like a man suddenly released from a horrible nightmare, it felt relieved, free, brave again, and aggressive. Vast fortunes, most of them from questionable sources, had been made during the war. Poor men saw the fortunes, noted that their sources seemed not to preclude their owners from being respected and honored, and resolved to keep an eye peeled for what was known in the parlance of the day as a "good chance."

The vast country beyond the Mississippi was now open and largely free to homesteading. A good part of western and northern Europe was arriving in ever increasing numbers. A sizable portion of the Eastern seaboard, especially

New England where agriculture could not compete with the new West, was moving westward. Eastern centers were filling up with new hordes of foreigners.

Any time of great and sudden movements of peoples is a time of opportunity, a time of good chance, for aggressive and clever men. Aggressively clever men were not lacking in the United States. All they needed, beyond their own abilities, was an acceptance by the people of the Republic of the doctrine of laissez faire. And this they got.

It is deplorable to report that the man who had greatest influence on the United States during the last third of the nineteenth century and the first third of the following century, was not Ralph Waldo Emerson of Concord, Massachusetts, but Herbert Spencer, an Englishman. Spencer, a genius who took the reflections of earlier British and French philosophers and the new theories o. Charles Darwin and pounded them into a philosophy of action exactly suited to the times, did not visit the United States until 1882, yet his influence had long been felt here, less through his books than through the efforts of three American philosophers. These men made Spencer a far greater influence in the United States than he was at home in the British Isles. Edward L. Youmans, writer and lecturer on scientific subjects, became a convert to Spencer in 1856, after reading the Englishman's *Principles of Philosophy*. First through his lectures, and later in the columns of the *Popular Science Monthly*, which he founded, Youmans beat a powerful drum for Spencer. The brilliant John Fiske—born Edmund Fisk [sic] Green, in 1842—was devouring Spencer at Harvard at an age when most Harvard students were more interested in the goings-on at the Howard Athenaeum, which is not a library; and he went on to drive Spencer's doctrines into generations of Harvard scholars so well that nearly all of them lived and died in the faith. Fiske was also one of the most popular lecturers in the United States and many a non-

MR. AND MRS. DRED SCOTT

FREDERICK DOUGLASS

LIEUTENANT BENNETT YOUNG RAIDED VERMONT

MARY A. LIVERMORE

HENRY BLOW

HENRY ROWE SCHOOLCRAFT

CHARLES T. HARVEY

WILLIAM DEMPSTER HOARD

STEPHEN M. BABCOCK

MR. HARVEY IN THE FIRST EL CAR, NEW YORK

MONTGOMERY WARD

HANS MATTSON

college man first heard of Spencer through Fiske and became convinced that laissez faire was as great a motto as
E pluribus unum, and doubtless as patriotic.

The business of the doctrine of laissez faire at Yale college was meanwhile in the cool and ponderous care of William
Graham Sumner, the Goliath of sociology, a man ready to
combat anything from soup kitchens for unemployed to the
government of the United States. Sumner was the declared
enemy of all restrictive legislations. Life, including business
and industry, was a matter of the survival of the fittest. No
fetters whatever should be applied to Commerce. Social evolu-
tion was more or less automatic, virtually unamenable to
control or even to direction. Monkeying with the natural flow
of business would lead only to destruction.

Free competition, Spencer had said—and Youmans and
Fiske and Sumner relayed the welcome news to young men
who were about to take over many of the reins of American
business—free competition was a natural law, the first law,
of economics. Free competition was the certain and the only
guarantor of community well-being. Socialism, paternalism
of any sort, would stem all human effort, stop Progress dead
in its track and lead, doubtless, to grass in the streets and
bats and owls in the farmhouse.

The truth is, said Sumner, and wealthy young men listened, that the social order is fixed by laws precisely analo-
gous to those of the physical order. The most that man can
do by his ignorance and conceit is to mar operation of the
social laws. David Ames Wells, an American philosopher
widely read in the eighties, put it all down on paper, and
he was even more specific than Sumner. "In point of natural
resources," Wells wrote, "Providence has given us all that we
desire. And that these resources may be made productive of
abundance, great and overflowing, to all sorts and conditions
of men, there must be, first, industry and economy on the
part of the individual, second, on the part of society, a
guaranty that every man shall have an opportunity to exert

his industry, and exchange his products, with the utmost freedom and the greatest intelligence. . . ."

A leading industrialist of the era, Andrew Carnegie, said publicly and to a great audience, that no matter how tough competition might be—and Carnegie had reason to know it could be tough—it was necessary because it was the best for the race, best because it insured the survival of the fittest in every department of life.

So much for the doctrines of Herbert Spencer, which were admirably suited to the place and the time—and the people. They could be cited against any and all reformers. They could be cited to "explain" the slums of American cities. They "explained" low wages. In fact, they "explained" just about everything needed to guide the United States on its way to becoming the greatest industrial nation on earth. That is, everything except for high tariffs which, it appeared from time to time, it was proper to ask the government to set.

In spite of the almost complete acceptance of the doctrine of laissez faire by the American people, there were a few native heretics who protested and set out, with almost indescribable courage, to refute it. Before getting on to these agitators and reformers, however, a low-brow disciple of Spencer ought to be mentioned. I refer to Horatio Alger, Jr., the man who made Spencer mean something to the rising generation of the masses of Americans, not the college men nor the intellectuals. It is to be gravely doubted that Alger ever read anything in Spencer. He was just not that kind of man. Nor did he consider himself a disciple of the great Englishman. Yet by indirection and literally tons of the most popular literature imaginable, he possibly did as much for laissez faire as all of Spencer's avowed followers together; and it was Alger who went beyond Fiske and Youmans and Sumner, for he was the man who put free and untrammeled competition on the side of the angels, and kept it there until well into the next century.

I do not recall having seen Horatio Alger's name mentioned before in connection with Herbert Spencer. Likely this seeming oversight is due to the fact that Alger operated on lower levels than did Fiske, Sumner and Youmans, and to mention him would thus seem a gross impropriety to most writers on sociology, who are very polite men; yet it was Alger, and Alger almost alone, who brought the philosophy of the whole Spencerian school to the proletariat of America and to the farms and backwoods as well. Alger did not call it laissez faire. He called it Upward and Onward.

Horatio Alger was born on Friday the 13th of January, 1832, in Revere, Massachusetts, the first son of a Unitarian minister who had marked his boy for the church. Early schooling at Gates Academy was followed by Harvard, where young Alger began a diary that was continued throughout his life and to which he confided virtually everything that happened to him. From the diary * we learn that the youth roomed in Cambridge at a Mrs. Curran's until that lusty female one day appeared before him in the altogether. "I shall have to move," says the diary, "to where there is more respect for decency." Move he did, and promptly. In his senior year he roomed at the house of Floyd Thurstone, an educated and amiable old eccentric who helped the youth with his lessons. The old man was trying to run a bookstore. He ran it into bankruptcy. Alger, learning of his friend's difficulty, worked furiously in an essay contest for which the college offered a first prize of forty dollars. Alger won it with a paper entitled "Athens at the Time of Socrates," and forthwith presented Thurstone with the money which, little though it was, permitted the old man to meet a mortgage payment and thus save his home.

Graduating in the class of 1852, whose shining light was Joseph H. Choate, young Alger faced one of two courses laid down by his father: he could enter divinity school, or he

---

* As quoted in Herbert R. Mayes's *Alger* (New York, 1928) the only serious biography of the man.

could go it alone with no parental aid. Horatio did not care for the pulpit. He rejected divinity for literature, and worked briefly on the staff of a short-lived periodical in Boston. He did some private tutoring. But it was a hard world. After going hungry for the best part of a week, the boy gave up the fight and entered Harvard Divinity School. He seems not to have been overly enthusiastic about his course, but he was graduated and certified as fit to preach in 1860.

Just at graduation time an astonishing event occurred. Mr. Thurstone died, leaving young Alger a ring, a nice stem-winding watch, and two thousand dollars in cash. Alger put on the ring, tucked the watch and cash into his pocket, and started on a European tour with two friends, both male. A brief and foggy pause in London was disappointing to the trio, who now called themselves art students. Arrived in Paris the two friends, but not Holy Horatio as he was known in college, went in for a major course in wine and women, minoring on the side with a little Art. But Parisian life at last caught up with Horatio in the form of one Elsie Montselet, an honest working girl who sang in a café.

After what seems to have been considerable effort on her part, the girl taught Horatio some of the facts of life, which appear to have been omitted at Harvard, and next day he addressed his diary with the only lines he ever wrote that ought to live: "I was a fool to have waited so long. It is not nearly so vile as I had thought." A bit later he penned another deathless line in the diary. His New England conscience had begun to boil, but he finally subdued it. "Genius has its prerogatives," he wrote in a good round hand; then he went back to Elsie.

Another charmer appeared, one Miss Evans, an alleged student of art, who took Horatio over and started to manage his life. He wrote in his diary that he should like to strangle Miss Evans, but characteristically, instead, he ran away and

got aboard a ship bound for New York. He didn't know Miss
Evans. On the first day out of Cherbourg, she appeared on
deck, as big as life and twice as domineering as before. When
the ship docked at New York, Horatio excused himself a moment, and as soon as he was out of Miss Evans's sharp eye,
he ran like the wind.

Broke now, and weighing exactly one hundred and ten
pounds as a result of his art studies, Horatio went home. At
the outbreak of the Civil War he went to enlist, fell, and
broke his arm. He drilled a home-guard company in Cambridge, then made another attempt to enlist, this time getting
into a train accident that put him back in hospital. In 1864,
feeling that God certainly had not marked him for Art, nor
Literature, nor War, he permitted himself to be ordained
minister of the Unitarian church in tiny Brewster, far down
near the elbow of Cape Cod.

For the next two years the Reverend Horatio Alger, Jr.,
retained his pulpit. This was the time when the urge to write
bloomed again, and most powerfully. He scribbled plots for
stories, and some of these he trustingly sent to William T.
Adams, editor of a goody-goody periodical for boys called
Student and Schoolmate.

Now, Editor Adams was also "Oliver Optic," already famous as a writer of juveniles, a man who knew good rich
tripe when he saw it. He at once sent Alger a most encouraging letter and wound up by asking him to contribute to the
magazine. In March of 1866 Alger, much like one of his own
future heroes, arrived at the Battery in New York City with
little cash and no knowledge at all of producing commercial
literature. But in his flowered carpetbag he had a great sheaf
of notes that became *Ragged Dick.*

Editor Adams took one look at *Ragged Dick* and rushed
it to his printers. It was an instantaneous success, a sensation, a story that Alger was to rewrite one hundred and
twelve times in the years to come, changing only the titles

and the names of characters.* It told of the rise to riches of a street urchin. It did more than that, much more. Ragged Dick and the horde of Alger heroes who followed him demonstrated beyond any doubt that the poor boy who worked hard and cheerfully, who was kind, decent, took baths, was respectful to his betters and elders, and was always more or less honest in his dealings, why, this boy was sure to become rich and honored. Nor did the Alger formula stop there. It went beyond the Spencerian promise and gave assurance that Ragged Dick and all his fellows were practically certain to marry the boss's daughter, who you may be sure was always beautiful and refined.

It was the crowd of boys who lived or hung out at the Newsboys' Lodging House over *The Sun's* offices in Fulton Street who started the cheering for *Ragged Dick* that soon spread countrywide and was to continue for more than three decades. Founded in 1853 by Charles Loring Brace, the House had a problem on its hands in the tough young drummer boys, back from the war, and thousands of other youngsters whom the war had set adrift. They had flocked to New York. The city fathers took no notice of them. The few charitable institutions in the city were feeble. About the only place for a homeless lad was the House, and the House was deluged, overrun. The influx had played havoc with discipline. When the superintendent, the kindly Charles O'Connor, came upon an installment of *Ragged Dick*, he knew it was what his boys needed. He ordered bundles, all he could get, of future installments.

The boys at the House simply ate up the story as it appeared. Faces shone with undictated washings. Politeness bloomed. Petty thievery stopped. Best of all, perhaps, was the fact that the boys got a hump on, as the phrase had it,

---

* Mr. Mayes's book and the Dictionary of American Biography credit Alger with 119 titles. Mr. Jacob Blanck, research editor of the Bibliography of American Literature, however, informs me (1944) that he has discovered no less than 135 titles, twenty-two of which are merely reissues under new titles.

and began to hustle, to pick up pennies and nickels and dimes for errands, shoeshines, matches, fireplace wood. O'Connor was so delighted with the incredible happenings that he went to see the author and invited him to make the Newsboys' Lodging House his base of operations. It was an inspired suggestion. Alger moved into the House, and there he rewrote over and over his one story, for the next thirty years.

Mark the Match Boy followed *Ragged Dick*. Both serials, once they had run their course, were put into book form and the presses had to work day and night to keep up, to turn out the immortal words that were to tell millions of young Americans that although Darwin might be wrong, Spencer was right. Alger went beyond Spencer, for the plain inference from Alger's stories was that the *poor* boy—that is, the poor boy who hustled—was far more likely to be a success than the boy born to money. Hearken to the Master as he sets the scene for *Herbert Carter's Legacy*:

"Is that the latest style?" inquired James Leech, with a sneer, pointing to a patch on Herbert Carter's pants.

Herbert's face flushed. He was not ashamed of the patch, for he knew that his mother's poverty made it a necessity. But he felt it was mean and dishonorable in James Leech, whose father was one of the rich men of Wrayburn, to taunt him with what he could not help. Some boys might have slunk away abashed, but Herbert had pluck and stood his ground.

"It is my style," he answered firmly, looking James boldly in the face.

And how does it go with patched but courageous and hustling Herbert Carter in the end? After 265 pages he is patently well through the worst of the jungle of free competition and coasting easily along the level hilltop marked Success. Says the Master in his final paragraph in this typical Alger book:

Herbert has undergone the discipline of poverty and privation, and prosperity is not likely to spoil him. He has done his duty under difficult circumstances, and now he reaps the reward.

If the meaning of an Algerian reward needs defining here, it can be done succinctly: Herbert Carter, like all other Alger heroes, was rewarded with $1,000,000, plus the boss's daughter, a priggish lass, perhaps, but beautiful and probably affectionate.

And the presses groaned and rumbled without stop. Endorsements of Mr. Alger's fine stories came in by the hundred, then by the thousand, from teachers, preachers, leading citizens, fathers, mothers, boys. Cynical printers passed ribald remarks on the copy they set, and laughed lewdly at the Alger heroes; but they kept on setting type and feeding the presses. Mr. Richard M. Hoe was none too early with his invention of the high-speed printing press. Larger and larger grew each subsequent impression of Mr. Alger's works.

Alger's writing habits, while eccentric, ran to a pattern. He outlined his simple plot in advance—although this was hardly necessary after he had compounded the first plot— and selected names for his characters. Choosing a title came before he wrote the first word of the story. Titles were important. But when he once got down to writing, he was a demon. Writing swiftly and with almost no revisions, he would sit at his desk ten, fifteen hours at a stretch, brewing strong coffee to keep him awake, the while inspired bilge flowed from his pen. He wrote so carelessly that his publishers made some attempt to correct the more glaring inconsistencies. For one thing, he could not always remember whether his current hero was Andy Gordon or Andy Grant or Bob Burton or Herbert Carter. Occasionally five or six heroes would appear in the same story, all obviously meant to be one and the same. As fame touched him, Alger took to writing absurd prefaces, often of 5,000 words in length, which his publishers usually managed to forget to include in the books.

For several years A. K. Loring was Alger's publisher, and in time he suggested to the author that he make a trip to the Pacific coast with the idea of writing a series of stories with Midwestern and Far Western backgrounds. Alger crossed the continent, getting ideas that soon became *The Young Miner, Both Sides of the Continent,* and other tales. On his return East he took lodgings in rural Peekskill, New York, a quiet, sleepy village that would be a fine place, so Alger thought, to write his Westerns. He couldn't have known it, but here in rustic New York both Drama and Romance were about to close in on him.

Shortly after his arrival in Peekskill, one Jeremiah Hardy, a well known villager, was found brutally murdered. His widow was arrested. She went into a hysterical turn during which she informed police she had seen a strange man in the neighborhood just before the murder. He was a small, dumpy, ineffectual looking person, she said, with mustaches. The local sleuths looked around and found, sure enough, a small, dumpy little fellow who wore a mustache and was growing bald. Questioned by the police, the little man said he was no killer, but Horatio Alger, Jr. The cops laughed heartily. "He's crazy as a loon, too," said the constable. "Thinks he's Horatio Alger, the great writer." They threw the protesting little chap into the town lockup, but within a few hours turned him loose. They wanted room for a man who had confessed to the murder. The cops apologized to Alger, and so did the Widow Hardy. She asked Alger to call, which he did, and things were going along nicely when Mrs. Hardy's sister, Una, showed up.

Una Smith, which was not her name, was about forty, pleasingly plump, and possessed, as it soon became apparent, of an ardent nature. She also had a husband, a traveling man, who must have been a particularly trusting soul. Within a short time Alger and Mrs. Smith took up lodgings, together, in New York City.

At this point, Mr. O'Connor of the Newsboys' Lodging House began to get worried about his good friend Alger. He noted that the author had all but ceased to write, that he showed little interest in the boys at the House. Alger's publishers were worried too. Here were the first hundred pages of *The Young Miner* all set in type and ready for serialization, but where was the rest of the story? Never before had they waited for copy from Alger. He ordinarily turned out 40,000 glowing words every week.

Mr. O'Connor, a pious soul, learned what was up and set about to break up the romance. Mr. Smith learned of his wife's liaison, doubtless either through O'Connor or through Alger's harassed publishers. In any case, Mr. Smith arrived and packed his wife off to Europe. And now Horatio was desolate. Day after day, while his publishers hounded him for copy, he sat at his table, mooning. Finally he gave up the effort to write and went to his publishers to tell them that he was about to sail for Europe and he wanted some cash for the voyage. But he had nothing coming in the way of cash. Keeping Mrs. Smith had been expensive.

Now Alger showed what he could do. He sat him down again and this time the imperishable prose of *Frank and Fearless* flowed from his heated pen, 80,000 words of it in fourteen days. He turned in his copy, took a brief stroll around Washington Square for exercise, then sat down to turn out *Upward and Onward*, another 80,000 words. Time: thirteen days. Collecting advance royalties on these two great works, Alger went to Europe.

In Paris, Horatio discovered that Mrs. Smith had cooled. She just was not interested any more. Horatio brooded. He tried to write, but could not. Months went by, and his frantic publishers cabled him for a story. With a superhuman effort Alger in a few days wrote *Walter Sherwood's Probation*. Then he fell into a fever that turned into some sort of violent

mental attack. One night neighbors heard terrific screaming. They called the gendarmes, who carried away to the
hospital a short, pudgy little man who fought like a trapped
raccoon.

When Alger had somewhat recovered he returned to New
York, so changed that O'Connor did not recognize him. He
had aged twenty years in one, said O'Connor. The devoted
O'Connor took Alger to his home and nursed him through
an illness of almost two years. Alger then resumed writing.
O'Connor died, and this all but finished Alger, for O'Connor
was the only adult male friend he ever knew.

Alger went back to New England, and started coughing.
He was put to bed, and word of his illness reached the Newsboys' Lodging House. The lads there drew up a splendid
resolution, in the form of a scroll, and sent a committee to
deliver it to the dying man. It was perhaps the greatest, the
fullest moment in Alger's life, and he wept tears of joy. A
few days later he turned his face to the wall and died. He was
buried on July 18, 1899, from the Unitarian church in
South Natick, Massachusetts.

Alger's books, all one hundred and thirty-five of them,
counting the reissues under new titles, continued to sell. One
man in the trade has estimated their total sales at 120,000,-
000 copies. Another set it at 250,000,000 copies. Whatever
the figure, it was enormous, probably larger than the sales
of any other American author. The impact of the gigantic
weight of Upward and Onward philosophy on Young America in the last third of the nineteenth century has never been
measured, but it must have been truly stupendous; and its
total effect was to certify the doctrine of laissez faire as right
and immutable. Although as literature Alger's writing is to
be dismissed as trash, the main thesis of it, namely that in
the United States a boy, no matter how patched his pants,
could rise from the slums or from the farms, to become a
capitalist, complete with plug hat and gold-headed cane,
happened just often enough in real life to give support to

the fictional narrative. Many a self-made man has not hesitated to name the Alger books as having had the greatest influence on his own life and success. It is more than possible that their influence was greater on the lives and times of growing Americans than the works of any other contemporary writer. Perhaps greater than all the others put together. Though the 1870's and the eighties and nineties saw dismal and widespread poverty in the United States, and though anarchists and socialists fomented strikes and riots, the Red Dawn never came up over the horizon. Too many Americans held the vision of Upward and Onward.

So, street urchins worked hard and long, never questioned the rate of their wages, and they went upward and onward—or, some of them did, and those who did not were more likely to blame their own shortcomings than to lay their failure to the System. The same was true of the many farm boys who went to live and work in the villages. Wealth, or anything approaching it, escaped a large majority of these would-be Alger heroes.

Wealth, however, was piling up in ever increasing amounts for an increasing number of Americans. And in time the more generous or more astute of the millionaires began to feel that great wealth carried with it a certain responsibility to the public. The immensely rich George Peabody gave generously to endow education in the South and also founded notable museums of natural history at Yale and Harvard and in Baltimore, and in Salem, Massachusetts. A great meat-packing family set up Armour Institute in Chicago. Jonas Clark established a fine technical school in Worcester. Ezra Cornell founded a great university. Rockefeller gave liberally to the University of Chicago. Leland Stanford founded a college on the Pacific coast. Carnegie poured many millions into libraries. All of this was welcomed by the hard-pressed preachers, often hard put to find something Christianlike in the Gilded Era; now they discovered that in Dives and his kind was the salvation of culture, if not of Civilization itself.

The great and unforgivable crime of these wealthy men, it seems to me, was not in their money, but in their personal tastes. Although Virginia and New England, at least, had many old and beautiful mansions to serve as inspiration, houses as fine and graceful as anything the world has seen, the newly wealthy considered them as native, hence too common for the American plutocrat. So while architects paled and shuddered, Pittsburgh millionaires and others insisted on pseudo-Norman castles, complete with moat and drawbridge, then added Japanese hothouses and New England weather vanes. One suddenly rich man was asked by his architect if he desired a porte-cochere in connection with his rising mansion. "Hell, yes," was the forthright reply. "Better put in five of them. And make sure they don't flush loud."

From Albany to Manhattan the Hudson broke out with dreadful piles of stone and stucco and wood. This mania for the grandiose began early in the 1870's and lasted to the century's end. Near Boston, monsters of brown shingle crawled on suburban lawns. In Saginaw, citizens saw and marveled at Florentine fronts ending in manorial windows, and at least one baron's wall around his great yard was composed of mortar and empty champagne bottles. Farther west, horrible monstrosities were assembled as banks and public buildings. Hotels, as Thomas Beer noted, resembled ennobled bathrooms without visible conveniences.

America's suddenly rich seldom considered American artists, although by 1860 many competent and a few inspired native painters were at work. Instead, the plutes became suckers for foreign art and they paid huge sums for faked Old Masters and for the inferior work of inferior French, Dutch, British, German and Italian artists. How very bad their choices were has become increasingly and embarrassingly apparent, as the sons and daughters of the plutes presented to museums the dreadful art their fathers had bought.

For the past forty years the cellars or attics of art museums in many of the larger Eastern centers have been growing heavy with these pictures, now seen no more.

Even worse, from the viewpoint of international respect and unity, was what happened only too often when the newly rich Americans went abroad to England and the Continent. There, by their vulgar displays, their crude manners, and their desire to marry their daughters to titles that were usually moth-eaten, they did the United States of America incalculable harm, an injury that has lasted down to the present moment: they gave the world the impression that all Americans had wealth—and almost nothing else. Let economists prove otherwise if they will, but I believe these crass Americans started the tradition of unlimited American wealth that has played a big part in preventing the United States from collecting just debts from foreign nations, debts that long since passed into the astronomical region of figures. They started, did these wealthy fatheads, the tradition among foreign nations that America's wealth should supply the rest of the world with what it needed, apparently, forever. In the intervening years, our country has done little as a nation to break the tradition.

Yet, for all its wealthy individuals, for all of its countless men who hustled but failed to become wealthy, the United States of last century harbored more idealists, more people who didn't give a damn for dollars, than any two, or perhaps four, other countries on the globe.

CHAPTER XII

Discontent: Mother of Progress

YEARS ago I knew an old anarchist in the Puget Sound country who operated a monthly journal of decided opinions and who tacked to the masthead of his little periodical a legend: "Discontent: Mother of Progress." It was his contention, and he marshaled notable proof in support of it, that most if not all social progress stemmed from a person or group of persons who for one reason or another were discontented, either with their own lot or with that of their fellows.

Wage earners in the United States had shown their discontent as early as 1806. That was the year when the Caulkers' Club of Massachusetts made formal demand for a ten-hour day when the common hours of labor were from twelve to sixteen. Again, in 1817, this union struck because employers had stopped the rum allowance. The Caulkers' Club dated back to pre-Revolution days—Samuel Adams's father was a member—and incidentally, our word "caucus," today applied to political plotting, is said to have been originally a mispronunciation of Caulkers. Small unions continued to plot for the next fifty years, and to die one by one. Among them were the Sons of Vulcan, the Knights of St. Crispin, the Knights of Industry. Railroad men, and a few of the trades such as printers, however, managed to survive as labor organizations. Then, in 1869, came a discontented man with an idea: a union of all laboring men.

He was Uriah Stephens. He was discontented with his own lot and that of wage earners generally. Born in New Jersey in 1821, he was studying to become a Baptist minister when the panic of 1837 brought woeful poverty to his family. He had to give up his schooling, and to earn his bread he became a tailor's apprentice. Stephens was a serious youth. He spent his few spare hours with books. He joined the Masons, the Odd Fellows, the Knights of Pythias. He taught school. He went to California, then to Philadelphia where he urged city workers to migrate to the West, where he said there were more and greater opportunities. More important was the fact that Stephens quietly organized the garment cutters of Philadelphia into a union.

In 1869 this union was wrecked and dissolved, chiefly through the pressure and hard-boiled tactics of employers. After some meditation Stephens came to the conclusion that the usual type of craft union could not successfully combat the organizations of employers; and in company with a handful of garment workers he formed a secret group first known as the Five Stars, which was to become the most powerful labor body of its day.

Stephens held that the new group should be sworn to secrecy, and he devised a sort of lodge ritual to go with it. He said that it should be a union of *all* trades—then a revolutionary idea—and that it should work for the education of all laboring men. Workers, said Stephens, did not know enough about the place of labor in everyday life. They did not comprehend their power as a group, nor appreciate fully how weak a worker was by himself. Stephens also wanted wage earners to know something of literature, of art, of history. He wanted them to achieve a culture as good as or better than that of the middle-class American, for he meant the Five Stars to be something more than just another union. Into this grand organization should go women as well as men, black workers as well as white. No race or religion nor any honest occupation should bar man or woman from becoming full members of the Five Stars.

The goal Stephens wanted was a sort of cooperative commonwealth in which the means of production would be owned and operated on a co-operative basis.

The new group made rapid progress, and in 1878 it dropped its name but not yet its secrecy and adopted the Knights of Labor as its style. Stephens apparently had no feeling of class consciousness; and although strikes by the Knights occurred, Stephens himself counseled use of the boycott rather than the strike as an economic weapon. In 1882 the Knights dropped their secret passwords and grips, and by then they were the biggest labor group North America had seen. Three years later the membership ran to more than one million. Then, in 1886, came the celebrated Haymarket Bomb in Chicago, a mystery not yet solved although men were hanged and other men imprisoned for it. The Haymarket Bomb was most disastrous to labor, and fatal to the Knights, who soon began to disintegrate and were for the greater part taken over by the rising young American Federation of Labor.

If any one man may be said to be the father of organized labor in the United States, it is Uriah Stephens, he who became discontented with an economic situation that prevented him from becoming a Baptist minister.

It would be more difficult, and probably impossible, to name either the father or the mother of what finally became Prohibition in the United States during the third decade of the twentieth century. Yet its birth was not by parthenogenesis, and midwives were busy with the matter as early as 1780, when the Methodist General Conference damned both the making and drinking of liquor. Because Prohibition, as it came to fullest flower between 1920 and 1932, was the most baleful and demoralizing event the United States has known since the Civil War, its halting but never ceasing progress through the years ought to be noted in any serious work about the Republic. Varied and often extremely weird milestones marked its way. At this same Methodist meeting in 1780 was a man who set up a milestone. He was the Reverend Ebenezer Sparhawk, founding father of the Prohibition literary school in its relation to physiology, and a man who could draw up an indictment that contained no loopholes and no qualifications. When the Reverend Ebenezer fired at the Demon, scarcely a sulphur spot was left. "Alcohol," cried he in vivid prose that has been copied by Temperance writers for more than a century, but never improved upon, "Alcohol puts the blood and juices into a most terrible ferment, and disturbs the whole animal economy. It vitiates the humors, relaxes the solids, spoils the constitution, fills the body with diseases, brings on meager looks, a ghastly countenance, and very bad tremblings; yea, when the abuse of it is persisted in, it quite ruins the health, destroys the strength, introduces decay of nature, and hastens death faster than hard labor."

The school physiology books of my day, and before and since, owe a good deal to the Reverend Mr. Sparhawk. They owe a good deal, too, to a forgotten and wonderful artist, Dr. Thomas Sewall, a progenitor of the Surrealist school, who is to Prohibition art what Sparhawk is to Prohibition prose. Doctor Sewall produced seven highly colored plates that allegedly depicted, and faithfully, the progressive hell through which the stomachs of rum-bibbers went their dreadful way from light pink to a deep purple covered with splotches of ominous brown and sinister black.

Let no one say that the United States did not produce an artist of influence on his country. Here in good Dr. Sewall's seven colored plates was an immensity of influence, immediate, widespread, lasting, and quite devastating in its impact. These plates were basically the material used ever since by most illustrators of American school physiologies; and they were jim-dandies, enough to frighten the young beyond compare and to give pause to all except confirmed and hopeless topers. Young boys blenched and girls fainted when they looked fair upon the results of rum as seen in the gorgeous stomachs produced in six colors by the art of Dr. Sewall. Both Parson Sparhawk and Dr. Sewall are to be reckoned with in American history, for they produced an art-plus-literature never before seen elsewhere on earth.

The ineffable Parson Weems, he whose biography of George Washington warped biography to the cause of piety, once took a hand at Temperance writing, but he was very mild compared to Sparhawk and others. Weems, in his charming *Drunkard's Looking Glass,* did not go all out for Prohibition. He counseled using a *little* wine for the stomach's sake, and "also cyder, beer, ale, etc." He announced that hot coffee in the morning was a good cure for dram-taking, and, when considered all together his work was merely against drunkenness and in favor of control of one's appetite for liquor.

The first serious and worthy study of the effects of alcohol on the human body by a competent person was that written just after the Revolution by Dr. Benjamin Rush. It was widely printed and quoted and also much read, making many converts, not to Prohibition, but to education in regard to alcohol and its effects.

One of the first organized groups against rum appears to have been the Moreau Society, formed in or about 1808 in the town of Moreau in up-state New York, characteristically enough, to keep liquor away from the greatest tribe of guzzlers the United States has known—the lumberjacks. Moreau was in the heart of the forest and was populated chiefly by loggers and sawmill workers. Many of them were married and had their families in the village. The men drank so much and so constantly that their womenfolk related their privations and discontent to the local physician, who himself had noted and was aghast at his charges' gargantuan appetites for strong drink. The physician persuaded a local parson and other more or less normal citizens to help him in founding a group pledged to use no distilled liquors and also to work for restriction of sale of drink to laboring men. The society was ahead of its time, and it seems to have quickly failed. It should be marked, however, that it was the lumberjack who first inspired an organized Temperance move.

Copies of the Moreau Society sprang up elsewhere in the Eastern states; and as the movement slowly permeated the country, the literary school founded by the aforementioned Parson Sparhawk was expanded by other tremendous liars, among the best of whom was Jonathan Kittredge of Lyme, New Hampshire. To Mr. Kittredge goes the honor of establishing in sober print a magnificent piece of American folklore—the story of the drunkard who went up in flames. Said this author in his *Address on the Effects of Ardent Spirits:* "Some drunkards are killed instantly; some die a lingering, gradual death; some commit suicide in fits of intoxication; and some are actually burnt up. I know of an intemperate man, a few years since, whose breath caught fire by coming in contact with a lighted candle, and he was consumed." Mr. Kittredge knew of another case, apparently a female old soak, who let go a hiccough near a candle and instantly started to illuminate. "Water was brought and thrown on the body in abundance," says the author, "yet the flame appeared more violent, and was not extinguished until the whole body was consumed."

Until 1840 the Temperance crusade was conducted for the most part by persons discontented with liquor tragedies in their own homes or families, but who themselves did not drink, or at least not publicly. Then, in 1840, in Chase's tavern, in Baltimore, six hard-drinking rounders one night suddenly decided to cease their practice and to convert all drinkers to sobriety. These were the first, or among the first, of the so-called reformed drunkards. They called themselves the Washington Temperance Society and set out to take the glad tidings of abstinence to those still living in depravity. They did not mention the Lord. They drew no long faces. They neither condemned nor abused anyone. They attacked the Demon with great gusto in speech and song, and they were a terrific success. In 1845 they published the *Washingtonian Teetotaler Minstrel,* a songbook stuffed with gems like "Mother, Dry That Flowing Tear." Attracted by the Washingtonians, who were now spreading throughout the states, was Timothy Shay Arthur, a journalist of commercially moralistic leanings. Shay wrote a widely distributed tract called *Six Nights With the Washingtonians* which became immensely popular, and soon followed it with the thundering success, *Ten Nights in a Barroom and What I Saw There.* First as a book, then as a play, this immortal work instantly became and has endured as the classic example of Temperance gone completely mad. Lurid as any melodrama, shoddy as any burlesque, and tinctured with music by an interpolation entitled "Father, Dear Father, Come Home," this piece of dramatic art kept an army of hams occupied for the next half century, and unquestionably spread discontent with the liquor business as it was currently conducted.

In the meantime, a former drunk named John B. Gough had become the most eminent of the Washingtonians. He tore into the purveyors of drams like a hurricane, he charged that drink filled all the jails and almshouses, he promised the hottest hell of all for makers of the stuff. He went through the Eastern states like a plague, converting, collecting funds. But the Washingtonians dissolved as quickly as they had come into being. It will be recalled that most members of the order had admittedly been inebriates. By 1843 backsliding among them had grown to such scandalous proportions that the survivors were happy to be admitted to the less spectacular societies, such as the Sons of Temperance and the Good Templars.

Of perhaps more influence than any other one man in the Temperance movement was Neal Dow of Maine. Discontent over the condition of the poor was what made a fanatic out of Dow. As overseer of the poor in his native Portland, Dow, a man of great energy and ability, became enraged at the lax administration of existing liquor laws. He thought that rum tended to fetter poverty on the poor and that rum was all too easily come by. In 1828 he set out to drive rum out of Maine. What he wanted was not Temperance, but downright Prohibition. He worked so ably that by 1846 he had got the Pine Tree Staters to vote a prohibition law that was strengthened by enforcement acts in 1851 and became the first recognizable prohibition law in the United States. Dow went to war a colonel in 1861, served gallantly, was commissioned a general, and returned home a hero. Until the end of his life he lectured for and contributed money, not to Temperance which he considered a feeble half-measure, but to brass-bound, double-riveted, Saharan Prohibition.

Although few states of the time gave any great indication of wishing to follow the lead of the Maine law, bands of militant women, most of them the discontented and miserable wives of confirmed soaks, were making life interesting for saloon keepers. They did not attack the saloons with ax and sledge, as a later drunkard's wife was to do. They simply gathered just outside a rum-seller's place of business and gave voice to their deep discontent by singing tearful songs. Occasionally they made so bold as to invade the rum sinks, which was very embarrassing to kindly bartenders and their customers, not all of whom were sodden. By 1873 these singing bands were a common sight, and a member of one of them, Eliza Daniel Stewart, had a new idea; she appeared in court, in Springfield, Ohio, to make an eloquent and moving plea on behalf of a drunkard's wife against a saloon keeper. The incident received wide notice in the papers, and later that year Mrs. Stewart formed in Osborn, Ohio, the Woman's League, said to have been the first local group in what presently became the Woman's Christian Temperance Union, a combination of nearly all of the anti-liquor societies that was to conduct the brunt of the battle under the leadership of Miss Frances Willard until the aggressive and more "businesslike" Anti-Saloon League took over and ran things on a considerably lower ethical level than was commonly occupied, even by the vile whisky interests.

The Temperance movement had a sizable by-product, for many of the White Ribbon ladies also became interested in what was called, with uppercase letters, The Rights of Women. Exactly what these rights were was not always clear, but discontent with woman's lot had been boiling, and often letting off steam, since Revolutionary times. The remarkable Mercy Otis Warren of Boston, a shrewd lady of really great intellect, had been treated almost as an equal by the male Revolutionary clique of New England, and also by Thomas Jefferson. Abigail Adams, wife of the second President, was another brilliant woman who in a later day would have been called a feminist. Mrs. Adams felt strong discontent with woman's place in the world, and in 1776 she sat down and wrote her husband that in drawing up a code of laws for the new Republic, the ladies should not be forgotten. Do not put such unlimited powers in the hands of husbands as they now have, she warned, for all men would be tyrants if they could. Abigail went so far as to say that women should not obey laws in which they had no voice or representation—which was one of the reasons why the colonies were at war with England.

The Founding Fathers, of course, were not anxious to allow women much say about things. The status of females in the new United States was not changed, and for a good part of the nineteenth century they were legally little more than chattels. Few young or middle-aged women in 1945 possess any knowledge of the status of their female ancestors of a century and more ago. The laws of the United States considered them perpetual minors. Spinsters were the wards of male relatives. Married women had no more rights in front of the law than a Jersey cow. No married woman could sue for her services. What she earned belonged to her husband. For all their mouthing about Freedom and Equality and such, the Fathers and their sons and grandsons took care that their women should remain much in the state they had been used to since man could remember, and beyond.

Perhaps the most engaging and certainly the most interesting of the early rights-for-women pioneers was a Scotswoman named Frances Wright. Coming to the United States for the second time in 1824, this restless and forever discontented female invested a small fortune in western Tennessee land and founded Nashoba, a utopia to be cultivated by boughten slaves who would there work out the cost of their freedom, be educated, and take their status as American citizens. As usual with utopias of any sort, Nashoba attracted an assortment of reformers, eccentrics, and lazy no-goods. Miss Wright herself had unorthodox ideas, one of which was that marriage was robbery and all but murder of the woman in the bargain. Miss Wright did not want matrimony, but she enjoyed male companionship very much, and soon what journalists of all times have called Free Love reared its attractive head at Nashoba. But Nashoba was a terrible failure.

Miss Wright next joined Robert Dale Owen in the New Harmony experiment, another utopia but on more pretentious lines than Nashoba. She not only joined Mr. Owen, but they lived together, openly and in sin, to the joy of all newspapermen of the time. By 1830 Miss Wright was pretty well, or at least widely, known, and she took to the lecture halls. Here she lambasted men for keeping women in slavery. She was lively on the platform and the men liked to hear her, even though she attacked them with a freedom and gusto not before heard. She made a great noise and doubtless started many a woman to reflecting on her melancholy status. But the free love business precluded Miss Wright from being very influential with her sisters.

A strictly home-grown rebel against man's inhumanity to woman was Margaret Fuller, the Yankee girl who made plain her discontent when she wrote *The Great Law Suit; or, Man* vs. *Woman,* perhaps the most logical and certainly the first plea for women's rights published in the New World. Miss Fuller was very much discontented with the subservient place of females, and made her views plain on every occasion. She left her mark on her sisters of the time, and on the men, too. She might have roused the women to action had she not lost her life in a shipwreck when she was but forty years old. Hers was probably the most brilliant intellect of any American woman of her century.

Catharine Beecher, elder sister of Mrs. Stowe, instilled no little discontent, in the young females attending her school, about women's rights; and at Troy, New York, Emma Willard, after undergoing ridicule and persecution that would have broken most women, at last established a city-endowed school that gave women the same educational advantages as men. Here at Troy Female Seminary, astonishingly enough in the 1820's, young women were exposed to history, philosophy, and the sciences. It was an unheard-of thing. It was also a great victory, and although Mrs. Willard was not particularly interested in votes for women, she wanted them to have as good an education as men. A few years later the example was followed at Holyoke, Massachusetts, by Mary Lyon. These two women cut a wide swath through male prejudices of the period, and their work is not to be overestimated.

Revolt was in the air, but it took brave women to lead the revolt; brave, and discontented. What appears to have been the first invasion of the American medical profession by a female occurred in 1849 when Elizabeth Blackwell was granted her M.D. by Geneva Medical School of Western New York. Dr. Blackwell had accomplished what must have seemed to almost everyone in the country the impossible; and in spite of a brilliant record in medical science, she discovered that prejudice was still so great as to prevent a profita-

ble practice.* Yet she was not merely a successful failure.
With the financial aid of Quakers she founded what became
the New York Infirmary and College for Women, entirely
staffed by women.

At the same time Dr. Blackwell was admitted to be a
competent person to practice medicine, the ghostly precincts
of the ordained ministry were invaded by Antoinette Brown.
Oberlin graduated her in theology in 1850, but was so ill
at ease about the whole matter that Miss Brown's name was
omitted from the class list. This piece of poltroonery, oc-
curring in so ordinarily courageous a college as Oberlin, indicates how strong must have been the feeling against the
heresy of female preachers. But preach Miss Brown did,
and she appears also to have given Lucy Stone her first
chance to air her views from a platform.

Lucy Stone weighed one hundred and five pounds with
all her clothes on and was a Yankee girl so discontented with
cooking, weaving, skimming milk and slicing apples that she
once cried: "Is there nothing that will put an end to me?"
There wasn't, and Miss Stone went to give aggressive aid in
putting an end to black slavery. She was no one-track woman.
In all of her abolition talks she added blistering strictures
about the non-existent rights of women; and when she got
around to marrying Henry Blackwell, a brother to Dr.
Elizabeth Blackwell, she made the ceremony a national event
that must have made Phineas T. Barnum regret it had not
taken place in his big tent. In a sort of marriage contract,
greatly publicized before the wedding, and which they
called a Protest, Mr. Blackwell and Miss Stone agreed that
she was to retain her own maiden name. It created a sensation. The papers played it up. Poets sang, wits performed,
and cartoonists had a wonderful time. Lucy Stone's name
became a by-word for strong-willed women, and she went
ahead to dynamite the prevailing male concepts about

* In 1945 a successful woman M. D. told the author that prejudice against
female doctors was still prevalent in the United States.

woman's place, and kept it up to the end of her life. She is perhaps the best remembered of the rights-for-women group, unless perhaps for Amelia Bloomer, née Jenks.

The wife of Dexter C. Bloomer is of course remembered for the garments that took her name. But dress reform was really the least of her many interests. From Seneca Falls, New York, where she edited a periodical revoltingly called *The Lily*, she demanded not only the usual legal rights for women, but downright suffrage, the vote, the vote in community, state, and national affairs. This was what was called whole-hog. Mrs. Bloomer had time for abolition, for Temperance, for new and "just" marriage laws. Votes-for-Women, however, was her favorite crusade, and possibly she was the first female to ask for suffrage. Certainly she was the best known, and this because she chose to wear "a bodice, short skirt, and full trowsers." Like Lucy Stone she soon became a newspaper celebrity, but her activities for dress reform enticed few of her sisters and she was ever indignant, or pretended to be, that she was known only for her "bloomers." *

At least one woman was permanently affected by Mrs. Bloomer's dress reform. This was Dr. Mary Walker, mentioned briefly in relation to the Civil War, who got her M.D. at Syracuse in 1855. Miss Walker, who never married, was teaching school in New York when she took to trousers. No bloomers for her. She went direct from skirts to male pants and a long flapping coat. Her fame did not touch that of Mrs. Bloomer until Dr. Walker's work as a commissioned assistant surgeon in the war, after which an appreciative Congress had a bronze medal struck in her honor. After the war she practiced medicine and lectured, now garbed in striped trousers, frock coat and silk hat. She conducted an erratic campaign for female suffrage, and when not otherwise

---

* The bloomers worn by Mrs. Bloomer seem to have little connection with the garment known by that name today; and an attempt at genealogical descent by the author proved futile.

engaged battled with what she described as the Nicotine Evil. Like Miss Stone and Mrs. Bloomer, Dr. Walker became a favorite newspaper subject, and the illustrated weeklies, such as *Harper's* and the *National Police Gazette*, delighted in showing Dr. Walker in the act of knocking a vile cigar from the mouth of some amazed male person. She carried a tightly rolled and stanch umbrella for the purpose.

Discontented with her ill health, discontented with doctors of the time, and with all medicine, was a New Hampshire woman, best known as Mary Baker Eddy, by all means the most dynamic American of her sex down to the present. In 1866 Mrs. Eddy founded the Church of Christ Scientist and, with a dictatorial will seldom possessed by man or woman, directed its steady progress with a sure hand through its formative years and beyond. In an era when the great majority of Americans were intensely interested in material things and very little in matters of the spirit, Mrs. Eddy came out with her creed, which was practically a denial of all the dogmas of the natural philosophers of the day. "There is no life, truth, intelligence, nor substance in matter," she wrote. "All is infinite Mind and its infinite manifestations. . . . Matter is mortal error. . . . Man is not material; he is spiritual."

The idea of the power of the mind over body was not original with Mrs. Eddy. A number of men, including Phineas Parkhurst Quimby, the mental healer of Portland, Maine, and perhaps a woman or two, such as Mother Ann Lee, the Shaker leader, had reflected on the effect of mind on the body. What Mrs. Eddy did was to synthesize the central doctrine of mental-healing with the more or less accepted belief in a supernatural Jesus Christ. Sickness, poverty, death, wrote Mrs. Eddy, were alike illusions and "errors" of mortal mind. Let mortal mind get in tune with Eternal mind, said she, and the illusions and errors disappear.

Healing the sick, she went on, is to be done through the mind rather than through matter (medicines). Her doctrines she put into a book, *Science and Health,* which appeared in 1875. In an America that seemed all but wholly engrossed with the desire to follow the natural philosophers such as Spencer to the shining goal ahead, Mrs. Eddy ignored the sacred doctrine of laissez faire, loathed the theory propounded by Darwin, and guided her new sect with startling success through the ridicule, abuse and persecutions which any new idea must pass, or die. By the turn of the century Christian Science had rich and flourishing congregations or societies across and up and down the American continent, and in many foreign lands. Its influence, however, has perhaps been more searching than appears in the number and size of its churches. Most doctors of medicine, though they naturally enough have never doubted the efficacy of material cures for human ailments, came to recognize, and even to admit, that the mind itself could do a great deal to cure the body.

The results of the early discontent of Mrs. Eddy probably did nothing to delay the steady advance of medicine on its way to new discoveries, and it unquestionably hastened what is today known and generally accepted as a branch of medicine, that of psychiatry.

The ways of discontent are often as strange as the ways of Providence. It was discontent with things as they were, both economic and social, that drove John Humphrey Noyes into founding Oneida Community, the utopia in up-state New York that had a wider and more lasting effect on life in the United States than is generally supposed. Oneida, in fact, was the only one of the varied American community utopias to leave its mark on the nation. Incidentally, it was Noyes who was the first American to promote consideration of eugenics in relation to the begetting of new Americans. "Who can say," he demanded in his famous *Essay on Scien-*

tific Propagation, published in 1873, "who can say how much the present race of men in Connecticut owe to the number-less adulteries and fornications of Pierrepont Edwards? Corrupt as he was, he must have distributed a good deal of the blood of his noble father, Jonathan Edwards."

Driven from Putney, Vermont, for his radical views, Noyes took his small group to Oneida and there for thirty years it flourished like the bay tree. He invented what he called Complex Marriage, which amounted to being promiscuity within the bounds of the Community. Mere dalliance was permitted without control so long as conception did not occur; but the begetting of children was under rigid rules. Noyes and a committee of elders had to pass on the physical and mental conditions of the man and woman who proposed, through their own free will, to become parents. Time has shown that the end-products of these eugenic marriages were of high caliber, well above average, both physically and mentally; and although it would be a bold or foolish judge who would say that Noyes was or was not on the right track, his Oneida Community belongs in American history, not be-cause of its marriage practices but because of its contribu-tions to American industry. They were two in number—the modern steel trap and silver-plated tableware.

An early convert to the Perfectionists, as the Oneida Com-munity referred to its members, was a gigantic woodsman of Brattleboro, Vermont, by name of Sewell Newhouse. New-house had hunted and trapped wild animals for many years. As dignified as an Iroquois chief, with the measured stride of a stag, Newhouse was said to look not unlike a sullen eagle. But he was gentle enough, only sot in his ways. He found the crude iron traps of the day faulty, so he started making his own. In so doing he discovered a method of tem-pering steel that made the Newhouse springs and jaws hold anything they had once clamped upon; and before long, so great was the demand for this product, he quit the woods and trap lines and set up in a small way as a maker of traps.

He was thus engaged when he and his wife were admitted to Oneida Community as members.

Like all utopias, Oneida was having financial troubles. When the Community larder got low, Newhouse went into the blacksmith shop and pounded out a dozen traps, which were sold for the benefit of the group. In 1854 Noyes took cognizance of the Newhouse traps as a possible source of Community income. He went to work on Newhouse. It required a vast amount of "communizing and the democratic power of inspiration" to get the old trapper to reveal his method of tempering steel, for he was as secretive as could be. At last he was prevailed upon to initiate a selected few of the younger Perfectionists into the secret. Then power machinery was installed and the shop enlarged. From here on the manufacture of Newhouse traps was the chief source of Oneida income for many years. By 1856 orders for traps far exceeded the possible output. A bit later a man from the great Hudson's Bay Company came to Oneida to attempt to purchase all the traps the Perfectionists could make. Imitators appeared, but the Newhouse-Oneida product was so superior it had no trouble in maintaining a fabulous reputation. All the way to the Rockies and beyond, both in Canada and the United States, men in buckskin shirts and coonskin caps swore by the stanch traps made by Perfectionist Newhouse; and in time "Newhouse" and "Oneida" became practically generic words to describe a steel trap. What Winchester and Remington had done for the rifle, Newhouse did for traps. Never again was Oneida Community in financial straits.

The Community as a whole became interested in plated flatware manufacture through members of its branch colony in Wallingford, Connecticut. Plated flatware had been made in the United States for some years. What the Perfectionists did was to make better spoons and knives and forks, and to give them patterns of some beauty. Until then, a plated spoon was utilitarian only. The Wallingford product was handsome and also well made; and before long making it called for large factories that were built at both Wallingford and Oneida. Oneida's tableware and Oneida's traps survived the Community and are still to be had.

The story of the break-up of Oneida Community has been told in detail.* Suffice to say here it was attacked and destroyed because of its eminently successful daring. It was different from anything else. It would not conform. Hence it must go, and go it did, a victim to Philistines and the Philistine press. In 1880 the Community was dissolved, and in its place appeared a stock company, Oneida Community, Limited. No other utopia, including the celebrated Brook Farm, had much influence on the Republic, but Oneida's influence is to be seen today.

As different from John Humphrey Noyes as could be imagined was Thomas J. Foster, yet the influence of both men on the United States came by indirection of their original efforts. Noyes wanted to convert the country to his ideas of marriage and breeding; instead, his contribution came from good traps and the mass production of excellent flatware. Thomas Foster wanted to prevent accidents in the mines of the anthracite regions of Pennsylvania, where he edited a small weekly newspaper; instead, his end-product was a wide and unifying influence on the foremen and keymen of American industry.

Editor Foster discovered that mine disasters in the 1880's were the chief source of news and of discontent in the coal-mining regions. A study of their origins led him to believe that they were caused by ignorance on the part of both miners and operators. In 1882 he started a question-and-answer column in his paper, a department concerned mostly with accidents and their prevention. The column obviously met a great need. Correspondence grew steadily; intelligent

---

* *A Yankee Saint*, by Robert Allerton Parker, New York, 1935.

HORATIO ALGER, JR.

URIAH STEPHENS

NEAL (MAINE LAW) DOW

SEWELL NEWHOUSE

THOMAS FOSTER OF THE I. C. S.

LORENZO COFFIN, AIRBRAKE FANATIC

FRANCES WRIGHT   MARGARET FULLER

MRS. EDDY

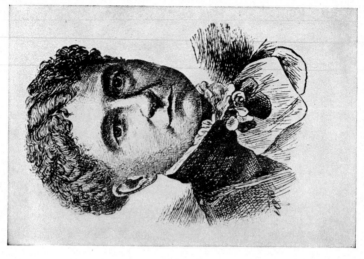

AMELIA BLOOMER

DR. MARY WALKER

miners were asking all sorts of questions about gases and
engineering. So, an idea came to Foster. In 1891 he started
the International Correspondence Schools, with headquarters in Scranton, and enrolled his first pupil, one Thomas
Coates, a miner.

Nine years later students numbered 251,310, practically
all of them men discontented with their places in industry.
The courses increased in number. So did the students. The
I. C. S. had touched off an American phenomenon that appears to be yet growing and of late years has been adopted
even by staid universities of the orthodox type. Education
by mail has influenced, and doubtless aided, millions of men
and women, many of whom are shy to admit the source,
though they have benefited thereby. Were Founder Foster
alive in 1945, he might be pleased to know that among his
students of the past few decades have been rather noted
men, among them John C. Garand, inventor of a rifle; Walter
P. Chrysler, industrialist; Philip Murray, labor leader;
Eddie Rickenbacker, flier and industrialist; and David Low,
world famous cartoonist of New Zealand, who had a four-
year course in drawing through the mails from I. C. S. Of
more importance, however, is the fact that I. C. S. has
trained in some degree more than five million men and women
who have played a part in American industry of the past
half century; and if American industry is as good as we
Americans believe it to be, then this huge alumnus body of
I. C. S. has had no small influence on the country.

A steady stream of new inventions flowed into American
life in the nineteenth century, many of them to change or
modify the lives and affect the characters of the American
people. The story of the effect of inventions had been ade-
quately told in many a book, but not so the story of a discontented man, a non-inventor, who gave the best part of
his life to clubbing recalcitrant railroads over their tough
heads until they had adopted inventions, ready at hand, for

the saving of untold American lives. Americans, indeed, when they have come safe and whole of limb to the end of a railroad journey, might give a moment's pause and thanks to the memory of Lorenzo Coffin, a man of one-track mind and grim determination, who probably saved more American lives than Moody and Sankey saved American souls.

In 1874 Coffin was a successful farmer in Iowa. In that year he witnessed an accident to a railroad brakeman who was switching freight cars. The man lost the two remaining fingers of his right hand. He had lost the others in a similar accident the year before. Coffin learned that few brakemen of any experience possessed all of their fingers; they were lost in the highly dangerous operation of coupling cars by the pins then in use. The brakemen had to stand between the cars being coupled, in order to direct the pin into the socket. This took a lot of fingers, many whole hands, and often lives. Even a greater number of brakemen were killed, from falls, while twisting at the old hand brakes.

The accident he had seen and the knowledge he had gained had a powerful effect on Coffin, by then a bearded veteran of the Civil War. Less and less he tended his farm. He was discontented to know that though a good automatic coupler had been invented and was on the market, and that although George Westinghouse had invented an air brake, railroads would not install them. Coffin brooded over this, then with the characteristic drive so often seen in fanatics, he went to work. His first job, as he saw it, was to arouse the public "to this awful wrong," this butchering of faithful railroad men who were serving the public at such fearful risk to life and limb.

It should be borne in mind that railroad travel on American railroads in the 1870's was at best a dangerous adventure. Rails were light, and of inferior quality. The signal cord through the train to the locomotive was comparatively new. Use of the telegraph was only twenty years old, and far from perfect. Time tables, when they existed at all, were more fiction than fact. A majority of railroad employees were hard-drinking daredevils who bragged of taking chances—with their own lives and the lives of others. The safety of passengers was hardly considered at all. From about 1850 until near the end of the century, wrecks caused by head-on collisions, by derailments, by falling bridges and trestles continued to be a national scandal.

Lorenzo Coffin did a great deal of traveling in the late seventies, all to a purpose. He wasn't going anywhere; he was getting an arsenal of facts, as he liked to call them, about how railroad employees were being needlessly killed or injured. Coffin gave little thought to the traveling public. What he planned to do was to save the lives of railroad men through the use of air brakes and automatic couplers.

The railroads were immune to Coffin's first suggestions. They feared nobody. They were buying the influence of United States senators and congressmen, just as they bought rolling stock. They operated trains when and where they pleased. They charged what they would for freight and passengers. In American railroads the policy of laissez faire was to be seen in all its flower.

By 1880 American railroads were probably the most arrogant corporations in the country; and Coffin, a lone bewhiskered farmer from Iowa, set out to tackle these giants single-handed. He became known as the Airbrake Fanatic. Railroad officials got to know him as either a bore, or a gadfly. Snubbed, often thrown bodily out of offices, Coffin turned to the press. He wrote pieces for the daily papers, whose editors tossed them into wastebaskets. The only outlets Coffin could find for his protests were the small religious, family, and farm periodicals, and into these dimly printed journals he poured his discontent with things as they were.

In direct and appealing language, often with quaint asides and Scriptural allusions, Coffin attacked both the emotions and the reason. He described in some detail, dripping with gore, the accidents, and he mentioned the tragedies brought

to so many families—in 1881 they numbered some 30,000—
by loss of their breadwinners who had been killed or maimed
for life because of accidents with hand brakes and coupling
pins. He took pains to describe these lethal devices, and he
shouted that the butchery was all unnecessary. Needless,
cried old Coffin, all needless tragedy! He said that Mr. Westinghouse had invented a brake that would do away with most
of this murder, but that because of the cost the railroads,
sweating golden dividends at every pore, would not install
it. He was right, too.

At last, in 1883, when he had passed sixty, Coffin's crusade
showed its first small results. He was made railroad commissioner of Iowa. Immediately he wrote, with his own hand,
thousands of letters to railroad officials, to newspapers, labor
union, lodges, Granges, societies of all kinds, and to individual men and women. He asked for moral support to club
the railroads into adopting two simple devices, both ready
at hand, which he said would greatly reduce injury and
fatality to railroad employees. He invited himself to conventions of railroad officials, and here he was as welcome as
leprosy. But he attended, when they did not stop him by
force, and once there he stood up and accused the railroads of
committing mayhem and murder.

Although the Westinghouse and other air brakes were
now actually in use, in a very small way, on the passenger
trains of a few lines, these were the exception; and air brakes
were not used at all on freights. Coffin soon discovered to his
amazement that the lines had no intention of generally in-
stalling either air brakes or automatic couplers. Cost too
much to maintain. "But I note," shouted Coffin in speech
and newspaper, "I note that the Chicago & Alton and most
other lines continue to pay their 8 per cent regularly."

The tall old fanatic with the grizzled beard took a new
tack. By almost superhuman effort he prevailed on the Master Car Builders Association to agree to a test of airbrakes

on a long freight train. The first test came in 1886. It was disappointing. The second trials were held in May of 1887, and this time Coffin persuaded George Westinghouse himself to attend. The tests failed once more, and again Coffin was denounced as a wild-eyed fanatic. But Westinghouse had seen the trials. He saw what his invention lacked. He returned to Pittsburgh, took off his coat, and personally went to work in his shops to perfect an air brake that would stop a fifty-car freight train.

Later in the summer of 1887 the third and what have since been famous in railroad history as the Burlington Trials were held on a long grade of track of the Chicago, Burlington & Quincy, eight miles west of Burlington, Iowa. Both Westinghouse and Coffin were present. The two men watched, said an eyewitness, while "the immense train was hurled down the steep grade at forty miles an hour." At a signal the air brakes were applied, and "the train came to a standstill *within five hundred feet* and with hardly a jar." It was wonderful.

Lorenzo Coffin, aged and weatherbeaten, stood close to the track and bystanders saw tears of joy stream from his eyes and run shamelessly down his lined leathery face. "I am," he cried with great emotion, "the happiest man in all Creation!"

It was an epochal day in American railroad history. Not before had a long heavy train of cars been stopped by air, quickly and without harm to men or equipment. Coffin, still naïve in respect to railroads of the time, thought his work was done. It was really just beginning, for the roads were no more anxious to adopt the new device than most railroads of the 1940's appear anxious to adopt the method of train control by radio.

Soon after the successful tests Coffin drafted the first railroad safety-appliance law ever written. It required that all trains operating in Iowa should be equipped with air brakes and automatic couplers. The act was made into state law. The roads disregarded it. Yet its passage and the flouting of it brought national attention to Coffin and his crusade. Then, in 1888, the Interstate Commerce Commission came into being. One of its first acts was to invite the state railroad commissioners of the nation to a meeting in Washington to discuss various problems having to do with the roads, chiefly traffic rates. Coffin was no longer a railroad commissioner, but he planned to attend the meeting. First he sat down and rewrote his safety-appliance law to fit the country as a whole. This he put into his pocket and went to Washington.

As soon as the large gathering was called to order, ready to discuss traffic rates, Coffin stood up, straight and tall despite his years. The old fire burned brightly still. He told the assembled experts, before they could stop him, more about railroad accidents than they had ever guessed, or wanted to hear. He piled horror upon horror. "These are cold facts," he said, his voice shaking. He painted scenes that made his listeners squirm, and left many of them, as they were later to admit, wet-eyed. He was eloquent, this old man from the tall corn country, and he knew what he was talking about.

Coffin's address to the group was superb, and it had a lasting effect on the audience, including the Interstate Commerce Commissioners themselves. But the time still was not quite ready. The meeting refused to approve Coffin's proposed national act relating to safety appliances. Coffin went back to his farm, not to weep but to prepare for the next attack. He raised a little money from his own resources, then returned to Washington, to stay for four years, leading a Spartan life in cheap boarding houses because he could afford no better fare. His Great Idea was now an act, a law, that if passed would cover every mile of every railroad in every state, a truly big conception. The act was to apply to all railroads alike, and it would impose on them what Coffin said was the absolute necessity of air brakes and automatic couplers. He worked hard on senators and congressmen. He rewrote his proposed law again and again. At last he managed to get a pretty good bill through the House. He hovered over it like a mother hen until it had passed the Senate; and on March 2, 1893, often called the greatest day in railroad history, President Benjamin Harrison gave it his approval, and the pen with which he signed the bill he gave to Coffin, ever thereafter the old man's ikon.

The Railroad Safety-Appliance Act brought immediate and striking improvement, reducing the accident rate to employees by more than fifty per cent, while the passenger accident rate, long a scandal, fell to almost nothing. The improvement in safety increased, and with it came an increase in railroad running speeds. Coffin had done his work well. One more fanatic had left his mark on American life.

Coffin had discovered his discontent out on the flatlands of the open country, where railroad trains came up the hill of the horizon, pounded across the visible world, then gradually sank over the earth's rim. Lillian Wald, a young woman of the open spaces of Ohio, found her discontent at the other pole from Coffin's. In the slums of Manhattan she discovered a fearful state of affairs, known to the city fathers but ignored by them: The indigent sick.

Although the Ethical Culture Society of New York had appointed a nurse to follow up dispensary treatment in the hellish tenements of the city, little else had been done when Miss Wald arrived from quiet Ohio, where family doctors took care of everybody. She was shocked at the casual cruelty of the unfeeling big city. Working with great good nature, in spite of the dismal scenes on every hand, and with tact and fine judgment, Miss Wald soon established the famous Henry Street Settlement House, organized what we call today public health nursing, and established the first municipal school for nurses. The Children's Bureau, established in 1902 by the federal government, was also Miss Wald's idea.* She worked as purposefully in the slums as Coffin worked in the open country.

* Neglected by historians and biographers, this remarkable woman became the subject of a heart-warming book in 1938, *Lillian Wald, Neighbor and Crusader*, by Robert Duffus.

CHAPTER XIII

Apostles of Protest

As THE old century waned and went into its final decade, discontent on a rising scale swept through the great manufacturing centers of the Eastern states. Wages were too low, both working and living conditions were too dreadful to stand without protest. Daniel De Leon, Eugene Debs, Samuel Gompers, and many other men, along with Emma Goldman and a few women, stirred the proletariat, and the strikes and riots were many and usually bloody. Though these protests in their total effect did have an influence in the rise of labor unions, and a greater public sympathy for the wage earners, yet they failed dismally to dissipate the general belief in the doctrine of laissez faire and the Alger myth of Upward and Onward.

The nineties belonged to the West, the West of the farms, the corn, the wheat ranches, the West of the hard-rock miners, the West of the lumberjacks. Out there where the sun sank into the flat earth or fell behind a white crested peak, the pioneers had for thirty years been struggling to make a living off land that had cost them, as somebody pointed out, nothing but sweat. And now late in the century they were sullen with discontent. The Grangers and Alliances and thousands of rank individualists were ready to wage the political war that was to result in the classic attitude of the West toward the rest of the country. A champion without peer was ready to lead them. In fact, he had been stirring their discontent for a quarter of a century before they were ready for

267

revolt. He was probably the most colorful political and literary character in our history, not excepting Andrew Jackson and Mark Twain. I refer to the Honorable Ignatius Donnelly of the synthetic and all but non-existent metropolis of Nininger, Minnesota.

Donnelly was rightly called a radical, and wrongly called a crank. A crank is a monomaniac. Donnelly was many-sided. His interests were intense and practically without limit, and his influence on the United States, together with its people, its institutions and its literature, was far greater, I think, and more lasting than the few historians who have even mentioned the man have seen fit to accord him. Political handles are easy to apply and not always are justified, but Donnelly earned the title applied to him in the nineties. It was the Great Apostle of Protest.

Donnelly was born in Philadelphia in 1831, and studied for the law, which he found quite dull. He had rather write poetry. He married, and in 1856 set out with his wife for Minnesota, a land considered by most Philadelphians of the time to be well beyond the moon. With a few partners Donnelly bought eight hundred acres of wild land on the west bank of the Mississippi and set out to build a city, a metropolis, which he christened Nininger City for one of the group. Although this was in an era when synthetic towns and all sorts of bogus real estate ventures were booming, Nininger was of a different stripe. Donnelly was no shark seeking to make a quick fortune by unloading a fake town on the gulls. Nininger City, to Donnelly's mind, was to be a community where artistic and intellectual pursuits went hand in hand with agriculture and industry.

But a city must have citizens, and Donnelly's first move was to establish *The Emigrant Aid Journal,* unquestionably the most intellectual periodical ever issued in the interests of real-estate promotion. Its masthead was magnificent, one of those teeming, old-fashioned trade marks one can study for an hour, like a Hogarth drawing, and still discover things.

This one depicted steamboats in the river, racing like mad for the great terminal of Nininger City; railroad trains belching smoke across the prairie; covered wagons creaking their way; men plowing, wheat growing, and fruits and vegetables of startling girth. Beneath this dazzling masthead was a question and an answer:

Dost thou know how to play the fiddle?
No, replied Themistocles, but I understand the art of raising a little village into a great city.

Nininger land was to be sold at cost, which Donnelly reckoned to be six dollars a lot, and only men who would settle on the land were wanted. No person could purchase unless he promised to begin improvements within six months and complete them within two years. Speculators were thus discouraged. Donnelly meant to have only men who had their hearts in building the finest, most intelligent commonwealth possible.

In December of 1856 Nininger City was abustle with new arrivals and a great noise of nailing and sawing. Men were erecting a hotel. *The Emigrant Aid Journal* was coming off the press in thousands of copies, and copies were being "placed in the reading rooms of all transatlantic steamers." By the spring of '57 the city was taking on physical and cultural form. The Handyside House, a bounteous hotel, was open and offering a menu containing nine kinds of meat and fowl, four kinds of pie, ice cream, blancmange and charlotte russe. In the Handyside's cellars were eight kinds of imported wines, including champagne. The Handyside must have astounded visitors to the raw West of the 1850's.

A literary society, called the Atheneum Company, had been formed. So had a musical society. And the erudite editor of the *Journal*, who was Donnelly himself, was indicating the sort of town its founding father had in mind. Between helpful accounts of how to make good butter and the care of farm machinery were interspersed a poem by John

Greenleaf Whittier, a blast against Spiritualism by Harriet Beecher Stowe, and an indictment of slavery by the Editor. Lavender farming was a subject discussed, and was followed by a rousing account of the recent Battle of Balaclava, and a scholarly obituary of James G. Birney, the abolitionist.

In another issue the Editor hailed the first number of a new magazine in Boston called *The Atlantic Monthly*. In another he announced formation of a co-operative society by which prospective immigrants of the British Isles could pay their fares—doubtless to Nininger City—in more or less easy installments. More indicative of things to come—aye, to come thundering across the prairies with the roar of revolt— were the Editor's dissertations regarding the economic philosophy of Adam Smith and a resounding damnation of all bankers to the lowest and hottest chambers of hell.

The year was 1857, and just as Nininger was beginning to bloom came the crash. A sharp and sudden panic hit the country. Banks closed, many not to reopen. Factories shut down. Wheat rotted in the fields. Nininger City began picking at the bedclothes.

One more winter was left to the new town; and it was a busy one. Despite the hard times the Atheneum brought many lecturers. Grand balls were held in the Handyside House. Donnelly himself gave talks on economic subjects, not forgetting the accursed bankers. Nininger's sawmills and gristmills ground on a while longer, but more feebly. The Railroad (always referred to with capitals) which Donnelly had expected to pass through his town, chose another route through near-by Hastings. Now it became apparent that most of Nininger's citizens preferred a railroad to culture. They picked up their houses and moved them to the unspeakable Hastings. The *Journal* breathed its last, and by May of 1858 Nininger's population, never more than one thousand, had departed. That is, all but Donnelly. That stouthearted man and his wife remained, to live on in the big rambling house they had built. More than a thousand prairie dogs returned to their old homes in Nininger's now empty lots, and the big harvest moon of 1858 revealed tall grass, high enough for hay, growing thick in what had been the town's main street.

Donnelly, as resilient as india rubber, had lost everything in the crash except his bounce. He leaped at once into state politics and was elected lieutenant-governor of Minnesota. In 1863 the Republicans of the state sent him to Congress, where he sat in the House and made an excellent record, attentive and faithful to the nation's business, and highly vocal.

In debates over conduct of the war Donnelly displayed a matchless power as an orator. Opponents came to fear his sharp wit. But more important to literary America than Donnelly's blasts from the floor were his efforts in his off hours. These he spent in the Congressional Library, engaged in becoming perhaps the most erudite man ever to sit in Congress. His interests were catholic and his memory as retentive, apparently, as a photographic wet-plate. All this was to stand him well, for his days in Congress were coming to an end. Minnesota's boss Republicans were finding Donnelly too hard to handle, to manage. They greased the skids for him, and he retired to his old home amid the melancholy ruins of Nininger City.* He attempted, quite unsuccessfully, to carry on as a farmer, and at the same time worked on a book that was to live.

In 1882 the House of Harper brought out a thick, solid volume entitled *Atlantis: The Antediluvian World*, by Ignatius Donnelly. This was no novel but a serious if popular study to demonstrate the truth of Plato's story of a sunken Atlantic continent. Donnelly held that the world's original

---

* Donnelly's house was standing in 1944. James Gray of St. Paul found it weatherbeaten, but stanch, on an exposed promontory surveying a superb sweep of the river valley. On the roof is the squared and railed platform, much like the widow's walks of Marblehead, Mass., but in this case a lookout station to spy the approach of Indians; and just under the eaves are the narrow slitlike windows through which guns could be fired in case of siege.

civilization had developed on Atlantis, the veritable Garden of Eden of the Bible, and thence spread to the other continents before Atlantis sank beneath the sea. With no ballyhoo by its publishers, *Atlantis* caught on immediately and within a few weeks Harper's knew it had something big on its hands. Before the year was out *Atlantis* was the talk of the country, and of England, too, for the great Gladstone himself commended the book publicly. Poems about Atlantis appeared. Gagsters picked it up. Highbrow monthlies and quarterlies printed essays pro and con. And with these stigmata of a great best seller apparent, the House of Harper put on a night shift in the press room.

Atlantis was so charmingly written and the whole theory of the sunken island made so plausible that the public devoured it and believed they were getting doses of sound archeology—as indeed maybe they were. In any case, Donnelly's book gave generations of men and women their first insight into the wonders of archeological theory and research. It introduced even the name "Atlantis" to hundreds of thousands of Americans who had never heard of Plato. Nor could any lay critic refute the book; too much real erudition had gone into it.

The sales of *Atlantis* put Donnelly on his feet, but did not change his life much. He remained amid the remnants of his ghost city, and in 1883 came out with *Ragnarok, The Age of Fire and Gravel*, in which the author attributed the world's deposits of clay, gravel, silt and sand to contact with a mighty comet in some remote time. This volume had a large sale, and meanwhile *Atlantis* was moving from press to reader like a river. Donnelly took to the lecture platform and became immensely popular. But a magnum opus was tormenting his restless mind. This was *The Great Cryptogram*, a weighty tome that stirred up an uproar to last for years. In this book the author set out to prove, by use of a diabolically ingenious cipher, that Francis Bacon wrote all of the works commonly attributed to Shakespeare. Never a man to do anything by halves, Donnelly also suggested, and gave "proof," that Bacon probably also wrote Marlowe's plays, Montaigne's essays, and old Burton's *Anatomy of Melancholy*—quite an order for anyone but Donnelly, who hardly got his wind up.

The better-known critics of the day either ignored *The Great Cryptogram* or jumped on it with both feet. Either method was dangerous with an author like Donnelly. He heaped sarcasm on the white-livered nincompoops who chose to ignore the book. Those who attacked it were given the Donnelly Treatment, which must have left them thinking they had been struck simultaneously by lightning and a blunt instrument. A literary war raged for several years, and Donnelly had able men on his side. Nor has the book been forgotten. Specialists still consult it.*

After a brief lecture tour of the United States, and another in England, Donnelly returned again to Nininger to write his first novel. He was now about to enter his apostle-of-protest period. The book was *Caesar's Column*, a work of the Utopian school which more than suggested that the times were not nearly so good as they ought to be, or could be, and pointed to sharply needed remedies, both economic and political. It also foresaw dirigibles with aluminum bodies, poison gas in warfare, television, radio, and other horrors since come to pass. But the story was basically one of social protest. Donnelly had never forgiven the bankers whom he believed responsible for many of the country's ills, and specifically for the crash of his dream city; and *Caesar's Column* startled and frightened Americans who had thought of Donnelly as a mere literary if eccentric gentleman. In this book they could see the hand of revolt against things as they were.

---

* Any reader of the book will be impressed not only by the immensity of the work Donnelly had to do to "prove" his theory, but also with the uncanny manner in which he applied a seemingly immutable cipher to the Bard's works and came out with the right answer. It has to be seen to be believed at all.

Donnelly had never ceased to think of himself as an agrarian. Times were hard on the farms in the 1890's, and now Donnelly re-entered politics and quickly became the leading figure, as well as the dominant one, in the new People's Party, whose members were called Populists. The People's Party was a sort of catch-all of discontented farmers, and to a lesser degree of city proletarians. Into it, through the genius of leadership shown by Donnelly and his henchmen, went the many singly impotent groups who wanted a different kind of a United States than they had known. Into it went the powerful Farmers' Alliance of Minnesota, the People's Party of Kansas and Indiana, the Independent Party of South Dakota, the Industrial Party of Michigan, the People's Independent Party of Nebraska, the Independent Fusion of Colorado, the Union Labor Party of Missouri. Out in remote Oregon, where William S. U'Ren was carrying the banner, the Grange, the Prohibitionists and the Greenback Party combined in a Union Party. Third-party groups also were active in Iowa and Illinois, and in Texas and Arkansas, although elsewhere in the South the discontented fought shy of third parties and concentrated on putting radicals into office within the sacred folds of the Democrats.

Paced and inspired by Donnelly, the National People's Party had become, by 1892, not a political party but a religion to millions of Americans in the West and South. The women were aroused. In Kansas, Mary Elizabeth Lease stumped the farms and crossroads to tell her hearers: "What you farmers need to do is to raise less corn and more hell." Tall and stately, with a deep and resonant voice that carried to the back of the hall and to the far edge of the field, Mrs. Lease fired many a rustic male with a desire to stamp out "the bankers," the favorite bogey-men of the Honorable Ignatius Donnelly.

Sarah Emery of Michigan wrote a pamphlet "Seven Financial Conspiracies" which the Populists distributed by hundreds of thousands and which made dull, unimaginative men see red. Annie L. Diggs left Prohibition to get along as best it could and turned to Populism, becoming very effective in towns of the Midwest. Prettiest of the female Populists was probably Eva McDonald-Valesh, a small and handsome siren, who stumped Minnesota and soon had all the farmers foaming and steaming all the way from Clay and Otter Tail to Winona and Pipestone counties.

Meanwhile, Donnelly kept up an ominous drumming, editing propaganda sheets, writing articles and pamphlets, making speeches, drinking the blood of bankers.

Ranging the cow and wheat country was Sockless Jerry Simpson, a terrific character with the voice of a slide trombone, who demanded government ownership or control of practically everything except cows, ensilage cutters, and farm land. On a higher plane was Populist William A. Peffer, Kansas lawyer, who could out-argue 'most anyone so long as the subject was kept away from pure emotion. And in the South Tom Watson and Pitchfork Ben Tillman were leading a revolt from within the Democratic Party.

In 1891 fourteen hundred delegates from thirty-three states and territories had met in Cincinnati. Representing every possible shade of reform, and with many conflicting ideas about how to achieve reform, this disparate mob of discontented was taken firmly in hand by Donnelly. With a tact matched only by his eloquence he worked out a skillful compromise which resulted in the National People's Party, and by the middle of the following year this group, as related, had become less a political party than a religion. But a political party it was, too, and it was to stage the last great revolt of the nineteenth century in the United States, a protest which though seemingly unsuccessful at the time was in reality one of the most influential protests in our history; for nearly if not all of the dreadful heresies of the Populists were to be made into national law during the next forty years, many of them by the New Deal, legitimate offspring and heir of the People's Party as formed in 1891.

The new party's demands in 1891 brought horrible fear to conservatives in both the old parties. The Populists demanded, you may be sure because Donnelly wrote the plank, the abolition of privately owned national banks; and the establishment of postal savings banks. It called for direct election of the President, the Vice-President, and Senators; for universal suffrage, for government regulation of railroads and telegraph companies, and a number of restrictions on the activities of business corporations generally; for high income and inheritance taxes; and urged a national law for an eight-hour day in respect to employees of industrial concerns. Donnelly counseled successfully against making an issue of Prohibition. He also urged, then and later, resolutions asking for some sort of subsidy to the farmers.

Other conventions of the People's Party were held. Then, on July 4, 1892, it held its great meeting in Omaha, called by an enthusiastic but unnamed journalist of the time "Our Second Independence Day." Under the inspired management of Donnelly, James B. Weaver of Iowa, a former Union general, was nominated for President, and for Vice-President James G. Field of Virginia, a former Confederate general. In the new party, to Donnelly's way of thinking, the Blue and the Gray should be woven into the same banner.

Now Donnelly turned to and wrote most of the new party's official platform, a document that may be read fifty years afterward not only for the clarity of its prose but also for a lot of common sense mixed with its naïve proposals to cure financial ills with fiat money. In general, it stated the same principles enumerated at the organizing convention in Cincinnati the year previous.

In the elections the National People's Party polled 1,027,-329 votes, better than ten per cent of the whole. But the significance was not in number. Its importance was that this fusion of agrarian and industrial groups congealed into an attitude which largely prevails in the West to the present day; and from this same attitude has come a great majority of the economic and political reforms brought about since 1900. Donnelly, the Great Apostle of Protest, and his henchmen—and henchwomen—surely have had far greater influence on the United States of the present century than has generally been accorded them. If the New Deal of the 1930's had any influence, then so had Donnelly. He proposed much of it half a century before.

As a distinct political group the Populists disappeared after the 1892 election. They went underground, to reappear four years later as Democrats, when the astute fixers of that old party listened, incredible at first, to a new drum, a "drum incarnate," that of William Jennings Bryan, and picked him to run and run again until the horrible wild Populists had been ironed out and lost their fire in the pseudo-liberalism of the great Christian Statesman. Bryan, and all his managers, were a pale substitute for Donnelly and his wild men; but a residue of Populist ideas remained, heaving turbulently under blankets, until it could be aired and finally given physical form in the next century.

With the collapse of Populism, it was apparent that industrial enterprise, rather than agriculture, was to dominate the United States; and along with the triumph of Business came a new emanation of a recurrent American notion which statesmen had begun to call Manifest Destiny.

Before the arrival of Manifest Destiny, however, there was time for the emergence of two unusual men, neither of them Populists, who added to the conviction of the discontented that all was not well with the operation of economic forces in the United States. One of these was Eugene Debs, the magnetic Socialist, Apostle of Protest, and leader of the Debs Rebellion of 1894. Debs has at last got into all modern American histories worthy the name, where his effect on his country is admitted and sometimes honestly appraised. The like cannot be said of William Hope Harvey, dead as recently as 1936. As Professor Coin, Harvey set fire to the imaginations of millions of his countrymen and injected into them, painlessly, what were doubtless more erroneous notions on monetary subjects than any hundred thousand of them could have thought up alone. He also scared the daylights out of all sound and respectable people.

In 1893 Harvey, who had been a real-estate operator in Colorado, published a curious little yellow-backed volume entitled *Coin's Financial School* that was destined, as the staid *Review of Reviews* said a bit later, and with a trace of fear in its editorial voice, to "sway public opinion from the Alleghenies to the Pacific and from the Great Lakes to the Gulf of Mexico." Yet this was no campaign pamphlet. It was written by a fanatic, an Apostle of Protest, who sought to change the world's monetary practices and who did not care which or what political party did the job he proposed. It did not accomplish its purpose, but it gave to millions of Americans the ideas about money which they held ever after, and among these Americans was nobody but William Jennings Bryan.*

The author of Professor Coin's little book was a native (1851) of Buffalo, in what later became West Virginia. He practiced law and speculated in mines and land. And he formulated a theory. In 1893, having purposely saved a little money to support him during his literary labors, he went to Chicago and there wrote the book he hoped would light up the world, show its mistakes regarding money, blast the outworn yet sacred theories, and bring about a "rational system" of coinage, credit, and banking. The immediate success of the book was known in those days as a corker. Be-

* Jerome D. Greene, the well known educational administrator of Cambridge, Massachusetts, informs me that the late Senator Joseph W. Bailey, Texas, related in his hearing that he, Bailey, was probably partly responsible for Bryan's ideas on money, including Free Silver. In the Presidential campaign of 1896, Bryan confessed to Bailey that he was totally ignorant of money matters and asked for some book that might be helpful. Jokingly, Bailey suggested *Coin's Financial School*. Bryan apparently read it well, for presently he became an expert on the money question—along the exact lines advocated by Professor Coin.

fore the year was out better than two million copies had
been sold. They were read, too; and half a century later
Harvey's intense personality glows from the dim type and
brittle pages.

The front cover of *Coin's Financial School* has a big
blackboard beside which stands a midget man, Professor
Coin himself, in dress suit and silk hat. Inside, one comes
smack up against Scripture: "I thank Thee, O Father, Lord
of Heaven and Earth, because Thou hast hid these things
from the wise and prudent, and hast revealed them unto
babes." Then comes the dedication: "To those trying to lo-
cate the seat of the disease that threatens the life of the
Nation."

Now Harvey, who appears throughout the book as Professor Coin, gets directly to work. His financial school, he
says, "opened on the seventh day of May, 1894. There was
a good attendance and the large hall in the Art Institute
was comfortably filled. Sons of many merchants and bankers
were present, and many journalists." All this and much more
is sheer fiction, but so graphically done that many readers
believed, and believe to this day, that Professor Coin did
operate a school to which came the great of Chicago to gain
wisdom in money matters.

Most of the book is in excellent dialogue. Professor Coin,
through his replies to questions, exposes what is either the
patent fallibility or the cynical casuistry of Editor Medill
of the *Chicago Tribune*, then a powerful figure in journalism. Then, Lyman Gage, president of a large bank, pipes up
to ask how two different metals, gold and silver, could remain at a fixed ratio to each other and also have the same
commercial value. That one might have posed many a
reformer, but not Professor Coin.

"That is the 'stock fallacy' of the gold monometalists," he
replies with what one can feel is Christian calm and for-
bearance in the face of abysmal ignorance. "All commercial
values," he continues, "are regulated by supply and de-

mand. If the demand for a particular commodity is rising, and the supply does not increase, the commercial value will continue to rise."

Right or wrong, Professor Coin's answer rendered Banker Gage speechless for the rest of the lesson; and there was even a round of applause from the other students, among whom were Leander McCormick, H. H. Kohlsaat, Levi Leiter, Potter Palmer, Phil D. Armour, Marshall Field, and Franklin MacVeagh, titans all.

Page after page of lively dialogue reports the school's classes. One notes first one, then another of those captains of industry and finance becoming gradually convinced of the Professor's amazing knowledge of all subjects relating to money. The book's illustrations are atrocious, and so simple that the dimmest-witted could grasp at once the ideas expounded. One telling picture is of a head, in fact an Average Business Man's Head. One can see it is filled with wheels and springs, and back of the head is a hand pulling a wire that motivates the machinery. The hand bears one stark word: Banker.

Another rousing illustration is a before-and-after theme. On the left is a scene of bouncing prosperity, "Bimetallism in 1872," with factories belching smoke, a happy workman receiving his full dinner pail from a daughter who can be described only as well-fed and rounded. But on the right is a truly ghastly scene, "Monometallism in 1894." Here the factories are shut, buzzards are in the air, and a horrible family of human skeletons is tottering about the foreground.

Millions read this book and millions believed it to be, not a fantasy of William Hope Harvey, but the reporting of actual fact. They believed, did millions of Americans, that big men of finance did attend Coin's Financial School and there learned the sound principles of scientific money use, even though for selfish reasons they would not adopt Professor Coin's theories. There were then, and there are today, countless folk who are wholly unable to distinguish a novel from a serious work of non-fiction, a short story from an article. One feels certain that many of Harvey's readers would have been incredulous if told they had been reading a fairy story.

Harvey's book was going great guns in 1896, when Bryan was opposing McKinley. Copies continued to roll off the presses in hundred-thousand lots. It cost 25 cents. Very likely between four and five million copies were sold. The author stated that he put all of his income from the book into Bryan's campaign; and Bryan significantly remarked of it that it was "safe to say that no book in recent times has produced so great an effect in the treatment of an economic question." But he never publicly admitted his debt to Professor Coin.

Out on the plains of the West, and in the mountains and beyond, Populists, Greenbackers, Anti-Monopolists, Alliance members, Agrarians, Patrons of Husbandry, Knights of Labor, miner Federationists, and Socialists, one and all they bought and read and studied *Coin's Financial School* as their fathers had studied the Bible. With Old Testament fervor they discussed it amid the corn shocks, in wheat fields, in mine dryhouses, up the arid gullies of Idaho and Utah, in the logging camps of Oregon and Puget Sound. And they forgot their assorted and conflicting dogmas once more to vote for Free Silver and the Boy Orator of the Platte—as men might vote for God. Yea, any treatise on American literature that so much as mentions Henry George's *Progress and Poverty*, or Edward Bellamy's *Looking Backward*, must in all decency give space to *Coin's Financial School*, or fail to give a true picture of influences of the period.

Incidentally, and although it was all anticlimax, Harvey's life after publication of his celebrated book ran true to form. He founded various monetary reform leagues, ran for President on the Liberty Party ticket in 1932, and erected at Mena, Arkansas, The Pyramid, a concrete monument sixty feet square at its base and 130 feet high, in which is buried "a history of our civilization and the Cause of its Downfall."

As for Donnelly, he died in 1901, aged seventy, too soon, by a few years, to see the first of his proposed reforms adopted. No doubt it would have made him happy to see the hated bankers somewhat regulated, even if not annihilated. What would have pleased him more, no doubt, would be to know that his old publishers, the House of Harper, in 1945 were planning to bring out another whacking big printing of *Atlantis* just as soon as paper restrictions permitted.

CHAPTER XIV

War in the Mauve Decade

IN THE fair springtime of 1898 the United States declared war on Spain. The war lasted all of ten weeks and was conducted, so far as we were concerned, by gorgeous improvisation. It was a war, too, as our most brilliant chronicler of it, Walter Millis, remarks, "entered into without misgivings and in the noblest frame of mind." * History has listed but few cases of plainer military aggression, and even fewer where the aggressor has labored under so profound a conviction of righteousness. We simply had to protect the honest and noble Cubans from their oppressors, and to make certain that all the Cuban virgins, who were said to be many and pretty, remained intact.

One of the results of the war was the damaging of a great many American reputations, both military and civil. Little doubt some of them needed public damaging, for every crisis produces eminent stuffed shirts who deserve deflation. And, of course, the usual scandals over government contracts rose high, higher than the stench of rotten beef which had laid a thousand American soldiers low to every one hit by a Spanish bullet.

But one good and faithful American suffered abuse and recrimination that was wholly unjustified. He was General William Rufus Shafter, quite likely the most cruelly ma-

---

* See his *The Martial Spirit,* accurate, realistic, and most readable.

ligned general officer of courage, competence and patriotism in our history. The record shows that General Shafter improvised and carried out one of the swiftest and most successful campaigns in American military annals. And while so engaged, to the glory of American arms, this gallant soldier's character and reputation were assassinated by a crew of arrogant and unbridled newspaper correspondents whom the General had treated in what they felt was a cavalier manner. If General Shafter is forgotten today, it is a sad thing. Neither soldiers nor men come in finer quality. It is long past time that he was brought out of the nameless limbo in which the United States has buried only too many of its good and gallant forgotten men and women, and given his rightful place, modest though it is, in history.

Shafter was born in 1835, the first white male child to see the light of day in Kalamazoo County, Michigan; of parents who had come from Windsor, Vermont, to settle the timbered frontier. The boy was given some casual education in Galesburg, then went to teaching school. He enlisted for war in 1861, and late that year was commissioned a first lieutenant in the 7th Michigan Infantry, taking part almost immediately in the battle of Ball's Bluff.

Shafter was a born soldier. He served with distinction at Yorktown, West Point, Savage Station, Glendale, Malvern Hill, and Fair Oaks. In the latter engagement he was severely wounded. With one tall boot filled with his own blood, the husky young man refused to leave the field but fought like a very devil and with such bravery and coolness that he was later awarded the Congressional Medal of Honor. He seemed to have the faculty of being with the regiment or part of a regiment which always saw the heaviest action. Promotions came steadily—he was made a major in 1862, then lieutenant-colonel, then colonel in command of the 17th Colored Infantry, which gave a fine account of itself in the fighting before Nashville in 1864. Shafter was again cited, and in 1865 was brevetted brigadier-general of volunteers.

In the postwar reorganization of the Army, and on the high recommendation of General George Henry Thomas, the Rock of Chickamauga, Shafter was appointed lieutenant-colonel and assigned to the 24th Infantry, perhaps the finest colored outfit in the service. Now followed a decade of isolated frontier posts and intermittent Indian campaigns, much of it in the Southwest, where Colonel Shafter's men gave him the title of Pecos Bill. Stories vary as to how he came by this nickname, but generally agree that it had to do with a long and terrible march. Shafter had told his regiment one morning that night must find them camped along the Pecos river. It turned out that the Pecos was far more distant than the Colonel had calculated. They marched and marched. Night fell. There was grumbling, even among the officers. But Shafter bade them to be of stout heart and to follow him— and around midnight, after a march that was ever after used as a comparison for all other marches, the outfit at last reached the river and encamped.

Men who served under General Shafter recall him as standing five feet eleven. Blue eyes peered out, grimly for the most part, from under shaggy and heavy white brows. His heavy head of snow-white hair was parted in the middle. His walrus mustaches were gray. His great body was long and set upon very short legs. He could swear, as the saying was, like a trooper; and under great stress, the profanity rolled out of his huge bulk like gathering thunder.

The one trouble with Shafter was that he never enjoyed a sense of what even the military of late years have come to speak of as public relations. Good-humored, even jolly in his intimate personal relationships, he presented a gruff and often downright grim front alike to soldiers and civilians, and to all politicians. He was likely to give short and blunt answers to questions. Yet he was quick to give credit to his junior officers when they deserved it; and he backed his men to the limit. "Shafter," one of his former non-coms remarked in 1945, "was a soldier and a man's man."

As a commander Shafter was aggressive enough when he thought he had a superiority of troops or when he figured that boldness was tactically called for. When he struck, he struck hard and fast. During his obscure years on the plains he gained the reputation of being a tough and able commander indeed. Yet, while Custer and Terry and Miles and others were gaining fame with the American public as great tamers of Indians, Shafter's abilities were little known outside Army circles. He just didn't give a damn about publicity. But his superiors knew and appreciated Shafter's great soldierly qualities. With them, Shafter stood at the top of the list. Made a colonel in 1879, he was put in command of the Department of the Columbia and the Department of California. And in 1898, with the outbreak of the Spanish-American war, General Nelson A. Miles, commander in chief of the Army, unhesitatingly chose Shafter to organize and lead the American expedition against the Spanish land forces in Cuba. Outside of Shafter's campaign, the rest of the war was wholly naval.

It is doubtful if any American commander since Washington faced a more heart-breaking job than that which faced General Shafter in April of '98. Our professional Army was tiny, hardly large enough to act as seasoning for the body of 70,000 men that President McKinley directed be raised and dispatched at once to Cuba. No such army existed, and even if it had, the Ordnance Department could muster but 67,000 rifles to equip it, and none too good rifles at that. (The Spaniards were armed with up-to-date German Mausers.)

As the National Guardsmen began to assemble at Tampa and Chickamauga, it was seen that they were armed, when they had any arms at all, with old-fashioned black-powder rifles. A number of soldiers in the Southern outfits appeared with percussion-lock guns, obsolete since the Civil War. The First Missouri showed up with many barefooted men in its ranks. Virtually all militia equipment such as clothing, shoes, cartridge belts and haversacks were in no condition for field service.

Beyond the general order to invade Cuba and take Santiago, the high command appears to have had no plan of strategy; so, General Shafter, following the common pattern of this strange war, improvised as he went along. He was an excellent improviser, for his years of Indian campaigns had given him practice. Establishing his headquarters at Tampa, he gathered his troops quickly, and by the middle of May was ready to embark. But the high command could not make up its mind, or could not get transportation. It would appear that both factors were present. Dressed for the most part in heavy blue all-wool uniforms, the men sweltered in the Florida heat and cursed the fate that had put them on the flea-bitten sand wastes.

The non-existence of Army staff work became more obvious by the day. Flour for bread remained hidden in unmarked box cars for weeks, and the cars were scattered over side tracks all the way from five to thirty miles from camp. Other supplies rested in other box cars on sidings between Washington, D. C., and Tampa. Orders to Shafter from the high command in Washington arrived only to be countermanded within a few hours. The camp swarmed with newspapermen who had suddenly become great military strategists. In their dispatches to their papers they laid the whole plan of campaign before the American people. They listed the troops by regiments and gave their numbers. They estimated the total number of troops to embark. They reported the arrival of a few transports. General Shafter had an old-fashioned idea of keeping the enemy in the dark as to an army's strength and plans, but he could do nothing with this crew of newspaper war experts. No restrictions were placed on the writing boys, so the General grumbled while his every move was reported to the nation.

Not until June 12 were ships assembled at Tampa to take the ill-equipped expedition, which numbered close to 20,000 men. On the 22nd Shafter started disembarking his men at Daiquirí, eighteen miles east of Santiago. It was during this process that the first of several unfortunate incidents involving Shafter and the press occurred.

Aboard the General's headquarters ship were a number of newspaper correspondents, among them Richard Harding Davis, probably the most brilliant if not the most accurate reporter of his time, and certainly the most widely known. Mr. Davis had been serving Mr. Hearst as Cuban correspondent in the exciting period just before outbreak of war; and had supplied the Hearst papers, in New York and California, with some pretty fine Spanish-atrocity stories.

Well, here was Richard Harding Davis, complete with felt hat with white puggree, a high white collar, handsome blue coat, trousers tucked into high field boots, binoculars slung —the very picture of what an American war correspondent should look like. He stood on the deck with General Shafter and others, watching the blue sea alive with small boats filled with men, rising and falling on the swells. It was not unlike a regatta, of which Mr. Davis had seen many, and Mr. Davis probably forgot for the moment the deadly seriousness of this attempt to land on an unknown shore fringed with jungle that might well hold an ambush. He certainly neglected to bear in mind that the dreadful responsibility for the entire campaign rested on the hoary head of sixty-three-year-old General Shafter, who weighed a little more than one-seventh of a ton and was a man of low boiling point who took his responsibilities to his country seriously and never for a moment thought of the Press as an adjunct of war.

"General," observed Mr. Davis, "I see that the order for disembarking directs that none but fighting men be allowed in the boats of the first landing party. This will keep the reporters back."

The General said Yes, that it certainly would; and went on to indicate how the terrain dominated the beach. For all Shafter knew the bushes were crawling with Spaniards.

Should the enemy oppose the landing, he said, he would need every American he could get ashore, to hold the position.

Davis was not to be put off so easily, and now he told the General that Richard Harding Davis was no mere reporter but a "descriptive writer." Old Pecos Bill let him have it: "I don't give a damn who you are," he growled. "I'll treat all of you alike."

Never afterward did Mr. Davis write a kindly word about General Shafter; and the incident, according to Colonel E. J. McClernand, Shafter's chief of staff, "doubtless materially affected the future reputation of the General." This was an understatement. Davis was very popular with most of the other newspapermen, one of whom later was honest enough to admit that "from that moment pencils began to be sharpened for General Shafter."

With the troops ashore, the advance over rough ground to Santiago started at once. General Henry W. Lawton, a Regular officer, commanded the infantry brigade, while Fighting Joe Wheeler, famous ex-Confederate cavalry general, led the division of dismounted cavalry. Lawton's outfit was to spearhead the advance; but Wheeler, in face of explicit orders to the contrary, secretly moved his troops around Lawton and attacked the enemy at Las Guasimas. He soon found the Spaniards more than he could handle. His men were being killed and driven back. Fighting Joe had to call on Lawton for help. Lawton responded with a charge, and the enemy broke and ran, while Fighting Joe shouted one of the most famous lines of the war. "We've got the goddam Yankees on the run," exulted the old Confederate.

But Wheeler's importunate attack endangered the American position and also threw everything out of schedule. Lawton got hot under his all-wool collar. He called Wheeler on the carpet to tell him that this was a war and not a political campaign; and General Shafter supplied a tart word or two of admonition.

There were other troubles. Lieutenant-Colonel Theodore Roosevelt and his Terrors, who by now were called the Rough Riders, were amenable to orders only part of the time. And one of the New York militia regiments gave way in action and went into a rout such as had not been seen since First Bull Run, back in 1861. Casualties were mounting; and now the War Department bombarded Shafter with queries as to whether it would be possible to secure the body of a soldier scion of one of New York's great families, to have it properly embalmed, and shipped back to the States. This in the midst of battle. If Old Pecos Bill rumbled a bit and chewed his great mustache, it is wholly understandable.

Then, there was what soon became known as That Balloon. This was a single observation balloon that somebody—not General Shafter—had thought to bring along as an experiment in jungle warfare. It proved a tragically costly experiment. The bag appeared first, and last, as the troops moved through the bush to attack a ridge that has come down in history as San Juan Hill. In the balloon was Colonel George Derby, towed by four enlisted men on a path through the woods, and he rode majestically above the tops of the trees, accurately marking our advance for the watching Spaniards on the ridge. The Spanish fire quickly became heavy, and deadly, for it was directed not at the splendid object in the air but at the terrain beneath it. American casualties piled up along the path under the swaying bag above the steaming jungle. Just when the punishment was getting beyond all endurance, a Spanish bullet punctured the balloon and it sank slowly to earth, while American soldiers blessed the "spik" who had shot it down.

Worse than these and many other unfortunate incidents was the vile food and polar equipment, and the swiftly advancing ravages of the dread yellow fever. All conspired to try the courage and determination of officers and men alike. General Shafter did not waver. His 310 pounds took a terrible beating in the tropic heat. Often confined to his field

COVER OF COIN HARVEY'S INFLUENTIAL BOOK

THE RIGHT AND THE WRONG OF MONEY, ACCORDING TO COIN HARVEY

WILLIAM S. U'REN   THOMAS J. WALSH

FRED WARREN   MARGARET SANGER

ANDREW S. ROWAN

GENERAL SHAFTER

J. A. WAYLAND

THORSTEIN VEBLEN

cot for short periods by severe illness, the old Indian fighter nevertheless pounded some idea of Army discipline into his militia troops. He badgered the War Department for better food, better equipment. And with the resources he had, he accomplished wonders.

Though the administration in far-off Washington had no idea of the difficulties Shafter was encountering, orders were sent him to attack Santiago at once, immediately, now, to-day, and capture it. What was wanted, at home, for political reasons, was a smashing land victory. Shafter withstood all pressure, while the part of the American press operated by Hearst and Pulitzer howled for his removal from command.* These papers insisted that Shafter charge head-on into the murderous barbed-wire defenses of the city. Shafter made no reply, either to the press or the war department. When he had placed his troops exactly where he wanted them, and not a moment before, Shafter sent a demand for surrender to the Spanish commander, General Toral. A few days later the city capitulated.

Shafter was a general who considered bloodshed to be an evil, if a battle could be won without it. His refusal to be hurried into a glorious and bloody assault unquestionably saved many hundreds of American lives. Personal glory did not, in 1898 or ever, enter into his calculations—and of glory he received little enough for his able work in Cuba. The bare record: Shafter moved an army of 20,000 men a distance of 1,500 miles by water, landed on an enemy shore in open boats—after making a feint at landing elsewhere; in ten days drove the enemy back to his last line of entrenchments in front of Santiago, and in fifteen days more compelled surrender of the city and an army of 24,000 men, an army larger than his own. The entire campaign, moreover, was

---

* The *New York Evening Post,* however, took Shafter's part and laid about furiously in attacking Davis and other correspondents by name, their newspapers, and especially the Yellow Press which, so the *Post* said, was largely responsible for the war itself.

carried on in the sickliest season of the year in Cuba. For speed and adept improvisation, Shafter's campaign has had few equals in our long military history.

With the surrender of the entire Spanish army, General Shafter's troubles, far from being at an end, were merely in midstream. All went well with the surrender itself, outside the city gates. After the brief ceremony the Spaniards filed into the town and stacked their arms in the arsenal. Then the Americans moved in, and as they advanced they noted the four strong, wicked lines of defense that encircled the city. An enormous amount of barbed wire had been used in these defenses, and many an American officer and man reflected aloud and unashamedly upon what would have been the casualties had an American attack been made. General Shafter's judgment began to look pretty good.

Into the city along with the American troops, but unknown to Shafter, went three up-and-coming promotion men of the New York *Journal*. The subsequent performance of this trio of yahoos is all but incredible today. These breezy agents of Mr. Hearst were no sooner within the city than they started to plaster it, as if for a circus, with highly colored lithographs showing the wreck of the battleship *Maine* —one of the many incidents leading up to war—with good and dead American sailors floating bloodily in the wreckage. At the top of these posters was a legend: "Remember the Maine," and at the bottom another classic legend: "Buy the Journal!"

It would of course be difficult to conceive of anything in worse taste than these posters, or more inflaming. As soon as Shafter spied one, he rumbled like a volcano and sent a detail of soldiers to tear down the offending posters, then to arrest the Hearst men and hold them for deportation.

At noon, thousands of Santiago's citizens, together with Spanish troops (unarmed) and American troops in full fighting order, surrounded the Plaza for the ceremony of raising the American flag. As American officers on the roof were awaiting the signal to hoist the Stars and Stripes, the chief correspondent for the New York *World*, Sylvester Scovel, noted that photographers were training their cameras to record the historic scene. Mr. Scovel was celebrated more in journalism for his ability to promote scoops than for his ability to report them. He at once sensed the importance of this flag-raising occasion. Simultaneously he reflected on what a wonderful news beat would be his if the *World's* famous correspondent appeared prominently in the foreground. He climbed to the roof. There Captain W. H. McKittrick, in charge of the flag, ordered him down. Scovel refused to leave. McKittrick leaned over the edge of the roof and appealed to General Shafter, who stood motionless, huge and oxlike, before his troops in the Plaza. The great body shook slightly, and out of its depths came a tremendous voice. "Throw him off," roared General Shafter.

Mr. Scovel came down before he was pushed. His great dignity had been hurt. The Press had been insulted by military autocracy at its most bestial. He advanced toward General Shafter and swung. The blow missed the commanding general of the American army in Cuba by a hair, and Scovel was put under arrest, and later deported.

Although the war was now about over, dispatches to the Hearst and Pulitzer papers became actually venomous in regard to Shafter. I have read enough of them to believe that neither Washington nor Lincoln suffered more vitriolic abuse than did this gallant old soldier. What the Yellow Press did to Shafter can be described only as assassination.*

---

* The poison concocted about Shafter permeated even the youth of the period, one of whom, Milton T. Dunten, was a 15-year-old lad in upstate New York. Mr. Dunten recalls, in a letter to the author in 1944: "The armchair strategists with whom generals from the days of Aemilius Paulus have had to put up began to operate: Why doesn't McKinley get that fat old s.o.b. of a Shafter out of there and put in somebody who'd DO something—Teddy, or Wheeler, especially Teddy, he'd SHOW 'em. . . . I gathered from my elders, too, that the Spaniards were about to attack upstate New York. That fear gradually subsided, and how our heads did

With the war done, Shafter was again placed in command of the Department of California and had his headquarters at San Francisco. In 1901 he retired, and went to make his home with his only child, a daughter, at Bakersfield, California. He died November 12, 1906.

Stewart Edward White, who knew the General intimately for six years and was his literary executor, describes Shafter as one of the few really noble men he has known. Deeply patriotic in the best sense, thoughtful, generous, and direct in all his dealings both private and public, the old soldier never once mentioned honor but was the soul of honor itself. Beneath the gruff exterior that he presented to casual acquaintances, he unquestionably was deeply hurt by the uncalled-for attacks of the jackal press. Yet never, says Mr. White, did he hear the General mention the name of any reporter or newspaper who and which had a part in defaming him. He probably believed, and with some reason, that the results of his last campaign, along with his services in the past, would be sufficient to defend his character. In this, however, he was mistaken. Most Americans who were old enough to read newspapers in 1898 seem to recall General William Rufus Shafter as a profane, cowardly, and incompetent soldier, a monstrosity of flabby flesh, who would never have taken Santiago had it not been for those brilliant and magnificent officers, Fighting Joe Wheeler and Rough-Riding Teddy Roosevelt. The public relations of military men have never won a war, but they have had their effect on history. . . .

Indeed, the public relations of military men have affected history in more than a negative way. If Shafter suffered from a hostile press, it was different with Theodore Roosevelt. As soon as he had helped to get the war under way, that brash young man resigned, as will be recalled, his position in the

swell when the war was won—and until the boys came home. These embalmed beef casualties gave us distressing news about the martyred Cubans. They seemed to consider the Cubans a pack of thieves, and worse; and regretted having interfered with Spanish rule, or misrule, of the island."

navy department and with Colonel Leonard Wood organized what went into history as Roosevelt's Rough Riders. This outfit was one of three regiments of United States Volunteer Cavalry recruited by a special act of Congress for the apparent purpose of pleasing Mr. Roosevelt, who had many influential friends. It is of interest to note that the other two regiments were never heard of, in the war or since. But the Rough Riders were wherever the headlines waved and the type was large and black. They were armed with the newest carbines, smokeless powder (very rare in the Army in 1898) and the best of equipment—and press relations.

The Roosevelt outfit was recruited from cowboys, college men, and the sons of wealthy or prominent people. From the beginning to the end they were seldom off the front pages of the nation's press. Mr. Roosevelt himself saw to that, for he was a combination of P. T. Barnum and Ivy Lee, and better at the trade than either of those masters. The Rough Riders did not ride anything, for they had no horses, and they were not particularly rough; yet to many Americans at home, it came to seem that the Rough Riders, and especially their Colonel Roosevelt, were winning the great war against Spain single-handed. Newspaper reports of the flurry of fighting that preceded the battle of San Juan Hill indicated that Colonel Roosevelt and his men had come upon the field at a critical moment and saved the day. Roosevelt was mentioned as in line for a brigadier's star. A few days later Roosevelt was again dramatized in the American press for his heroic charge on the Spaniards up San Juan Hill. He was seen there, waving his big hat, giving orders, apparently the only American officer in the whole neighborhood, and perhaps the only one in all Cuba.

Another military genius had been made by American newspapers of a man who knew as few others have known the sterling value of printer's ink in copious doses.

Theodore Roosevelt had so much real ability and energy that it is quite likely he would have become President of the United States without the Spanish-American War as a starting point. But the paper reputation he achieved in that conflict made him a national military hero and unquestionably started him for the White House.

The one other hero besides Roosevelt and Admiral Dewey to come out of this war was Richard Pearson Hobson, whose brave feat in attempting to block the entrance to Santiago harbor is solidly embedded in our history.

The forgotten hero of the conflict was Lieutenant Andrew Summers Rowan. Nearer the truth, perhaps, would be to say that Rowan is not only forgotten but was never known. He was the man who took the famous message to García; and for obvious reasons any mention of García must bring up the name of Elbert Hubbard, the odd genius who immortalized the name of García, yet did nothing for the man who took that gentleman the celebrated Message.

In 1899, Hubbard was the long-haired editor of *The Philistine*, a monthly magazine written wholly by himself and in which he commented on life, literature and the arts, and generally attacked orthodoxy in all its many forms. He was first of all a good business man, for at the age of thirty-six he had retired fairly well-to-do from his sales promotion job with a manufacturing concern in Buffalo, New York, for which he had devised the Larkin Club Plan for selling soaps and other goods by mail to groups of women.* After a tour of England, where he spent some time with William Morris, the poet, artist, printer, and reformer, Hubbard established at East Aurora, New York, a sort of community of printers and other craftsmen. Here he wrote and published *The Philistine*.

In February of 1899 Hubbard needed a piece to fill the March number of his magazine. He had just been reading an item which told, now that the war was over, how one

---

* Most middle-aged Americans whose childhood was spent in the Lake States or farther east will remember the Larkin Soap Orders by which groups of women pooled their orders for things they thought they needed, and received "premiums" from the company. These premiums account for much of the surviving Morris-type furniture.

Lieutenant Rowan had carried a message from Washington, D. C., to Cuban insurgents, just before the start of the war. Inspired, Hubbard sat down and within the hour had dashed off *A Message to Garcia*. Hubbard was a facile writer, and one of the most inaccurate ever in practice, and in this instance he had President McKinley calling Lieutenant Rowan secretly to the White House, where he gave him a letter "sealed in an oilskin pouch" which Rowan "strapped over his heart." This letter was to be delivered to General García, the insurgent leader already mentioned in this volume, who was "somewhere in the mountain fastnesses of Cuba," and a reply brought back as quickly as possible.

Characteristically, Hubbard got nearly all of the facts wrong; but it mattered little, anyway, for after a couple of paragraphs devoted to getting the Message delivered, the author dropped the matter entirely and went into an attack on slipshod office workers. The rest of the article is merely a preachment to careless employees, anybody's employees, admonishing them to snap out of it, to be alive, to work for the good of their employer, to take pride in their work and duties, no matter how lowly.

The "Message" was exactly what thousands of American employers had been waiting for. The March *Philistine* was a sudden sell-out, and orders for reprints started to roll in, one for 100,000 copies from the New York Central Railroad, which distributed them to employees, then ordered half a million more copies. Industrial concerns, department stores, churches, schools, lodges, all kinds of societies except labor unions took up the demand. Hubbard's Roycrofter Press had to work nights to supply more "Messages." A decade after its appearance John Wanamaker's stores asked for 200,000 copies, and in World War I millions more reprints were called for by Do-Good groups of various kinds, who inflicted them on soldiers, sailors, munition workers, and school children. Not even the Roycrofters have been able to estimate with much accuracy the number of "Messages" that have been printed and distributed, but the total is thought to have reached at least 100,000,000 copies.

The booklet went abroad. Before the revolution the Russian railroads had the work translated and printed and a copy given to each employee. During the Russo-Japanese War, Japanese officers found copies of the "Message" on so many Russian prisoners that they thought it must be pretty important. So, typically enough, the Japs translated it and had it printed for every employee of the government. It is said to have been printed in at least twenty languages.

Well, Lieutenant Rowan's name did appear once or twice early in the story, but Rowan was not the reason for the pamphlet; he was merely an allusion, vague, ghostly, a mere symbol for the "Message." García was no more than a be-whiskered foreigner in a Cuban jungle. Hubbard was a business man. The "Message" was for business men—and their employees. Few who read the "Message" could remember, an hour later, even the name of the courageous soldier who braved the jungle in an enemy land.

Andrew Summers Rowan was born in 1857, in Virginia. He was graduated from West Point twenty years later, then assigned to the 15th, and later to the 9th, Infantry. For some reason or other he took an interest in Cuba and, although he never went there, wrote a book about the country. This book was probably the reason he was summoned by his chief, Colonel Arthur Wagner, twelve days before war was declared on Spain. It is questionable that President McKinley ever heard of Rowan until later. Wagner gave Rowan no "sealed oilskin pouch." He did not even give Rowan a letter. Orally he ordered the young officer to find General García in the Cuban interior, learn how many troops he had, observe their morale and equipment, discuss with García what plan of action he might have for co-operation with American troops. Rowan was also to learn, if possible, the number of Spanish forces on the island.

Rowan's mission was going to be just as perilous as Hubbard made it appear. Dressed in civilian clothes, he sailed to Jamaica and got in touch, secretly, with Cuban insurgents there. They put him in a closed carriage and drove him seventy miles to a remote spot on the coast where the driver, also a sailor of parts, uncovered a small boat. Into it went Rowan, the sailor-driver, and an interpreter. Cuba was better than a hundred miles distant, but the little craft made it in thirty-six hours, although not without a bad moment. The craft was hailed by a Spanish patrol boat, but Sabio—the cabby-sailor—made out that he was a lone fisherman having hellish luck. He was allowed to sail on.

On the day the United States declared war on Spain, the party landed in Oriente bay, in Cuba. Here Rowan was met by Cubans who, mysteriously enough so far as Rowan could learn, knew of his coming. For the next six days they guided the American through the jungle. When food ran out the first two or three times, the guides would presently stop, look around a bit, concentrate on a spot, then dig up a fresh supply of edibles that obviously had been cached for this occasion. But finally the caches seemed to have petered out, and the rest of the journey was accomplished pretty much on a fare of sweet potatoes. "I thought of Marion and his men in the American Revolution," Rowan said later in telling the story of the trip. "They had fought their battles on a like diet, and through my mind flashed the idea that as Marion and his men had fought to victory, so also would these Cubans."

It was a rather frightful trip for Rowan. The heat was intense, and damp. Bugs of all sorts were biting. One day the party fell in with several men who said they were Spanish deserters, and Rowan asked that they be carefully guarded. One attempting to escape was shot and killed. Another tried to get at Rowan with a long knife. He was decapitated by one of the Cubans.

On May 1 the tired party reached General García, who was found besieging the village of Bayamo. There ensued the business of scrutinizing Rowan's credentials, and he discovered that he had been described in a letter written by a Cuban not as a man of confidence but as a confidence man. But García accepted the phrase as it was meant, and not as it sounded to the amused Rowan. They discussed matters, and the Cuban told the American that he needed artillery and muskets and ammunition for both. After a conference lasting most of one day, Rowan was guided to the north coast of Cuba, a five-day trip even worse than the trip in, and Rowan and party got into a tiny boat having gunnysack sails. Two days later they landed on Nassau in the Bahamas; and after telling monumental lies to the British authorities there, Rowan was permitted to sail to the United States.

On May 13, exactly one month from the day he left, Lieutenant Rowan reported back to Colonel Wagner in Washington. His courage, resourcefulness, and all-around ability gave him a captain's bars at once. But there was no public to-do, no heroism party, for the affair was kept secret till the war's end. Then, with three authentic heroes—Roosevelt, Dewey, and Hobson—already enshrined and immortal with the public, and with the excitement of war evaporated, there was no interest shown in Rowan or his brave achievement by the American public.

Nor did Hubbard's booklet create any interest in the man. He remained to his dying day a mere name in a pamphlet.

Rowan went on to serve with distinction in the Philippine Insurrection, and was cited for gallantry in the attack on Sudlón Mountain. He continued in the Army until 1909, when he resigned on account of ill health. He was retired with the rank of major and spent much of the remainder of his life in California. Only one flurry marked the obscurity of his retirement. That was in 1922 when, through the offices of Senator Samuel Shortridge of California, he was awarded the Distinguished Service Cross. A movie company, at last catching up on History, at once approached the old soldier with a demand that he appear in a film based on his exploit in Cuba, but when he learned that pretty Cuban girl dancers would be a feature of the drama, he declined savagely. Hollywood went ahead, anyhow, and made a film about *A Message to García,* in which the actor playing Rowan falls in love, you may be certain, with a lush Cuban beauty. Rowan indignantly refused to see the movie.

The man who actually took the message to García lived to be almost eighty-six years of age. He died January 11, 1943, in San Francisco, but not before he had let go one historic line. It was at a dinner. One of the gushing type of females was sitting next to the old soldier, and she brightly spoke up to ask him: "Colonel, what *was* this message to García, anyway?" Said the gallant Colonel: "It was, madam, an invitation from President McKinley to an old-fashioned New England boiled dinner at the White House."

As for General García, he did not pan out very well. Most military students of the war appear to believe that it would have been much better had no message reached him. After the naval engagement of Santiago, García's insurgents amused themselves by shooting at Spanish sailors who were clinging to the ghastly wreckage for their lives. García refused to put a stop to the butchery until General Shafter sent word that if the amusement was not stopped at once, he would open up with his artillery on García's camp.

García gave little aid to the Americans. He also allowed some two thousand Spanish troops to march through his lines and join the defenders of Santiago city. General García died while on an official visit to Washington in 1899 and, seemingly oddly enough, was buried with military honors in Arlington cemetery.

The man who made the "Message" famous, and received an estimated $250,000 in royalties for his trouble, went down with his second wife on the *Lusitania,* May 7, 1915.

CHAPTER XV

Muckrakers & Other Critics

With one notable exception the administrations from the death of Lincoln to the death of McKinley had shown no outstanding abilities, nor any great imagination, save Grant's two, which were as imaginatively corrupt as anything France or Spain could offer. The single exception was Cleveland's first administration, which was extremely able and courageous. Cleveland has at last been given his just due in American history.* From Grant to McKinley the White House had otherwise been occupied by honest, well-meaning and generally amiable men who as chief executives left no indelible marks on the American scene. Year by year their shadows fade, and they become merely names in books and bewhiskered figures in steel engravings.

Theodore Roosevelt was a new kind of President. He, too, has been accorded, even more than Cleveland, a notable space in our history, for he has inspired a truly immense number of books. What has seldom been pointed out, at least in general histories, is that Theodore Roosevelt, the President, was pretty much "made" by a crew of rambunctious writing men and women.

The first Roosevelt quickly became in office one of the most effective leaders ever to stir the enthusiasm of the common people. On a lower level he would have been termed a demagogue—as indeed he was, anyway, by the more case-hardened

---

* For instance, *Grover Cleveland*, by Alan Nevins, New York, 1932; and *Grover Cleveland* (2 Vols.) By Robert McElroy, New York, 1923.

ogres of capital and big business. But he was anything but a radical. He loved his country deeply, intensely, and with his whole heart. He liked its economic system as it basically was, and had no desire to change it. He liked the system so well, so much more intelligently than the business leaders of the time, that he felt certain it must be modified if it were to survive. One very keen observer who knew Roosevelt well, both as man and as President, Lincoln Steffens, summed up his character and place in our history with great shrewdness and brevity: "Roosevelt was not a reformer in the White House; he was a careerist on the people's side."

Roosevelt saw, or rather had them pointed out to him, the cracks and leaks in the American economic system, and set about with great energy and as much noise as possible to patch them. He was a statesman-plumber who believed that the old pipes could be fixed, that no new installations were necessary. For eight years he carried on this patching brilliantly, putting on the best show since the days of Old Hickory. He clubbed the trusts with his celebrated Big Stick, but he had no thought or desire of killing them; and they survived and remained vigorous, if more polite. The powers of the important Interstate Commerce Commission were greatly enlarged, the methods of packing meats were investigated, so was the processed food industry generally; the drug business was looked into, especially in its relation to advertising, and the federal parks and forests came into being.

Roosevelt was perhaps less a leader in the exact sense of the word than he was a director. He was intelligent enough to know that a leader leads almost nobody until a majority of the people are ready to be led. Bryan, Roosevelt's long-time opponent, was a prophet, not a leader. Bryan, the true Old Testament prophet, lacking only the beard, was crying aloud for things that really needed doing—things the Populists had put into his mind—but not yet were a sufficient number of people ready to fight for those things. Determination was lacking. Bryan was ahead of his time, just as the Populists had been ahead of their time. Roosevelt, the superb timer, was never for an instant ahead of his time. He was gloriously of the present moment. And so were the group of snooping writers who unquestionably inspired Roosevelt to many if not most of his patchwork reforms and who in any case took the public's deep if vague discontents and put them into words that were indictments of specific wrongs or abuses. The reforms indicated by these wrongs were offered by Roosevelt with the exciting din of his matchless showmanship.

The snoopy journalists who inspired and encouraged Roosevelt and supplied him with practically all of his ammunition are usually identified with Samuel Sidney McClure, the genius of the American cheap magazine. And McClure, although he said in later years that the crusades he had fathered were not planned but merely "happened," may well have got the idea from an earlier editor, Benjamin Orange Flower, the talented, courageous and now forgotten man who in 1889 founded the *Arena*, a periodical that set out to expose corruption in American business and politics. The *Arena* did expose corruption, but in general terms. McClure took the *Arena* formula and made it apply to specific business men and firms, and the same to politicians great and small.

S. S. McClure had come to America from his native Ireland in his youth, and in 1893 founded a monthly magazine bearing his name. *McClure's*, price ten cents, catered to the masses with romantic fiction, illustrated articles, and broad humor. It was an immediate success. Soon McClure began forming a stable of capable investigators and writers, among them Ida Tarbell and Ray Stannard Baker, who started a series of sensational exposés of big business. Standard Oil and the railroads were raked over and presented to the public as octopi. *McClure's* circulation leaped to more than half a million copies. Other publishers quickly saw what was doing. They aped McClure, and soon half a dozen magazines were printing exposés of one thing and another. The *Cosmopolitan* had "Men Behind the Pool Rooms" by Josiah Flynt. In

Everybody's Percy Stickney Grant was asking "Are the Rich Responsible for New York's Vice and Crime?" and in the same magazine William Hard wrote about "Making Steel and Killing Men." In *Hampton's* Charles Edward Russell discussed "Scientific Corruption of Politics." In *The Independent* "The Greatest Insurance Wrong" was related by Louis D. Brandeis. In the *American* Burton J. Hendrick described "The Gould Fortune" and told how it was accumulated.

One writer of fiction was meditating on the same corruption. He was Upton Sinclair, freshly graduated from college. With $500 given to him by the *Appeal to Reason*, of which more later, he lived for several weeks among the workers in the stockyards of Chicago, then wrote a novel *The Jungle*, which was published serially in the *Appeal* and subsequently put into book form by a publishing house. This book should be too well known to need description here. I will risk pointing out, however, that Sinclair made clear the connection between government and business by describing how diseased cattle were butchered, marked by the government inspectors as rejected, then ostensibly taken away to be burned. But they were not burned. Instead, the diseased carcasses were carted back again, mingled with the healthy meat, treated to remove the signs of disease, and sold as top quality.

Sinclair was adept at revolting descriptions, and in *The Jungle* he wallowed in them. They were so effective that a goodly portion of the United States became, for a period, vegetarian.

The effect of Sinclair's novel and of the many exposés by the fact-writers in *McClure's* and other magazines was to awaken the public to current abuses and to give President Roosevelt a number of fine menaces to work on. Investigations of railroads, insurance companies, packers, distillers, brewers, stock jobbers, banks, and a variety of business and industrial concerns were followed by new federal laws in many cases. Although he gloried in the uproar and made capital of every bit of it, Roosevelt quickly forgot the sources of his inspiration and aid. In 1906, after five years during which he had acted again and again on the exposés of the magazine journalists, he denounced them publicly as a pack of muckrakers, a term which Ellery Sedgwick, no muckraker, had lifted from Mr. Bunyan's *Pilgrim's Progress.*

The muckrakers, naturally enough, felt a bit hurt. Roosevelt had invited Ray Stannard Baker to dine with him more than once, to discuss corruption and abuses. He had consulted with Lincoln Steffens more than once. He had corresponded with others of the muckraking school. Now that he had denounced them unequivocally, Steffens called on Roosevelt the next day and told him rather bluntly that it had been the muckrakers who had made Roosevelt. The President denied that he had meant Steffens and his colleagues, but his explanation of whom he did mean was so vague that no one was ever able to discover the guilty party. The epithet "muckraker" stuck, and in time it came to be one of honor.

While the muckraking magazines were hitting at this and that, Edward Bok went after the patent-medicine manufacturers in *The Ladies' Home Journal.* The advertisements for Lydia E. Pinkham's Vegetable Compound intimated that Mrs. Pinkham was still alive and giving wonderful advice to many women. Bok ran the Pinkham advertisement and alongside it a photograph of Mrs. Pinkham's grave, with the legend cut into marble that the good woman had gone to her reward twenty-two years previously.* Bok also printed chemical analyses of more than a score of highly popular patent medicines, showing them to contain morphine and other poisons.

---

* For many years Mrs. Pinkham wrote, in her own hand, a reply to every letter from the women who used her Compound, and they ran to the thousands. Her letters were, on the whole, says her biographer, Robert Collyer Washburn, quite sensible and probably of real value to the neurotics to whom they were sent. Incidentally, in 1876, if never again, Mrs. Pinkham advertised her Compound as "good for all weaknesses of the generative organs of *either* sex" (the italics are mine).

In *Collier's* Samuel Hopkins Adams tore the lids off other so-called remedies. He reprinted a federal order forbidding the sale or even possession of Peruna on Indian reservations, where it had lately been widely used as a successful intoxicant. He reported the verdict of a coroner's inquest showing that a child died from an overdose of Doctor Bull's Cough Syrup. He ripped into alleged medicines which "eradicated" asthma with sugar and water, "relieved" heartache through the agency of heart-impairing coal-tar drugs, "dispelled" catarrh by cocaine mixtures, and "cured" tuberculosis, cancer, and Bright's disease with concoctions of whisky, gin, and jalap.

One remedy of the period that really did work was a Secret Liquor Cure, sold by mail-order houses. The advertisement pictures Mother slipping the cure surreptitiously into Daddy's coffee, and said that after a few such treatments Daddy would cease going out nights and helling around. The Secret Cure kept Daddy at home, all right. The cure was a powerful narcotic that put Daddy to sleep right after supper; and pretty soon, sure enough, Daddy was a liquor hound no longer. He was a confirmed narcotic addict.

Muckraker Adams, his bilious eye scanning the advertisements of the food processors, happened on one for Postum, a coffee substitute, that interested him. It related three cases of people who were dying from drinking coffee and were saved by turning, as few people were surprised to learn, to Postum. Adams looked up the source of this alarming information, finding it to be a dubious medical journal that had failed. But he discovered the "doctor" who had been quoted in the coffee tragedies. He happened to be a printer, not an M.D., and also a fanatic about coffee, which he held to be poison. This printer, name of Underwood, told Adams that he had written to Mr. Post, the Postum man, about the ill effects of coffee on his three friends. Mr. Post had replied and said he would gladly pay "Doctor" Underwood if he could get his account of the hellish work of coffee into a magazine. Underwood got it into the fake medical journal, and Mr. Post had paid him.

Adams printed the story of "Doctor" Underwood in *Collier's*. Mr. Post sued *Collier's*, but lost when Underwood, whom Post had never seen but whom he vowed to be "a reputable and eminent physician," was called to the stand. Underwood appeared as a shabby, strange old man who had never pretended to be a doctor. Incidentally, *Collier's* also printed an editorial ridiculing a Post advertisement which claimed that one of its cereals, Grapenuts, was a cure for appendicitis. Post then published advertisements saying that *Collier's* was attacking him because he would not place advertisements in its pages. To this *Collier's* replied by publishing letters it had received from the Post company offering advertising matter, and its own rejection of the advertising. The days of the muckrakers must have borne down hard on the copy-writers of the budding advertising agencies.

Much of the exciting rumpus over foods and drugs led from and back to an until then unsung chemist, Harvey Washington Wiley, one of the most influential Americans of the twentieth century to date. Born a Hoosier in 1844, Dr. Wiley served in the Civil War, taught school, then became state chemist of Indiana, and in 1883 accepted the post of chief chemist in the United States Department of Agriculture. Here he performed valuable work in the study of sugar cane and sugar beets; but his greatest contribution was to what soon was known as the pure food movement.

Wiley had known for a long time that many prepared foods were adulterated. Sausage contained coal-tar dye and borax, canned pork and beans contained formaldehyde, maple syrup was contaminated with cane syrup. Wiley wanted this information printed on the labels of the food packages. He had reported his findings in various government bulletins which, then as now, were little read except by farmers, and farmers were more interested in stopping the sale of oleomargarine as butter than anything else. The muckrakers came along just about then, and they were what Wiley had been praying for—writers who would take his findings about adulterated foods and drugs and make them into exciting articles that the public would avidly read.

Wiley furnished the muckrakers with bombshells of catsup loaded with sinister-sounding chemicals, of bread freighted with alum, of pickles containing dangerously poisonous coloring matter, of drugs that had been diluted into ineffectualness. And he himself took to the lecture platform to arouse the public. A giant in stature, filled with a crusading spirit, he knew how to lecture dramatically. He formed what he called his "poison squad," a group of men in his department who volunteered to act as guinea pigs for his experiments with foods containing harmful preservatives. He reported on these human guinea pigs from time to time. Meanwhile the muckraking magazines were beating a terrible warning on their drums. At the St. Louis Exposition in 1904, too, there appeared a booth displaying samples of practically all of the canned and bottled foods made in the United States. At the same place were displayed pieces of wool and of silk which had been dyed purple and pink and yellow and green—all with dyes that had been extracted from the foods on display in the booth. Placards explained the connection between the brightly dyed cloths and the foods, to the gaping wonder and horror of the monster fair crowds. The booth was a sensation that few who saw ever forgot, and it added to the growing uproar.

Two years later, and due in large part to the hammering of Dr. Wiley and the muckrakers, a Food and Drug Act was at last made into law. Primarily this law sought to regulate the labeling of products. "Tell the truth on the label," Wiley said, "and let the consumer judge for himself." The law was immediately attacked by powerful combinations of food and drug manufacturers, and the same groups attempted to impeach the professional character of Dr. Wiley. The old Puritan—for Puritan he was, said his friends—fought back and at the end of five more years he had successfully vindicated his reputation and the work of his Bureau of Chemistry. The Food and Drug Act remained on the books, and it has been strengthened in the years since its passage.

A striking example of one effect of the Food and Drug Act is to be seen in a comparison of almost any of the big mail-order house catalogues. In 1905 they carried page upon page of quack cures of all sorts. Two years later there are notably fewer pages of these quackish items; and in 1915 two of the largest concerns had but one page each of medicines, and these were mostly of such simple things as epsom salts, aspirin, and so forth.

In 1912, after twenty-nine years of active service during which he probably made more powerful enemies than all of the Presidents of the United States of the era combined, Dr. Wiley resigned his post. American stomachs and insides generally have been better than they would have been had Wiley not lived and labored. He died in 1930, and his memory should not entirely fade so long as drugs and canned foods are made to carry honestly descriptive labels.

What the muckrakers accomplished, say, in the first decade of the new century was to rediscover for the mass of Americans the social conscience that had been lost since the Civil War. Although the muckrakers had no philosophy of their own, they did make it patent to all but the dimmest-witted that the corruption in American politics was in no small part the child of business interests. And they dramatized the paternity by laying on the doorstep of Business, as Vernon Parrington pointed out in a famous line, the lusty and growing bastard. It seems likely that the muckrakers, by their persistent and careful exposures of abuses, raised by a good deal the whole tone of American business. And they did, I believe, do much for the historical stature of President Theodore Roosevelt.

While the muckrakers were being read and discussed in all walks of life, American intellectuals were being disturbed and excited by the reflections of Thorstein Veblen, one of the oddest geniuses ever to come out of Wisconsin, which has supplied more than its share of original thinkers to the nation. The son of Norwegian parents, who had exposed him to Carleton College at Northfield, Minnesota, young Veblen taught school, attended William Graham Sumner's class in social theory at Yale, and turned up at Cornell in 1891, dressed in rustic corduroys and a coonskin cap. A year later he was at the University of Chicago, and here he remained for a dozen years. Here too he simmered and also distilled the vinegar of his soul into a book, *The Theory of the Leisure Class* (1899), without doubt the most savage attack any American ever made on the plutocratic attitude and on the business class in general. Five years later he published *The Theory of Business Enterprise*, a more direct attack and analysis on and of the *mores* and methods of business men.

Veblen's first two books fairly shook the thinking of countless professors, scholars, editors, and journalists, and gave them new and sometimes uneasy ideas on the nature of corporate promotion, of the use of credit, of the influence of business ideas and pressures upon politics and law, and above all the pecuniary values, both avowed and masked, of the well-to-do and wealthy business classes.

The general public, of course, never heard of Veblen in his day, any more than they have heard of him today (1945), years after his death in 1929. But the influence of his writings—he was an exceptionally poor speaker—has been a live force during the first forty-odd years of the new century. Veblen, perhaps as much as or more than any other man, prepared the intellectual leaders of the United States for the trend toward social control which continued from the days of the Populists down to 1932, and then became a fetish.

The new century saw new crusaders take up the banners of old campaigns that had been unsuccessful, and carry them to victories in varying degrees. One such crusade was designed to win recognition of the right to control conception. Abner Kneeland and Dr. Thomas Knowlton, it will be recalled, went to jail in the 1830's for their attempts to disseminate information regarding the subject. For the rest of the nineteenth century birth control was little discussed in public. Then, in 1900, Dr. Abraham Jacobi opened the subject with a favorable article in the *Journal* of the American Medical Association. Six years later old Moses Harmon, editor of *Lucifer*, went to prison despite his seventy-five years for an article on birth control published in his periodical. But the movement languished for want of vigorous leadership. Margaret Sanger, a visiting nurse on New York's East Side, came forth to supply it.

Mrs. Sanger, a short, slight, good-looking woman, possessing great courage and excellent judgment, had seen the effects of continuous child-bearing in the New York slums and had became convinced that the poor would surely always be with us, and sickly as well as poor, so long as they continued to bring huge families into the world of their poverty and degradation. After several years of study and reflection, she issued in 1914 the first number of *The Woman Rebel*, which proposed to give information as to birth control. It was barred from the mails. Later it was admitted to the mails, then barred again, and at last suppressed; and Mrs. Sanger was arrested and jailed. In 1916 she was arrested again, this time for conducting a birth control clinic in Brooklyn. She appealed, and although her conviction was sustained, the decision really was a victory, for it opened the way for physicians to give birth control advice in New York for the "cure and prevention of disease."

Several small groups interested in the subject now joined to form the American Birth Control League, through which, despite strong opposition from the Catholic Church and other bodies, the movement was to continue and gradually to establish a large number of birth control clinics in many states. The crusade to accomplish this much had required almost a century.*

A champion of most reforms proposed in the nineties and after was a periodical that is never mentioned in general or even in literary histories, yet no account of the rise of "radicalism" or "social consciousness" in the new century is complete without an understanding of the tremendous influence of *The Appeal to Reason*. The *Appeal* scared the daylights out of industrialists and business men and middle-class white-collar people who never heard of Veblen; and it made "radicals" of millions of young and older men and put them in line for the protest vote, whether the candidate was Bryan, La Follette, Debs, or Norman Thomas. It seems odd that literary historians have ignored a sheet that occasionally printed four million copies to an issue, that was packed with some sort of social dynamite in every column, that was seriously noticed by at least two Presidents of the United States.

The *Appeal* was the child of Julius A. Wayland, a Hoosier tramp printer who, unlikely enough, made some money out of a real estate speculation in Colorado, then lost it in financing a Socialist colony, known as the Ruskin Commonwealth, first in Tennessee, then in Georgia. Gradually the comrades drifted away, some to the Fairhope Single-Tax Colony, some to Home Colony on Puget Sound, while a few, including

---

* In 1944 Mrs. Sanger told me that any account of birth control crusades, no matter how brief, should mention the names of Leonard Abbott, Dr. E. B. Foote, Dr. Robert L. Dickinson, and William J. Robinson, editor of *Critic and Guide*, "all of whom," says Mrs. Sanger, "did fine educational work." A recent milestone in the crusade was passed in 1937 when the American Medical Association, after long meditation, came out for birth control under medical supervision.

Wayland himself, were quite cured of community living.

But Wayland had a lot of steam left over from the Ruskin layout. Going to Girard, Kansas, he broke out on April 3, 1897, with the first issue of the *Appeal to Reason*. Wayland announced that his paper would kill you or cure you inside of three months, and that no man was rich enough or great enough to get the paper on credit. The dimes came rolling in, many of them from hard-shell Populists, with which the West was still infested. The paper was radical in all ways and considered itself Socialist. Citizens of Girard did not like their Fundamentalist village to harbor such a snake in the grass as the *Appeal*. Wayland and his printers often worked behind strong, closed shutters, to protect them from the glass that flew from the impact of heaved bricks. Wayland's wife was ostracized, his children hooted at by other kids. The families of heretics usually suffer worse persecutions than the heretics themselves.

The *Appeal* had a time of it to weather the Spanish-American War, when most of America was cocky and hot for imperialism, but it did survive; and now one Fred Warren, a typesetter on the paper, began to push his weight around. Wayland had been prone to give his subscribers good solid doses of straight Socialism, doctrinaire and rather dull. Warren suggested leavening the columns with lighter stuff, possibly lurid, always connecting the item with a curse against the Capitalistic System, or pointing a moral leading toward Socialism. So, soon the *Appeal* carried news items, then whole articles, about the White Slave Traffic. This deplorable profession was shown to be a direct outgrowth of The System, but it was also described in some detail and with more than a little imagination.

The *Appeal* also laid in a stock of vermilion ink, which Warren used to fine effect. Black studhorse headlines, interspersed with brilliant red titles and borders, soon made the paper inflaming even to illiterates. It was the first to publish Sinclair's *The Jungle*. Every week it tied into Capital, both general and specific. It attacked the rich on every score, including a number of indictments that even Veblen had not thought of. The paper under Warren was never heavy. It got in most of its licks at The System by indirection. In the middle of a wonderful exposé of some pornographic incident in the life of some man, who for present purposes was always labeled a Capitalist, the *Appeal* would pause to remark that "we do not relish digging into this muck of filth and degeneracy, but we owe it to the victims of a corrupt System to tell this story in all its hideousness."

Warren, who gradually came to take over the *Appeal*, making Wayland a sort of emeritus and Grand Old Man of Socialism, never lacked for a good juicy Menace. For weeks on end the menace was the Boy Scout movement, which Warren said was "a diabolical and sinister attempt to debauch youth." The city of Sodom was mentioned in connection. Other and more serious menaces were treated by Eugene Debs, who made highly incendiary attacks on Theodore Roosevelt, the Supreme Court, the Tariff, and practically every American institution.

When any one of the *Appeal's* thousands of volunteer subscription agents was insulted, or attacked, the paper came out with a rousing Martyr story, in which the agent was pictured as a Christian at the stake, with the unholy Philistines, or Romans, lighting the fires around him. If the agent was in jail, as was occasionally the case, a Martyr Defense Fund was started. How many of these defense funds were operated by the *Appeal* is beyond knowing. Hundreds of thousands of dollars were raised in this manner, and no doubt some of the cash was actually spent in attorney fees, although more of it went into getting new subscriptions to promote the Red Dawn.

In 1906 the *Appeal* made an attack on Roosevelt that got under the President's hide. He defended himself in *The Outlook*, terming the *Appeal* a "vituperative organ of pornography, anarchy and bloodshed"—which pleased its editors very much. A bit later President Taft took occasion, when pardoning Editor Warren who had been sentenced to six months jail and a fine for sending threatening printed matter through the mails, to read the editor a lecture. Incidentally, because it was so characteristic of the *Appeal*, it is amusing to know that Editor Warren, on receiving the pardon, refused to accept it because he could find no union printer's label on the pardon form. Subscribers went into ecstasies over this neat thrust by their hero at the Ruling Classes.

Wayland must have at least tired of being Emeritus. One night in November of 1912, he read a few passages in Bellamy's *Looking Backward*, then blew out his brains with an automatic pistol. The *Appeal* could even apply this tragedy to its editorial policy: it promptly and enthusiastically charged that the Grand Old Man of Socialism had been hounded to his death by the slavering hounds of Plutocracy.

Swiftly the *Appeal's* circulation list and sales mounted—one million, two million, three million, three million five hundred thousand copies, were run off and mailed from little Girard, Kansas, every week. A new post office had to be built by the Capitalistic Government. Now and then for some special Cause or other, the paper put out an edition of four million copies, and once or twice the total run was four million one hundred thousand. They were read, too. In Puget Sound and Minnesota logging camps, in Butte and Keweenaw mine boarding houses, and all over the prairie on farms and ranches, "the Little Old *Appeal*," as it was affectionately known, was literally read into pulp—and believed, every word.*

---

* Ernest Haycox, currently perhaps the best known writer of Western stories in the country, but in 1914 a youngster just starting out to make his way in Portland, used to sell the *Appeal* in Lownsdale Square in the Oregon city. Mr. Haycox tells me that he does not believe that any other paper ever had such a fanatically faithful and all-believing audience. A huge stack of *Appeals* would be sold out so quickly as to amaze young Haycox, and the manner in which the customers fondled the paper, folded it, or spread it out to read on a park bench, was virtually a religious rite. "Those men felt," says Mr. Haycox, "that this was the one and only periodical that spoke for them."

It is of course impossible to measure the effect that the *Appeal* had on its millions of readers, but I am not alone in believing that its influence, not only at the time but in years since its readers reached middle age, has been enormous. Although it was never considered as one of the muckraking sheets, it antedated them and they drew much from its exciting technique, although the muckrakers were carefully factual, while facts were the last thing to trouble either the editor of the *Appeal* or its reporters and article writers.

Taken all together, these periodicals supplied whopping big Menaces of abuse, corruption and other skulduggery in business and politics to Theodore Roosevelt, La Follette and other politicians, including Woodrow Wilson, and prepared the great mass of the public for social controls that have come in since the century's turn and were still coming in 1945.

World War I, with its attendant patriotism and prosperity, started the *Appeal* on its downbeat. In 1918 a controlling interest in it was bought by one of the *Appeal* employees, E. Haldeman-Julius, the Little Blue Book man, who let the paper die quietly in 1922. No periodical has quite taken its place.*

In the field of race relations, Booker T. Washington had long been preaching the salvation of the Negro through education and hard work. A younger group of colored Americans came to believe that the Negro was not making the progress he should because he was not given an even chance to earn his way, nor anything like—at least in the South— equality before the law. This new group made its protest in 1905, when it called a conference at Niagara Falls and issued

---

* Not all so-called radicals, however, believe that the *Appeal* and other periodicals of protest had much effect. Archie Sinclair, the former I.W.W. leader, writes me, in 1945, that "agitators from John the Baptist to Earl Browder have made a lot of noise but accomplished little. Social change comes about by the acceleration of energy conversion. My vote for the man most responsible for social progress goes to Henry Ford. He eliminated distance and brought city and country dwellers into close communication."

a "statement, complaint and prayer" to the American public. The time was not ripe, and the Niagara Movement failed. It had brought to the front, however, an exceptional man, William Edward Burghardt Du Bois, a Massachusetts mulatto of high intelligence who had been educated at Fisk and Harvard, and had received a degree of Doctor of Philosophy from the latter. With other young Negroes he helped to found the National Association for the Advancement of Colored People, and he soon became its major force through his able editing of a periodical, *The Crisis*. From the founding of this organization the condition of the Negro in the United States has steadily improved; and in 1945 no domestic problem—not even the resumption of the making of pleasure automobiles—received more attention than the welfare of the colored people of the United States.

Incidentally, many Southerners resent "the agitators," both white and colored, who they say are teaching Negroes that the Southern white people are their cruel oppressors but do not also divulge to the Negro that "his poverty is the result of a Federal economy that drains the wealth of the South to the North." * The real oppressor of the Southern Negro, say these Southerners, is not Jim Crow laws or poll taxes but poverty, and the poverty is not natural but artificial and is saddled upon the entire South by the North, through the application of tariffs, railroad rates, and other discriminations. Right or wrong, this belief is doubtless held by a majority of white Southern people; and it would seem that it will have to be considered in any attempt to solve the "race problem" in that region.

The quest for social justice for all Americans, a quest that stems so greatly from the Populist uprising, was a constant thing in the first decade of the new century. Robert La Follette of Wisconsin supplanted Bryan as the standard bearer

---

* See "The South and Its Adopted Children," by Lloyd E. Price, in *The Southern Weekly*, March 17, 1945.

of protest, and this he did very well indeed, and with the finest of dramatics, for Old Bob was as good an actor as either Roosevelt or Bryan. Coincident with those three men was another, a man who had, and has, absolutely no sense of publicity, yet whose influence has been as great as or greater than that of Bryan or Roosevelt or La Follette. William S. U'Ren, still living as these words are written and the sole surviving leader, or director, of the great days of Populism, Single Tax, and other fermentations, is the man; and he has seldom got into any book of wider scope than a monograph.

Born in Wisconsin, U'Ren worked on farms there and in the Far West, studied law in Denver, and went to Oregon to practice. His reading included Henry George's *Progress and Poverty*, and this book merely gave impetus to the ideas of social protest and reform that already were motivating the young attorney. He quickly became the most powerful political figure in Oregon, though he did not care for office and was uncommonly shy for a reformer. Persuasive, a quick thinker, and a strategist with few peers, this slight, soft-spoken little man was unquestionably the driving genius which gave Oregon the Australian ballot, the registration law, the initiative and referendum, the direct primary, the corrupt practices act, and the recall. Most of these reforms, now so prevalent that they are generally accepted nearly everywhere in the United States as part of the scenery, were original in Oregon, and were chiefly the work of U'Ren, the man who wanted the single tax most of all but was realistic enough to work for such reforms as he thought were possible of acceptance. But he seldom got his name in the papers, and if it did appear there, it was none of his work.

Still active in 1945, in his eighties, Mr. U'Ren, bright-eyed, silver-haired, straight as hickory, and very keen, is one of the wholly unknown historical figures who had tre mendous influence on his time.

CHAPTER XVI

In Praise of the Harding Era

It has been much in style in the United States, since around 1939, to praise the democracies of the world and especially our own. Strong men have became tearful and their voices have broken with emotion as they reflected, aloud and often too loud, that we are a nation in which any man may become President, that we achieve our laws by discussion, and that the rights of our minorities are often respected. These ponderous and occasionally strident writers and radio orators have sounded as if they had only then discovered what a truly wonderful place is the United States of America; and I should like to reiterate what I have said elsewhere about this tub-thumping.

All of this shouting has left some of us rather calm and collected, and quite uninterested, for some of us have never since birth thought otherwise than that our country, for all its imperfections, was the finest place on earth. I have never been able to read far in any of the many books written by Americans these past few years which would tell me of the boons of American democracy, nor to finish any of the many magazine and newspaper articles that would tell me the same thing. I have as much need of inspirational reading, or listening, about American democracy as I have of a book that will tell me the Sun rises in the morning and sets in the evening.

These special pleaders for America, it seems to me, have merely been doing some second-guessing and are in a great sweat to put down on paper, or to charge the air waves with, statements of things that were obvious truths to many of us when we were ten years of age. We did not have to learn them, either, for we drank them in with the air we breathed, and have since never had cause to doubt them, not for a moment, not even during the administrations of Harding, Coolidge, and Hoover.

I suspect that many of these suddenly patriotic pleaders for democracy must at some time have lost faith in the Republic, or had never understood it anyway; and, like repentant sinners at a revival, hurried down the sawdust path to stand at the testimonial bench and give cry to their conversion and salvation. In no other way can I understand the vehemence, the authoritative manner, and the curicus and to me pathetic naïveté with which they stress the marvels and glories of democracy as practiced in the United States.

It seems to me that one need know only the trials through which our country has successfully passed to believe it so basically stout and secure that only the wear of centuries and the evolutionary forces of time can lay it low. A nation comes through its every trial either weaker or stronger for the experience. Up to the present writing I believe the United States has emerged from every crisis with increased national intelligence and ability to operate a vast and complex nation in a fairly competent manner. And if that is true, then it is enough.

That is why I believe the administration of Warren G. Harding to have been one of the most valuable the Republic has ever had. It demonstrated our strength as a nation, our lasting qualities, in a manner that left no doubt. If we Americans could live through *that* period, and those of Coolidge and Hoover, including the long horror of Prohibition—if we could pass through those trials and find our system still workable, then he is a skeptic indeed who doubts that the United States continues to have a future.

It has been remarked a number of times, I believe, that the Harding administration was "the most corrupt since those of Grant." This is merely a lame attempt at whitewash. The brief regime of President Harding was filled with more corruption than Grant's two terms put together. It was far and away the most corrupt administration in our history. It was more corrupt than the France of 1870. It is likely that no South American country has equaled it. Nor has Spain. Only in Gibbon's melancholy report on the ancient and Holy Roman Empire is there anything to compare with it.

Corruption on such a mighty scale automatically assured the Harding regime of a safe place in any history of the United States. But the historical importance of Harding himself rests on a firmer foundation. He was unique in at least two ways. For one, he seems to have been the only President who neither in private nor public ever gave utterance to anything that could be called an idea. For the other, he appears to have been the only candidate for the office who said he did not want the job—and really meant it. He preferred to remain in the Senate, where he was liked if not respected, and which he thought of as a rather nice club. His character, which was kindly, genial and completely honest, was summed up best in a too-little-known line attributed to his own father: "If you were a girl, Warren," remarked the old man, "You'd be in the family way all the time. You can't say No." *

Nor was Harding elected through any personal merit, for the American people, except for Ohioans, had never heard of him. But that mattered not at all. What elected Harding was the fact that the people were voting against a man who was not a candidate—Woodrow Wilson. A moral slump had set in. Men could no longer hold to the lofty plane of idealism they professed, and to some degree actually maintained, during the war years. Disillusion had come down like soaking

---

* Quoted in *The Incredible Era,* a rousing account of the period by Samuel Hopkins Adams, Boston, 1939.

rain. A League of Nations, or any participation in world affairs, was a bogey to be plowed under. So men voted in savage resentment against the memory of Wilson, and Harding was elected.

Perhaps this would be a good place for a sort of interlude in which to consider that a number of presidential elections have been won or lost because of very minor things, mere incidents at times, none of which had any connection with the business in hand but which did turn out to have a great influence on the elections. Campaign years in the United States are always periods when skepticism on the part of the electorate should come to the fore and prevail in great strength until the most remote counties have been counted. Skulduggery is likely to be afoot, in various disguises; sometimes it works, sometimes not. Let the glories of the Harding administration wait briefly while we look at the odd or deplorable happenings in a number of our presidential election years.

For instance: In the midst of a savage campaign one hundred and forty-five years ago, a small and startling news item appeared in the *Baltimore American*. It reported without comment "the death of Mr. Jefferson at Monticello after an indisposition of forty-eight hours." No other details were given. Mr. Jefferson was of course the Republican (old style) candidate. The campaign was bringing out the most vicious and scurrilous personal attacks imaginable. Jefferson was described, in so many words, as an atheist, a revolutionary, an embezzler, and a propagator of Negro children. His opponent, John Adams, running for re-election, was treated almost as badly. There have been few more bitterly personal campaigns.

The canard about Jefferson's death first appeared on June 30, 1800. On July 2 the *United States Gazette* printed the item and remarked editorially that it "appears to be entitled to some credit." The New York *Commercial Advertiser* on the same day gave the item prominence. By the 7th the Hartford *Courant* had it, but cautioned its readers against implicit belief. The *Massachusetts Mercury* of Boston and the *Spy* of Worcester both ran the *Courant* story and warning. On July 9 the Boston *Centinel* ran it, with no note of caution.

Next, the Philadelphia *Aurora* told its readers that Jefferson was very much alive and in excellent health, that the story of his death was "a Federalist trick." So, no doubt, it was. One should bear in mind that news traveled slowly in 1800 and that it took a long time to refute properly the canard that one of the most prominent of Americans had died. It is not difficult to understand the confusion such a report, in the midst of a hot campaign, must have caused. The report was refuted, however, and Jefferson was elected. And in time an investigation brought out what appears to have been the basis—if it could rightly be called a basis— for the false report. An aged Negro, slave of the master of Monticello, had died in late June. Like so many slaves of the period, he bore his master's name, Thomas Jefferson.

Just what campaign manager turned the old Negro into a candidate for the President is not to be known.

How swiftly changes in political preferences can be brought about in the Republic by wholly unimportant things is well known, and no better example is to be had than that of the great Billiard Table Affair of John Quincy Adams, one of the celebrated political incidents of all time, now forgotten. It is difficult to understand how the clever political managers of the day could have made a sybarite and a debauched gambler out of such stiff and prim material as the younger Adams, but it was accomplished nevertheless, and it had something to do with relegating John Quincy to the quiet of his home near Boston.

Early in 1828, it appears from the records, President J. Q. Adams ordered, for his own use and own personal account, one billiard table, price $50, a set of balls at $6, and a chess set at $32.50. These were duly installed in the White House.

By an extremely unfortunate error, for Adams was too astute as well as honest a man to have bought the items at public cost, the bill for the hellish articles was included in a requisition for the White House by Adams's son, who acted as a sort of clerk and bookkeeper for his father. Although the error was soon cleared up and was forgotten by all immediately concerned, such was not the case with the opposition, the Jackson party. They were merely hoarding the incident.

President Adams, as related, was running for re-election in 1828. Things were not going too badly for him when suddenly a barrage of billiard balls rained down on the frosty head and stiff back of the man from Massachusetts. In the House, up rose Congressman Samuel P. Carson, to stand and inquire:

"Is it possible that it was ever intended by Congress that public money should be applied for the purchase of game-tables and gambling furniture? And if it is right to purchase billiard tables and chess-men, why not also purchase pharo [sic] banks, playing cards, race horses, and every other necessary article to complete a system of gambling in the President's Palace and let it be understood by the People that this is a most splendid gambling administration." And so on into the late hours.

The Honorable Samuel Carson set the tone for what followed. Speeches, broadsides, pamphlets, all described with pious horror the ascetic Yankee President, probably the last person in the United States to be accused justly of light entertainment and gambling, as a degenerate "monarch" of the Bourbon-Orleans type. The ever careful Charles Warren, historian of the Supreme Court and much else, estimates the Billiard Table Affair to have contributed largely to Adams's unpopularity and subsequent defeat.

A similar political example of smear-technique was the Gold Spoons business in the campaign of 1840, when Martin Van Buren was running for re-election. This, it will be recalled, was the famous Log Cabin and Hard Cider campaign, when Van Buren's opponent, the well-to-do William Henry Harrison, was pictured by his supporters as being a sort of combination hillbilly and hero, who had been born in a log cabin—which he had not—and drank nothing but hard cider, which he loathed.

The Gold Spoons smear was started on May 6, when Van Buren was renominated by the Democratic convention. The opening gun was fired by Charles Ogle, a Whig of Pennsylvania, who made in Congress a most extraordinary speech lasting several whole days in which he related in great detail, and with drooling relish, what he termed the squandering of appropriations by Van Buren. Ogle even had a pretty fine title for his interminable speech: "The Regal Splendor of the President's Palace." Here is a sample of what he gave to Congress, and through the Whig newspapers to the people of the United States:

". . . a palace, sirs, as splendid as that of the Caesars. . . . Let us enter this palace and survey its spacious courts, its glittering and dazzling saloons with all their magnificence and sumptuous array of gold spoons and silver plate, of crimson and orange, of blue and violet. . . ." Four days later, when Congressman Ogle ceased speaking and sat down, all Americans who read the Whig papers knew that Martin Van Buren was a snob, an aristocrat, an imitator of kings, a man who loved gold spoons and splendor above all else. (Whig papers of course described his opponent as a poor and honest and plain and capable man possessed of one shirt and no gold spoons.)

The Whig pack took up the Gold Spoons cry, and throughout the campaign, which most historians believe to have marked the lowest ebb in campaign taste, they rang every possible change on Van Buren's love of expensive show. The Gold Spoons issue was in fact one of the main causes that led to Van Buren's carrying only seven of the twenty-one states and receiving only sixty electoral votes to two hundred and thirty-four for that old synthetic backwoodsman, General William Henry Harrison.

No smear, but a little-known oddity in a later campaign, that of 1848, cost Daniel Webster the loss of his most cherished desire, that of the Presidency. He was offered the candidacy of vice-president to run with Zachary Taylor. Black Dan'l refused the insult with the deep and flashing indignation of which the New Hampshire orator was capable. It must, he said, be the Number One position, or nothing. Taylor died within eighteen months of taking office. One wonders futilely what the Master of Marshfield reflected on the matter, as he brooded at his farm and wrestled with his big ram, Goliath, when Millard Fillmore succeeded to the Presidency.

Once, at least, sheer ridicule was used to defeat a candidate. Nominated in 1852 by the Whigs, General Winfield Scott had a long and fine record as a soldier and army administrator; but he had the unfortunate habit of writing letters. Scott's literary phraseology often lent itself to easy ridicule; and when the campaign got under way, the opposition dug up several samples, two of which became Democratic heavy artillery in blasting Scott's chances.

These letters had been written many years before, during the Mexican war, in which, incidentally, Scott had performed wonders despite incredible political interference. But now the war was over, and a political campaign was on. One of the old letters published showed Scott complaining to President Polk of the interference of congressmen and senators with the Army. "I have," wrote General Scott, "a fire upon my rear from the men in Washington, and the fire in front, from the Mexicans." A phrase from another Scott letter, also to Polk, contained the line: "Your letter, received as I sat down to take a hasty plate of soup, demands a prompt reply."

Those were the damning lines used to wreck Scott's political career. For reasons that now would seem impossible to understand, the phrase "fire upon my rear" and also the line about the "hasty plate of soup" seemed so uproariously ridiculous to Americans of the day, that Democratic campaign managers quoted them again and again, in speech and broadside, and with dreadful effect. These two lines, taken from ancient correspondence, constituted, in fact, the chief campaign literature of the Democrats. And they mowed old Scott down.

General Scott was a pompous sort of man. He was large physically, pretty wide of beam, which is to say, rear. His appetite was notoriously voracious; he liked ten-course meals, gout or no. Perhaps these facts had some bearing on the national laughter occasioned by the fire-upon-my-rear and hasty-soup letters. In any case, the letters were used with telling effect and Scott met an inglorious defeat at the hands of an obscure party hack named Pierce.

Not ridicule but attempted praise by a prominent supporter is what probably defeated James Gillespie Blaine in the campaign of 1884. The incident should be too well known to call for more than a brief reminder. Blaine was opposing the Democrat, Grover Cleveland, and had every reason to believe himself headed straight for the White House until, at the very end of the campaign, a Blaine henchman, the Reverend S. D. Burchard, in a speech at the Fifth Avenue hotel in New York, referred to candidate Blaine as fighting the Democratic party as "the party whose antecedents have been rum, Romanism, and Rebellion."

This expression was not merely unfortunate for Blaine; it was his murder. Coming too late to be explained away, and accepted by a majority of the country's electorate as coming from Blaine himself (whose wife was a Catholic) instead of from Burchard, it unquestionably alienated many Roman Catholics. New York was the key state in this election. The race in New York was very close. A mere 600 votes would have turned the election in favor of Blaine. He lost them, and so lost his chance. But in this particular election, the

American people by losing Blaine were not given a nonentity like Franklin Pierce, but one of the strongest Presidents the country has had.

Such have been a few of the incidents which have affected the outcomes of elections. Mr. Harding needed no fortuitous or planned incidents to be elected. The public did not vote for Harding, but against idealism. Harding said that a return to normalcy was his goal, thus incidentally becoming America's most eminent solecist. He also remarked that "No man's life ever gave me greater inspiration than that of Alexander Hamilton"—a line every Hamiltonian has a right to forget.

Harding was probably the handsomest man ever to hold the office of President. Straight, well built, graceful, liked by men and women, by strangers and acquaintances, his dark eyes contrasted with a full head of white hair. In total, he was obviously the simple and sincere and typical American as conceived by most Americans.

Not illiterate in a strictly technical sense, he was widely unread and, happily, also ungrammatical, and his periods of oratory, composed mostly of resounding platitudes and odd solecisms, never in the least tried the minds of his listeners. H. L. Mencken declared that Harding's English was the worst he ever had encountered. William McAdoo thought that Harding's speeches left "the impression of an army of pompous phrases moving over a landscape in search of an idea." The search, he added, was ever futile.

Of ideas in the abstract, Harding had no suspicion. Nor was he guilty of harboring ideas on specific things like taxes and money and social reform. A fair sample of his knowledge was reported in an interview by Bruce Bliven. Asked about the tariff, Bliven's startled ears heard the President of the United States say firmly that "we should adopt a protective tariff of such a character as will help the struggling industries of Europe to get on their feet." The dazed Bliven left the room speechless.

It has been remarked here that Harding really did not want to be President. He often said, and with no false modesty, that he was not of a caliber to hold that office. Harry Micajah Daugherty, however, thought otherwise, and Daugherty was a man of great drive and ability who had come up through the ranks to become Ohio's most powerful and officeless politician. Starting 'way back in the 1890's, when he first met Harding, Daugherty had it in mind to put the handsome Marion lad into the White House. And it was Daugherty, more than any other one man, more than any other ten thousand men, who did just that.

In a Republican convention at which all of the leading candidates were far abler men than Harding, Daugherty, by well timed and directed efforts, put his man on top. The only discernible issue in the election seemed to be Internationalism vs. Isolation, and Candidate Harding could handle that one; he told the people with great sonorousness that he Favored America First. Thus assured they were not getting another Wilson, the people gave Harding a good majority over James M. Cox.

One of the most interesting things about the Harding regime was not the fact that the Ohio Gang moved upon the ramparts of the Republic to take over, but the speed with which they moved. Like a flight of dark buzzards they winged swiftly up out of the most obscure places imaginable and headed for Washington, where the body politic, as somebody remarked, was expiring of a surfeit of idealism. Almost but not quite all of the Gang were corrupt, and those who were not corrupt were vastly unfitted for the positions that were parceled out like so many door prizes at an Elks lodge.

One of the fattest jobs, that of superintendent of federal prisons, was removed by Harding from the civil service list and conferred on the Reverend Heber H. Votaw, the temporarily jobless brother-in-law of the President, and a man whose peculiar fitness for the duties, as Samuel Hopkins Adams pointed out, consisted of ten years of service as a Seventh Day Adventist missionary in Burma.

To be controller of the currency—and later governor of the federal reserve—Harding appointed an old friend and neighbor, one Daniel R. Crissinger, a small-town lawyer of no qualifications for either post.

To be director of the mint Harding appointed another friend of his boyhood, Edward F. Scobey, who had gained his knowledge of fiscal affairs as high sheriff of Pickaway County, Ohio.

Albert D. Lasker was made chairman of the United States Shipping Board. This old sea dog's nautical experience came wholly from many years in an advertising agency.

William J. Burns, an already notorious private detective, was put in charge of the federal bureau of investigation.

To boss the important Veterans' Bureau Harding appointed one of the great rogues of all time, Charles R. Forbes. Alongside Charlie Forbes, Jesse James looks saintly, and even so low a scoundrel as Benedict Arnold looks better than he deserves.

There was, of course, a cabinet. There *had* to be a cabinet; but there is little need to go into that of Harding, except to cite the fact that Daugherty was made attorney general; and Albert B. Fall, an all-around dubious character from New Mexico, was made secretary of the interior. And perhaps Edwin N. Denby, Harding's secretary of the navy, should be mentioned.

Holding neither cabinet nor other discernible appointments were two characters who ought never be forgotten by writers of history books. Into Washington with the Ohio Gang went Howard Mannington, a minor politician and friend of Harding, and Jesse W. Smith, son of a Marion, Ohio, department store man, and an intimate of Daugherty. Jesse W. Smith, if no other of Harding's Gang, deserves some sort of monument, perhaps of brass, and of a design that would remind all Americans what Normalcy meant in the Harding era.

The first thing Smith and Mannington did on arrival in Washington was to set up a kind of trading post at 1625 K

Street, soon to become widely known as the Little Green House. This was not only a trading post but also a relaxation center for the administration underworld. It was here that the Ohio Gang traded in appointments to office, illegal concessions of all sorts, in pardons, paroles, special privileges, in protection for bootleggers and distillers, and especially in liquor withdrawal permits, which as many Americans may have forgotten, was one of the big industries of the time.

Mannington, with the help of a stooge named Caskey, ran the Little Green House. Jesse Smith did not live here but with Daugherty, yet Smith was here a good deal and with the other two men named formed the best known triumvirate in the administration. If a citizen of the Republic wanted something or other "fixed" he went to the Little Green House. Did some gangster want to get another gangster out of one of the federal Big Houses? Call at the Little Green House. Did some shady merchant want to buy fine bed sheets worth $1.37 for 26 cents? The Little Green House. Did some 'legger know of a thousand gallons of genuine Old Crow gathering dust in a bonded warehouse when it could be moved into the trade? Call at 1625 K Street.

Mannington ran the K Street joint and handled the loot. His aid Caskey did the paper work necessary to orderly corruption. Jesse Smith called in every night or so to skim the profits. Jesse had an old song he was constantly humming, "Good God! How the Money Rolls In."

There was no key to the Little Green House. It cheerfully kept open for business day and night. It was here that one M. P. Kraftmuller, operating as a go-between, dealt in liquor withdrawal permits through Mannington. For one of these permits the General Drug Company paid Kraftmuller the sum of $20,000. He retained one-third as commission, turning the remainder over to Mannington, who gave Caskey a mere $1,500, keeping the rest for himself and for certain accommodating agents of the Treasury Department, who had issued the permits.

Jesse Smith's specialty was the sale of pardons and paroles, for which he had a price list that might fluctuate, according to the prominence of the thug to be pardoned or paroled and the venality of the judge who had to be bought. It required constant attention from Jesse, but he managed to attend to it, and later branched out into bigger time that included the disposal of federal judgeships. A Cincinnati bootlegger named Remus testified that he had paid Smith more than $250,000 for immunity from prosecution.

Normalcy was here, as the President remarked; and the President's friend, good old Jesse W. Smith, echoed the remark with his little song.

Although business was the leading activity at the K Street house, relaxation from the heat of the day was not forgotten. Up to the house in broad daylight rolled great express trucks, and case after case of goods plainly marked liquor were unloaded. This whisky was not for sale but for social purposes of Smith, Mannington and Company, and their many friends, customers, and clients. During the evenings more or less friendly games of poker, and more or less acquiescent ladies, combined with the constant flow of excellent liquor, in a period when most Americans were drinking hair tonic, to make a pretty scene of normal conditions within the Harding regime.

In the meantime, of course, gigantic corruption was at work in the higher reaches of the administration, but this particular graft was not uncovered until after the death of the President, on August 3, 1923.

The Harding outfit began blowing up on March 11, 1923, with the suicide of Charles F. Cramer, legal aid to Forbes of the Veterans' Bureau. Cramer knew what was just ahead. Forbes himself left hurriedly for Europe, and the whole Harding shebang started to reveal its complete putrefaction. The results of an investigation of the Veterans' Bureau served to make cynics of thousands of disabled veterans who had been told "there is nothing too good for you boys." What they got, instead, was Charlie Forbes, and what he did to the boys and their hospitals would have shamed Boss Tweed. And Forbes cost the taxpayers $200,000,000 in straight graft.

Forbes's first contribution to government, after his appointment, was to make a drunken junket across the country and back, during which he let contracts to build hospitals without regard to price—except the amount of graft for himself. Then, there was the income from supplies. A typical item was $70,000 worth of floor wax, sufficient to last until that day when wars shall cease and there will be no longer need for veterans' hospitals. Forbes got rakeoffs on all or nearly all of his purchases. He not only bought but sold. A typical sale was of 75,000 towels bought at nineteen cents, sold at three cents. It was the same with sheets, cots, other supplies and equipment for which the hospitals—and ill or wounded veterans—had sore need.

Among other items, good old Charlie Forbes, as Harding called him, sold 100,000 pairs of pajamas, which had been made and donated by the American Red Cross, for thirty cents a pair and pocketed the money himself. This happened at a time when men in hospitals were forced to sleep in their underwear. "Nothing too good for you heroes," Forbes told them in one of his magnetic speeches. And when surgical departments of many veterans' institutions were greatly in need of gauze, Forbes peddled 45,000 rolls of it at twenty per cent of its cost to the government. "I used to be a soldier myself," said Director of Veterans' Bureau Forbes, who was soon on his way to Leavenworth for fraud.

Very soon Mr. Harding's alien property custodian, T. W. Miller, was found to be making quite a fortune. He was convicted of conspiracy to fraud, and was sent to prison. In the same mess Mal S. Daugherty, a brother of the attorney general, was indicted, tried twice by juries that failed to agree on anything, and finally freed—but not before the government showed Mal Daugherty to have gone to his brother's bank and taken out and burned the ledger sheets covering his own accounts there, and his brother's account, and another account significantly known as "Jesse Smith Extra." (This was none other than the God-how-the-money-rolls-in man.)

Jesse Smith, indeed, had a hand in almost every piece of graft in the whole rotten caboodle. History cries for a monograph of this Jesse Smith, for he was superbly of his time. In him flowered to the fullest the Americanism of Normalcy. Just as sure as some new investigation got under way, an event that occurred every week or so after the Harding crew started to crack, soon or late the name of good old Jesse Smith turned up. And in time it must have got on his nerves, for, handsomely enough, on Decoration Day, 1923, Jesse was found on the floor of Daugherty's Wardman Park hotel apartment, his head in a metal waste-basket flowing with blood and brains. Either just before or just after he died, Jesse or somebody else destroyed a titanic mass of papers that otherwise might have gone into history as the Jesse Smith and Harry Daugherty papers and become of intense interest to researchers in the science of government.

Thus passed the boorish and unlettered political pimp who doubtless knew more about the vast underworld of the Harding administration than anyone else, not excepting Harry Daugherty. I regret that the biographical bits about Jesse Smith are not larger. They indicate him to have been the town cut-up, the card, of Marion, Ohio, the drugstore sport, the kind of young man who enjoyed wearing a "23-Skidoo" button in his lapel. I have no doubt but that in his youth he sent away for a booklet that told him how to be the life of the party. Taken to the nation's capital by the new attorney general and given unlimited powers to graft as he would, it was just too much for what passed for his mind. He had splurged like a movie star for a brief and wondrous heyday. Then, even he saw what was coming and, unlike Forbes and some of the other yeggs in office, he felt that he could not face it.*

One by one the Harding appointees killed themselves, went to prison, resigned under fire, were ousted for malpractice of one kind or another, or simply disappeared and were heard of no more. The Veterans' Bureau was in disgrace. So was the alien property custodian's office. So, very soon, was what somebody called the department of easy virtue—meaning the department of justice. The department's FBI, it will be remembered, was headed in the Harding administration by the fragrant William J. Burns. Under Burns the bureau was turned into a smearing weapon, used against senators, congressmen and others who sought to find anything wrong with the administration. One of its sweetest violets was Gaston B. Means who, on wages of $88.33 a week, rented a Washington mansion at $1,000 a month, owned an expensive car, had a chauffeur in livery, and lived very well indeed. Means, among other things, acted as go-between for Burns and good old Jesse Smith, handling the important matters of pardons, paroles and such. Means also could be depended upon for a smearing job now and then. He wound up, as many more of his co-workers deserved, in jail.

The aroma was getting fairly stout when Harding died, but it was attar of roses compared to the stench that permeated Washington within a few months. This came from the Teapot Dome and Elk Hills oil scandals, about which a large library of books already has been written and which need only be mentioned here in order to round out the picture of Mr. Harding's normalcy; and also to revive the largely forgotten name of Thomas James Walsh.

On April 29, 1922—Harding was still alive—Senator Robert M. La Follette of Wisconsin introduced a resolution calling on the committee of public lands to investigate the

---

* It is still believed by many that Jesse Smith did not commit suicide but was murdered, because he knew too much. In his careful account of the period, however, Samuel Hopkins Adams makes a strong case for suicide.

leasing of naval oil reserves in California. Because he believed that the chairman and a majority of the members of this committee were not in sympathy with the inquiry, La Follette asked Senator Thomas J. Walsh of Montana to take charge of the investigation. There was a momentary flash of public interest, then complete apathy, and Walsh was left to pursue the trail—and what a trail it was—undisturbed and forgotten.

For eighteen months this competent and determined man dug into a heavy jungle of conflicting facts and brought forth a story as incredible as it was startling and true. Briefly, Mr. Walsh learned that Mr. Harding's great friend, Albert Bacon Fall, secretary of the interior, had secretly and without competitive bidding leased government oil reserves to Edward L. Doheny's Pan-American Company and Harry F. Sinclair's Mammoth Oil Company. For this consideration Secretary Fall, who always posed as a kindly, drawling, rough-and-ready man of the Great Open Spaces—an Honest John if ever there lived one—for this consideration Secretary Fall received from Sinclair some $260,000 in Liberty Bonds and from Doheny a "loan," without interest or security, of $100,000.

While the department of easy virtue sought to discredit Walsh and his co-committeemen, and to harass him in every way, and while great newspapers called him a "Montana Scandal Monger," Senator Walsh calmly and methodically exposed this colossal roguery in high places. Secretary Fall went to prison. Doheny and Sinclair, by some quirk of the law of evidence not to be comprehended by any mind but a lawyer's, went free. But Secretary of the Navy Denby, who had amiably acquiesced when Fall transferred the oil reserves from the navy to the interior department, was driven from office by newspaper criticism. The leases were voided.

Senator Walsh's contribution to exposure of the last rottenness in the Harding gang should stand as one of the greatest public services ever performed by an American public servant. Yet his exposures were met, so far as the mass of the public was concerned, with a monumental indifference. The flight of a mechanic in a plane to France, the goings-on of a female evangelist, the suit of a gold-digging moron against a senile millionaire—those were the things that really counted with the public while Walsh was ripping apart the government of the United States.

On the death of Harding Calvin Coolidge became the thirtieth President of the United States of America.* He quietly sat out the rest of the term, was elected President, then sat quietly for four years more, doing nothing that can readily be recalled and delivering himself of but one comment on affairs that is worth remembering. When asked if in his opinion the war debts of foreign nations should be paid, he replied: "They hired the money, didn't they?"

During Mr. Coolidge's years in office the stock market rose to what the financial analysts termed "a permanent high plateau," which indicated a gross misunderstanding of the meaning of "permanent." Some genius labeled this condition Coolidge Prosperity. Coolidge did not deny the implication. He took time off to help with hayin' on the home place in Plymouth, Vermont, and America was happy to see pictures of this great and wealth-giving man at work on the stony acres with three-tined fork and bull-rake.

To follow the rustic Mr. Coolidge, and on the explicit understanding that he was to continue the Prosperity named for his predecessor, Herbert Hoover was elected. Hoover was a man of strong character, and also one of the most unfortunate men ever to hold the office of President. Under him,

---

* Known very favorably as Silent Cal, Coolidge said nothing publicly because of one of two possible reasons: Either he had no ideas on public affairs, which seems reasonable; or he was too timid to voice them. But in private Coolidge was garrulity itself. Philip Parrish, newspaperman of Portland, Oregon, once went to what he fondly thought would be an interview with President Coolidge, but for two hours Mr. Parrish was harangued on everything from trout fishing to the cost of cigars and, though he tried diligently, never once managed to get in a question.

while he and the United States watched with incredulous eyes, the great shoddy structure of Prosperity trembled, rocked, heaved most dreadfully, then collapsed.

Neither Harding nor Coolidge nor Hoover had any great influence on the history of the period between 1920 and 1932. For the most part it was an era of complacency, for as I have mentioned, even the exposé of the Harding Orgy failed to disturb our smugness. Cheap ballyhoo operated as never before. Above all, it was a period when the herd-mind became ascendant. To conform was the thing. So, a nation of one hundred millions of people went mad over a Chinese game called Mah-Jong. The very same people who played Mah-Jong presently went wild over a form of autotherapy known as Couéism. No man was a success unless he at least dabbled in the stock market. Everybody bought a radio, and all successful families owned two cars, although not *two* books. A backwoodsman of Kentucky got stuck in a sand cave and took a long time in dying, while newspapers, giving the public what it wanted, blew the incident into an event calling for Second Coming type, which is even larger than Studhorse type.

But Jesus Christ was not forgotten in all this tremendous uproar about nothing. An advertising man named Barton took firm hold of The Lamb and brought him forth as the Great Businessman, a go-getter, a president of Rotary, an Elk on a tour. The Gospel of Service, easy to understand but difficult to define, supplanted the Gospels of the New Testament. True hundred-percent Americans were assuredly the chosen people.

Meanwhile, Prohibition, which had been the first corruption to interest the Harding administration, grew into a gigantic, costly, and tragic farce. By the end of the Coolidge era, the manufacture, transportation and sale of hard and light liquors was the biggest business in the United States. Distilling and bootlegging called for "protection" from the law, and protection was to be had for a price all the way from high federal officials down to the sheriff and judge of the most sparsely populated county in the nation.

Hounded by fanatics like the Anti-Saloon League and the Methodist lobby, the federal administrations tried vainly to stop the flow of booze. The lowest type of thugs were employed as prohibition agents and many of them made fortunes, not from their salaries. Lawyers specialized in liquor cases. Judges, juries, police officers, all were bought, every day, everywhere. The government at last forced makers of industrial alcohol to douse it with lethal poisons; but still it continued to flow into the bootlegging trade where it was treated to remove the deadly federal dosing.

Although year by year the farce of Prohibition became steadily more apparent and its corruptive effects more sinister in their influence than any civilized country had ever known, few voices were raised publicly in protest. Here was a great nation that had prided itself on its sturdy individualists, now harassed and badgered, arrested, slugged, beaten, shot, often killed, made to drink slow poison behind locked doors or in furtive places, meanwhile cursing impotently the powerful organized minority which had brought them the boon of Prohibition and were making it stick.

In all of this futile protest there was one voice which made itself heard to some purpose. This voice belonged to Henry Louis Mencken of Baltimore, unquestionably the greatest and most effective critical force released in the United States since the turn of the century.

Mencken, it might be remarked for the benefit of those who came in a little late, was a Baltimore newspaperman. In 1923 with Alfred A. Knopf as publisher and George Jean Nathan as co-editor, Mencken founded *The American Mercury*, a monthly magazine of chaste appearance but of viscera composed of equal parts of dynamite, cyanide, and blue vitriol. The *Mercury* burst on smug America with a literary explosion not before seen or heard.

While most Americans and nearly all editors had been reading in the Gospel of Service, Henry Mencken had been delving deeply into the books of the Apocalypse. As early as January of 1920, when writing for the *Sun* of Baltimore, Mencken predicted without qualification that Prohibition, just then descending on the country, would make of America the most corrupt nation on earth. From that day until Repeal, a dozen years later, Mr. Mencken never ceased his slashing attack on Prohibition. He did for repeal of the dry laws what Garrison had done for Abolition, in reverse, and did it with something of the same berserker rage, though Mencken added sardonic ridicule to his attack.

Every issue of the *Mercury* was an attack on Prohibition and the kind of people who actually believed it to be a noble experiment; but that was not all. Every issue of the *Mercury* was also an attack on some other American myth, or merely on the smugness that had congealed into belief. No such command of invective had been displayed by an American before, not even by Samuel Adams or Theodore Parker or Eugene Debs. Mencken struck with ax, club, rapier, and brass knuckles. He attacked the higher education in America. He early ridiculed Coolidge Prosperity, saying it was hollow and that a reckoning would come. He blasted at Wall Street. He blasted at current literary criticism as namby-pamby. He went after bad writing and speaking. He badgered mountebanks of all sorts, religious, political, financial. He praised sound American writers who were then known to but few Americans. He encouraged hoboes to write for his magazine, and Negroes, priests, atheists, and anarchists. Together with Co-Editor Nathan, who was also engaged in drubbing shoddy American plays, Mencken collected absurdities perpetrated by Americans and listed them under mordant headings in the magazine's *Americana*.

Here at last was a force, strident, bombastic, iconoclastic, lambasting the puerilities of Mencken's fellow Americans, applying the birch to lesser evils such as Uplift and Service, and always using his heaviest artillery on Prohibition and its attendant evils. Editor Mencken quickly attracted a number of discontented Americans to write for him. One issue of the magazine might contain a piece ridiculing the New Humanism, another ridiculing Buchmanism, a satiric story on civilization in the South, a sardonic article about a big businessman posing as prophet, a horse-laughing essay on the would-be expurgators of literature—and always a vitriolic denouncement of Prohibition and all of its catchpoll minions.

The *Mercury* never reached a circulation of more than 100,000 copies, yet its influence was soon felt by millions of Americans who had never heard either of Mencken or of the magazine. It was read by editorial writers on newspapers and by all rebels who wrote or spoke or merely thought. The *Mercury's* influence opened the eyes of thousands of persons to the world of literature, not of written trash. It did more than any other magazine to bring a native realistic literature to the mass of the public—not through its columns but through its influence. For a time it stood almost alone for a breaking of the Victorian bonds on ideas and language. And always each month it thundered at Prohibition.

Almost overnight Mencken and the *Mercury* became a sensation to American literates. And in a little its influence could be seen in the rising tide of protest against Prohibition in the editorial pages of newspapers, which had previously been more than timid of the subject.

It is not to be said here that Mr. Mencken was the sole cause for repeal of the 18th Amendment to the Constitution. What I do mean to assert is that Mencken was the one great personal influence that was felt in that respect; and he should go into our history as the rambunctious Galahad who never once ceased attacking Prohibition until it was in the discard. His influence on criticism and literature in the United States was probably just as great as his effect on the dry laws. In 1927 Walter Lippmann termed Mencken "the most powerful personal influence on this whole generation of educated people." It was not too much to say of the Sage of Baltimore.

Mr. Mencken's place as an authority on language is assured, I think, by his monumental work, *The American Language*, and its supplementary volumes. And all future historians who are honest must consider him in relation to Repeal and as the greatest single force for a native Literature with a capital letter. In the 1940's, many of the younger generation know Mencken only as a name. Let them know and reflect upon it that they may drink their beer or their cocktail openly because Henry Mencken once led a twelve-year charge against Prohibition.*

It appears, too, that a number of older Americans, many of whom write books and pieces for the magazines and pretend to be social historians, now tend to dismiss Mencken as a mere fad. This is condescension, which is a form of attack used by literary fatheads.

For the sake of the record, Henry Louis Mencken is a stocky man, five feet seven inches tall, who moves and speaks quickly. His dark hair, thinning at last, is parted almost in the middle. He is always dressed immaculately, and as conservatively as any of the bankers he has so often derided. His wide face reveals strong character, and belies the large, round, china-blue eyes which gaze intently at one, as though they were constantly astonished at the imbecilities they had witnessed these past sixty years and more.

The man talks as brilliantly as he writes. His intellectual curiosity is immense and seemingly unlimited. He is as friendly, big-hearted and sentimental as any of the boobs and simple simons and gaping primates he had belabored all

---

*When I was reading proofs of these pages, in 1946, Howard Mumford Jones, Harvard professor, cried aloud in amazement that his charges in Cambridge had never heard of Mencken.

these years.* Out of print he is a gentleman in the best sense. In ink, he is a savage, except for his three volumes of memoirs, which show him in a mellow mood of nostalgic tolerance for all the impossible people and things he has known. But he *was* savage when he struck at smugness and phonies and Prohibition. He was savage when he opened the way for fresh and independent thought in this country and insisted, with great vehemence, that the thought be genuinely American. Like the biblical leaders and prophets of olden time, Mencken chastised his fellows to make them better men.

Although as early as March of 1926 Henry Louis Mencken was exploding the Coolidge myth of permanent prosperity, little happened to shake the faith of a majority of Americans for the next three years. Then, in Hoover's mid-term came the first rumblings of the debacle ahead, to be quickly followed by the thunders of downright collapse. Try as he would, and Mr. Hoover tried hard, nothing could be done to stem complete destruction of the American economy. He went out of office to the jeers of hundreds of thousands of disinherited who were living in packing-box settlements known as Hoovervilles.

---

* And don't think that Mencken's "gaping primates" did not strike back. He was the most abused man of his time. Here are a few samples from the record, which is entitled *Menckeniana, A Schimpflexikon* (New York, 1928): "This maggot, this ghoul of new-made graves, this buzzard." Eugene L. Pearce, in Tampa *Times.*—"A pole-cat." San Francisco *Chronicle.*—"He is, as a fact, far inferior to the average Southern Negro." Tampa *Tribune.* —"The Boy-Pervert from Baltimore." New York University *Daily News.*— "He is so damnably dirty, so vile and degenerate, that when his time comes to die it will take a special dispensation from Heaven to get him into the bottommost pit of Hell." Jackson (Miss.) *News.*—"Let him leave the country for the country's good." C. E. Stone in the *Nation.*—"Mr. Mencken is no writer at all, but a brick factory." The *New Republic.*—"Mencken is frankly a diabolist." Manchester (N. H.) *Union.*—"Mencken is an outstanding, disgusting example of what constitutes a poor American." Richmond *Times-Dispatch.*—"Who is he that he has any right to criticize any American, no matter who?" C. B. Langston in St. Paul *Pioneer-Press.*— "When H. L. Mencken attacks the Rotarian of today he is attacking the American people." Rabbi L. Binstock in Charleston (W. Va.) *Gazette.*

The average unthinking man laid the Depression squarely on the shoulders of poor Mr. Hoover; and there, so far as millions of Americans are concerned, the blame still rests. What caused the Depression has been the subject of more books than bibliographers could keep up with. They run to learned tomes filled with references to paper-credits, paper-profits, inflated values, inflated credits, and a hundred more terms highly thought of by economists. All of these books, even the more radical, discussed almost everything to do with the subject except that which to many men looks to have been the chief reason for the collapse—specifically, that too large a part of the national income was going to and being retained by an extremely small percentage of the whole population.

No professional economist, of course, would dare to admit that the basic cause of the debacle was so simple as that. Yet, no other reason intelligible to non-experts in economics has ever, so far as I am aware, been propounded. The whole thing thus remains in the realm of metaphysics.

There was nothing metaphysical in the manner in which President Franklin Roosevelt acted when he took over the helm of the sinking ship of state from the palsied hands of Mr. Hoover. Facing Mr. Roosevelt was a greater task than any since 1860. He moved swiftly to meet it, and with great daring. He closed the banks, both those that were tottering and those that merely shivered. He formulated what he called the New Deal, much of it taken over bodily from the almost forgotten Populists of the nineties, then began to carry it out.

The New Deal spent money on public roads and various public projects, some of them nonsensical, primarily to make work for the unemployed. It changed banking practices. It hired writers and artists and actors and musicians, and put them to work. It set about reforming the stock market. It set prices under farm produce. It made loans to industrial enterprises. It devalued the currency. It called in gold. It set young men to conservation work in the forests and on the plains. It brought something approaching order to the chaotic coal and oil industries. It started water-power projects. It broke up the great holding companies, it formulated codes of fair practices to eliminate wasteful competition in business. It raised the income tax rates. It passed laws designed to speed the organization of labor into unions.

At first, both press and public welcomed the New Deal, for people were frightened, dazed; and then, as the clogged arteries of business and agriculture began to function again, attacks on the administration started—and continued, often to the extent of gross personal abuse of the President. It was the old case of sick men fearing the Devil, but forgetting the Devil with the first glimmer of returning health. That the New Deal made countless mistakes, many of them ludicrous, was soon obvious. It put many mountebanks into appointive office. It probably got less of actual labor and finished goods for the cash it spent than any other administration. But the New Deal also brought the United States out of its greatest depression without violence, and with what in retrospect appears to have been as much speed as possible.

Roosevelt's domestic program was presently influenced by events abroad, both in the Orient and in Europe. War began in 1939. From that point on, much of the Roosevelt program was designed to put the country into a position for defense. Either that, or to put the nation into the war on the side of Great Britain, France, Russia and China. It will of course be many years yet before a sifting of documentary evidence will permit historians to say exactly what the United States was preparing for in the period after 1939—and even then, a century hence, perhaps, there is sure to be disagreement.

In any case, the wars grew greater, and the United States worked faster to make arms, and soldiers. Then, at two minutes past seven on the morning of December 7, 1941, Private Joseph Lockard of the United States Army's Aircraft Warning Regiment on the Island of Oahu, Territory of Hawaii, stood at his listening post and heard a far-off drumming. At five minutes past seven he reported to his duty officer at the information center that a large flight of planes was 132 miles distant and coming in fast.

Private Lockard gave his warning promptly and accurately. What happened to that warning remains something of a mystery four years afterward, although the official Pearl Harbor report says that the warning was "ignored." In view of subsequent events, "ignored" is not too strong a term.

Let Private Lockard go into all of our history books henceforth. His warning, even though it was ignored, was more important than the word Paul Revere carried. Nor let any American ever forget how dreadfully accurate it was. Fifty minutes later, fifty minutes that could have been used to change the course of events down to the present day and beyond, an armada of enemy planes came in over the mountains to catch the American army and navy in a condition in which no American force had been caught before. It was a truly ghastly tragedy, those wasted fifty minutes.

Remembering that fifty minutes as criticism, however, is more valuable to the United States than all of the unmeasured praise that is piled layer upon layer on our country by the professional trumpeters of democracy. Give us plenty of criticism, both from within and without, and we Americans will continue to live in the most agreeable country on earth.

ACKNOWLEDGMENTS AND
BIBLIOGRAPHY

MUCH of a book such as this must of necessity come out
of other books, and out of pamphlets, documents, periodicals,
and newspapers. Finding just the right source is not always
a simple matter, for bibliographies, even the best—and
praise to them all—cannot indicate exactly the content of
the source named. Thus, a man must often consult perhaps a
dozen books to learn how a certain event occurred, or perhaps
a score to learn the color of hair and eyes, the physical
stature and weight, the political and theological leanings of
some person of long ago. I happen to think it is important
to know that Captain John Smith had red hair, that John
Greenleaf Whittier was as swarthy as an Indian, that
Dorothea Dix had smoldering blue eyes, that the Reverend
Alexander Young was a most devout Whig.

Once the source has been found, then the rest is easy—or
comparatively easy. Finding the right sources took me to
Columbia University, where I was given generous space amid
handsome surroundings for many months; to the American
History Room of the New York Public Library; to the
Widener in Cambridge, to the Boston Public, to the New-
berry and the Chicago Public, to the Peter White Memorial
at Marquette, Michigan, the Wisconsin Historical at Madison, the Minnesota Historical at St. Paul, the Portland
Public in Oregon, the Seattle Public and the University of
Washington, and the State Library at Olympia, Washington. In each and all of these places I was accorded the great
aid and courtesies that are extended, apparently without
effort but with the best of cheer, to all of us who wish to

look into books. I never cease to marvel at the good nature and the wide knowledge of librarians, and I am in their debt beyond any payment.

To Sylvester Vigilante, of the New York Public Library staff, on whom the burden of my search rested particularly heavily, must go a special degree of thanks. I owe much, too, to Miss Nell Unger, Miss Katherine Anderson and Miss Louise Prichard of the Portland Public Library in Oregon; to Stewart Edward White of Palo Alto, California; to Allan Nevins and Henry Steele Commager of New York City; to George T. Springer of Minneapolis, Robert S. Monahan and Joseph Henry Jackson of San Francisco; to Lloyd Lewis of Chicago; and to Mrs. Alta Grimm, Miss Mary Hall, and Mrs. Pearl Yantis of Olympia, Washington.

The material listed below proved especially useful.

Adams, James Truslow, *Provincial Society*, New York, 1927.

Adams, John Quincy, The *Writings* of, New York, 1927.

Adams, Samuel Hopkins, *The Incredible Era*, Boston, 1939.

Allen, Frederick Lewis, *Only Yesterday*, New York, 1931.

Allen, Gardner W., *A Naval History of the American Revolution*, Boston, 1913.

Aptheker, Herbert, *American Negro Slave Revolts*, New York, 1943.

Ashley, Clifford W., *The Yankee Whaler*, Boston, 1926.

Ashmun, Jehudi, *The Liberia Farmer; or, Colonist's Guide to Independence and Domestic Comfort*, Philadelphia, 1835.

Atkeson, T. C., *Semicentennial History of the Patrons of Husbandry*, 1916.

Bates, Ernest Sutherland, *American Faith*, New York, 1940.

Beach, Seth Curtis, *Daughters of the Puritans*, Boston, 1905.

Beard, Charles and Mary, *The Rise of American Civilization*, New York, 1933.

Beddard, F. E., *A Book of Whales*, New York, 1900.

Beer, Thomas, *Hanna*, New York, 1929.

———, *The Mauve Decade*, New York, 1926.

Berry, Robert Elton, *Yankee Stargazer*, New York, 1941.

Blackwell, Alice Stone, *Lucy Stone*, Boston, 1930.

Blegen, Theodore C., *Norwegian Migration to America*, St. Paul, 1940.

Bonsal, Stephen, *The Fight for Santiago*, New York, 1899.

Bowers, Claude G., *The Tragic Era*, New York, 1929.

Bradford, William, *Of Plimouth Plantation*, Boston, 1898.

Brooks, Van Wyck, *The Flowering of New England*, New York, 1936.

————, *New England: Indian Summer*, New York, 1940.

Burlingame, Roger, *March of the Iron Men*, New York, 1938.

Calhoun, A. W., *A Social History of the American Family*, Cleveland, 1917.

Carnegie, Andrew, *Triumphant Democracy*, New York, 1893.

Cash, W. J., *The Mind of the South*, New York, 1941.

Channing, Edward, *History of the United States*, New York, 1905.

Clark, Thomas D., *Pills, Petticoats and Plows*, New York, 1944.

Cloud, D. C., *Monopolies and the People*, Davenport, Iowa, 1873.

Cochran, Thomas C., and Miller, William, *The Age of Enterprise*, New York, 1942.

Cohn, David L., *The Good Old Days*, New York, 1940.

Cole, Arthur Charles, *The Irrepressible Conflict*, New York, 1934.

Commager, Henry Stee'e, and Morison, Samuel Eliot, *The Growth of the American Republic*, New York, 1940.

Commons, J. R., *Races and Immigrants in America*, New York, 1920.

————, and Associates, *History of Labor in the United States*, New York, 1918.

Continental Congress, *Journals* of, Washington, 1909.

Curti, Merle, *The Growth of American Thought*, New York, 1943.

De Crevecoeur, St. John, *Letters of an American Farmer*, New Haven, 1925.

De la Rochefoucault, Duke, *Travels Through the United States of North America*, London, 1799.

De Voto, Bernard, *The Year of Decision 1846*, Boston, 1943.

Dexter, F. B., *Biographical Sketches of Graduates of Yale College*, New Haven, 1912.

Dictionary of American Biography, 21 vols., New York, 1928–1944.

Donnelly, Ignatius, *Atlantis*, New York, 1882.

———, *The Great Cryptogram*, New York, 1888.

Dorsey, Florence L., *Master of the Mississippi*, Boston, 1941.

Earle, Alice Morse, *Home Life in Colonial Days*, New York, 1898.

Eddis, William, *Letters from America*, London, 1792.

Faulkner, Harold U., *The Quest for Social Justice*, New York, 1931.

Faust, Albert B., *The German Element in the United States*, New York, 1927.

Fish, Carl Russell, *The Rise of the Common Man*, New York, 1941.

Forbes, Esther, *Paul Revere and the World He Lived In*, Boston, 1942.

Fox, Dixon Ryan, and Kraut, John Allen, *The Completion of Independence*, New York, 1944.

Fox, George, *Journal of*, 1672–1673, in *Original Narratives of Early American History*, New York, 1910.

French, Allen, *The Day of Concord & Lexington*, Boston, 1925.

———, *The First Year of the American Revolution*, Boston, 1934.

Frothingham, Richard, *History of the Siege of Boston*, Boston, 1849.

Gould, E. W., *Fifty Years on the Mississippi; or, Gould's History of River Navigation*, St. Louis, 1889.

Greenbie, Marjorie Barstow, *Lincoln's Daughters of Mercy*, New York, 1944.

Greene, Evarts Boutell, *The Revolutionary Generation*, New York, 1943.

Gurley, R. R., *Life of Jehudi Ashmun*, Washington, 1835.

Hamlin, Talbot F., *The American Spirit in Architecture*, New Haven, 1926.

Hansen, Marcus Lee, *The Atlantic Migration*, Cambridge, 1941.

Harlow, Ralph Volney, *Samuel Adams*, New York, 1923.

Hart, Albert Bushnell, ed., *The American Nation: A History*, 28 vols., New York, 1904–1918.

Haynes, F. E., *Third Party Movements Since the Civil War*, Iowa City, 1916.

Headley, J. T., *Washington and His Generals*, New York, 1847.

Helper, Hinton Rowan, *The Impending Crisis of the South: How to Meet It*, New York, 1857.

———, *Negroes in Negroland*, New York, 1868.

Hicks, John D., *The Populist Revolt*, Minneapolis, 1931.

History of Fort Dodge and Webster County, Iowa, Chicago, 1913.

Hohman, Elmo Paul, *The American Whaleman*, New York, 1928.

Holbrook, Stewart H., *Iron Brew*, New York, 1940.

Ivins, Lester S., and Winship, A. E., *Fifty Famous Farmers*, New York, 1924.

Jackson, Helen H., *A Century of Dishonor*, Boston, 1885.

Johnson, Amandus, *The Swedish Settlements of the Delaware*, Philadelphia, 1911.

Johnson, Gerald, *American Heroes and Hero Worship*, New York, 1943.

Johnson's Wonder-Working Providence 1628–1651, in *Original Narratives of Early American History*, New York, 1910.

Kelley, Oliver Hudson, *Origin and Progress of the Order of the Patrons of Husbandry*, 1875.

Kimball, Fiske, *Domestic Architecture of the American Colonies and of the Early Republic*, New York, 1922.

Knollenberg, Bernhard, *Washington and the Revolution*, New York, 1940.

Krout, John Allen, and Fox, Dixon Ryan, *The Completion of Independence*, New York, 1944.

Langdon, William Chauncy, *Everyday Things in American Life*, New York, 1937.

Leech, Margaret, *Reveille in Washington*, New York, 1941.

Livermore, Mary Ashton Rice, *My Story of the War*, Hartford, 1889.

Lossing, Bernard J., *Pictorial Field-Book of the Revolution*, New York, 1855.

Lovejoy, J. C., *Memoir of Rev. Charles T. Torrey*, n.p., 1847.

McCabe, Joseph, *Biographical Dictionary of Modern Rationalists*, London, 1920.

Maclay, Edgar S., *A History of the U. S. Navy 1775 to 1901*, New York, 1901.

McMaster, John Bach, *A History of the People of the United States*, New York, 1912.

Mann, Hermann, *The Female Review: or, The Life of Deborah Sampson*, Boston, 1866; a reprint, with corrections and additions and comments of the original that was issued at Dedham, Mass., 1797.

Marshall, Helen E., *Dorothea Dix*, Chapel Hill, S. C., 1937.

Matthews, Lois K., *The Expansion of New England*, Boston, 1909.

Mayes, Herbert R., *Alger*, New York, 1928.

Mencken, H. L., *The American Language*, New York, 1936.

Miller, John C., *Sam Adams*, Boston, 1936.

Miller, Perry, *The New England Mind*, New York, 1939.

Millis, Walter, *The Martial Spirit*, New York, 1931.

Minot, George R., *History of the Insurrections in Massachusetts, in the Year 1786, and the Rebellion Consequent Thereon*, Worcester, 1788.

Morison, S. E., *The Maritime History of Massachusetts 1783–1860*, Boston, 1921.

Murdock, Harold, *The 19th of April 1775*, Boston, 1923.

Muzzey, David S., *Readings in American History*, Boston, 1915.

Myers, Gustavus, *History of Great American Fortunes*, New York, 1907.

Nevins, Allan, *The Emergence of Modern America*, New York, 1927.

Nordhoff, Charles, *The Communist Societies of the U.S.A.*, New York, 1875.

O'Connor, William D., *Mr. Donnelly's Reviewers*, Chicago, 1889.

Osborn, Chase S., and Stellanova, *Schoolcraft, Longfellow, Hiawatha*, Lancaster, Pa., 1942.

Paine, Thomas, *Works of*, New York, 1925.

Parker, Robert Allerton, *A Yankee Saint*, New York, 1935.

Parrington, Vernon Louis, *Main Currents in American Thought*, New York, 1930.

Paterson, Isabel, *The God of the Machine*, New York, 1943.

Paxton, F. L., *History of the American Frontier*, Boston, 1924.

Regier, C. C., *The Era of the Muckrakers*, Chapel Hill, 1932.

Remsburg, John E., *The Bible*, New York, n. d.

Rhodes, James Forbes, *History of the United States from the Compromise of 1850*, 8 vols., New York, 1890–1919.

Richards, Laura E., *Samuel Gridley Howe*, New York, 1935.

Rochester, Anna, *The Populist Movement in the United States*, New York, 1944.

Rohan, Jack, *Samuel Colt*, Boston.

Sanborn, F. B., *Dr. S. G. Howe, the Philanthropist*, Boston, 1891.

Sanger, Margaret, *An Autobiography*, New York, 1938.

———, *My Fight for Birth Control*, New York, 1931.

Sawyer, C. W., *Firearms in American History*, New York, 1910.

Schlesinger, Arthur M., *New Viewpoints in American History*, New York, 1922.

———, *The Rise of the City*, New York, 1933.

———, *The Colonial Merchants and the American Revolution*, New York, 1917.

———, *Political and Social Growth of the American People*, New York, 1941.

Scudder, H. E., *Noah Webster*, Boston, 1881.

Sears, Clara Endicott, *Bronson Alcott's Fruitlands*, Boston, 1915.

Shepard, Odell, *Connecticut, Past and Present*, New York, 1939.

Shurtleff, Harold R., *The Log Cabin Myth*, Cambridge, 1939.

Smith, Capt. John, *Generall Historie of Virginia*, London, 1624.

Spencer, Herbert, *Principles of Sociology*, Vol. 3, New York, 1896.

————, *The Man vs. The State*, London, 1884.

Stokes, I. N. Phelps, *The Iconography of Manhattan Island, 1498–1900*, New York, 1926.

Sullivan, Mark, *Our Times*, 3 vols., New York, 1926–1930.

Sumner, William Graham, *Folkways*, Boston, 1906.

Thacher, James, *Military Journal During the American Revolutionary War*, Boston, 1823.

Thompson, Charles Miner, *Independent Vermont*, Boston, 1942.

Tiffany, Francis, *Life of Dorothea Dix*, Boston, 1890.

Turner, F. J., *The Frontier in American History*, New York, 1920.

Turner, L. D., *Anti-Slavery Sentiment in American Literature Prior to 1865*, Washington, 1929.

Tyler, Alice Felt, *Freedom's Ferment*, Minneapolis, 1944.

Van de Water, Frederic, *The Reluctant Republic*, New York, 1941.

Van Doren, Carl, *Benjamin Franklin*, New York, 1938.

————, *Secret History of the American Revolution*, New York, 1938.

Van Slyke, J. D., *Representatives of New England*, Boston, 1879.

Veblen, Thorstein, *The Theory of the Leisure Class*, New York, 1931.

Washburn, Robert Collyer, *Prayer for Profit*, New York, 1930.

————, *The Life and Times of Lydia E. Pinkham*, New York, 1931.

Walker, Jonathan, *Trial and Imprisonment of*, Boston, 1845.

Ware, Henry, *Memoirs of the Rev. Noah Worcester, D.D.*, Boston, 1844.

Washington, B. T., *The Story of the Negro*, London, 1909.

Webber, A. R., *Life of John Baldwin, Jr.*, Cleveland, 1925.

Wecter, Dixon, *The Hero in America*, New York, 1941.

Wertenbaker, T. J., *The First Americans*, New York, 1927.

Wilbur, Sibyl, *The Life of Mary Baker Eddy*, Boston, 1907.

Wheeler, Townsend, *The American Rifle*, New York, 1918.

Who Was Who in America, Chicago, 1942.

Wildes, Harry Emerson, *The Delaware*, New York, 1940.

Williams, George W., *History of the Negro Race in America*, New York, 1883.

Williams, Ralph D., *The Honorable Peter White*, Cleveland, 1907.

Winship, A. E., and Ivins, Lester S., *Fifty Famous Farmers*, New York, 1924.

Winsor, Justin, *The Memorial History of Boston*, Boston, 1883.

Wormeley, Katherine P., *The United States Sanitary Commission*, Boston, 1863.

PAMPHLETS, AND ARTICLES IN PERIODICALS

Anonymous, *Record of Charles T. Harvey*, New York, n. d.

Barrett, William, "Ephraim Bull," *Memoirs of the Social Circle in Concord*, 4th series, 1909.

Brainard, Dudley S., *Nininger, A Boom Town, Minnesota History*, June, 1932.

Branch, John, Sr., *The St. Albans Raid*, a reprint of newspaper accounts, St. Albans, Vt., n. d.

Commager, Henry Steele, "The Blasphemy of Abner Kneeland," *New England Quarterly*, March, 1935.

Deane, Silas, Correspondence of, *Collections* of Connecticut Historical Society, Hartford, 1870.

Dunten, M. T., "The Worker Through the Ages," *Four L Lumber News*, Portland, Ore., 1931–1932.

Ford, Miriam Allen de, "The Amazing Ignatius Donnelly," *American Parade*, Vol. 11, No. 2, Girard, Kansas, 1929.

Gale, Dr. Benjamin, letter to Silas Deane 9 Nov. 1775, *Collections* of Connecticut Historical Society, 1870.

Griswold, Charles, letter to Prof. Silliman, *American Journal of Science*, Vol. 11, No. 2, Nov. 1820.

Hicks, J. D., "The Political Career of Ignatius Donnelly," *Mississippi Valley Historical Review*, VII, 1921.

Holbrook, Josiah, "The American Lyceum or Society for the Improvement of Schools and Diffusion of Universal Knowledge," n. p., 1829.

House of Representatives, Document, 25th Congress, 2d Session, Rep. No. 159, Benjamin Gannett, Dec. 22, 1837.

Hubbard, Elbert, "A Message to García," *The Philistine*, March, 1899.

Jenks, Williams L., "History and Meaning of County Names in Michigan," Michigan Pioneer and Historical Collections, Vol. 38.

Jones, J. L., "Samuel Gridley Howe," *Charities Review*, Dec., 1897.

Knowlton, Charles, Obit. of, *Boston Medical and Surgical Journal*, Sept. 10, 24, 1851.

Lefèr, Hugh Talmage, "Hinton Rowan Helper, Advocate of a White America," in *Southern Sketches*, Charlottesville, Va., 1935.

McDermid, Jeff (E. R. McIntyre) "Oneida County Salute," in *Better Crops*, Washington, D. C., October, 1943.

Milburn, George, "The Appeal to Reason," in *American Mercury*.

Pargellis, Stanley, "The Judgment of History on American Business," The Newcomen Society, 1943.

Peabody, A. P., "Boston Mobs Before the Revolution," *Atlantic Monthly*, Vol. LXII, p. 321.

Shafter, William Rufus, Papers of, now in Library of Stanford University, Palo Alto, Ca'if.

Tudor, Frederic, Miscellaneous Papers, in Baker Library, Cambridge.

Wach, Henry Wellington, "Personal Recollections of a Great Baconian, Hon. Ignatius Donnelly," *American Baconian*, Nov. 1923.

FILES OF NEWSPAPERS AND PERIODICALS

American Mercury
The Appeal to Reason
The Arena
Boston Transcript
Chicago Inter-Ocean
Connecticut Courant
Emigrant Aid Journal, Nininger, Minn., 1857
Eastern Argus, Portland, Maine
Harpers Weekly
Hoard's Dairyman, since 1885
Niles Weekly Register, Baltimore

INDEX